CHRISTIAN**U**

FRESHMAN YEAR

Memoirs of a 1980's

Christian University Student

JOHN C. KWASNY

DEDICATION

To my best friend and love of my life, Martie (who I only dreamt
that I could meet in college)
To all my children and grandchildren

A special dedication to my birthday-sharing daughter,
Emmalyne for being my first reader

PREFACE

Don't you have to be famous to write a memoir? Probably. But I just so happened to journal every single day of my college career over forty years ago. With all that content, why wouldn't I publish my experiences? Hopefully, my children and grandchildren will be interested in what I was like as a college student. Then, there are all the people who went to college in the 1980s who may like a walk down memory lane (even if these are not their memories). And what about people who just like a good origin story?

So, why did I decide to begin journaling my life on August 12, 1984? Good question. I didn't journal in high school; but, I did write a lot of stories. I even tried to write the great American novel at one point—but never finished. I really don't know why! I do remember a sermon application from the pastor of my youth that encouraged journaling to grow our love for and gratitude towards the LORD. I certainly wanted to grow in my relationship with God and understand my purpose in this world. Whatever the true motivation was, I threw myself into this daily habit with vigor.

As I put this first year of university life together, I originally thought I would skip the uneventful days. But even those days continue the story in some way, so I decided to keep them in. If nothing else, those "boring" days give the reader places to skim over to move on to the interesting stuff. The truth is that every day is a day the LORD has made, and He is always at work even when we don't recognize it.

Unlike a typical novel, there aren't just a few major characters for the reader to keep track of in this memoir. Since I was at a large university (by Christian college standards), I interacted with lots of people. I chose not to change any names, but purposefully left out surnames to protect the innocent! As the year unfolded, people move in and out of my life, as it is for most of us during the late teen years. By God's providence, certain people become more and more consistently present—and I am thankful that they were in my life.

Hopefully, the reader will get a taste of what life was like in the 1980's at a typical Christian university in the heartland of America. They were interesting times to be alive, in many ways. But more importantly, the events, decisions, and relationships recorded here were used by a sovereign and loving God to shape one of His child's future. I am thankful for how it all transpired—the good and the bad, the challenging and the even more challenging. Even if I didn't recognize it in 1984, I truly believe that all that God ordains is right!

John C. Kwasny, October 5, 2025

II

PROLOGUE

I grew up in a Christian family in the south suburbs of Chicago. My parents were not Christians when they married. I was their firstborn, followed twenty months later by my sister, Amy. When I was four years old, they divorced. For three years, my sister and I lived with our mother most of the time, with every other weekend with our dad. Then, the first known miracle happened in my life: my parents remarried each other. Yes, you read that right: I was a witness at my parents' wedding, along with a Baptist minister and his wife. My duty was to read 1 Corinthians 13, often referred to as the "Love Chapter."

My life changed dramatically after that. We started attending a little Baptist church in Dolton, Illinois. I professed faith in Christ soon after, being baptized by the same pastor who married my parents. I was enrolled in second grade at Calvin Christian School in South Holland, Illinois. So, now I had the Bible taught to me at home, school, and church. So, that's what I mean by growing up in a Christian home. My dad even became an elder, and both parents were leaders in the youth ministry.

Upon eighth grade graduation, I went to a significantly large Christian high school: Illiana Christian High School in Lansing, Illinois. As the name implies, it was located on the border of Illinois and Indiana, fed by Christian elementary schools in both states. My first three years were pretty insignificant in my mind, as I was relegated to the "nerd" class of high school life. But everything changed my Senior year. For a variety of reasons, I was no longer "John," but "The Kwas." I made it to the popular crowd, gaining friends and influence. I would like to say I was growing spiritually, but that wasn't the case. My two best friends were Bry and Peck. We wanted to be friends for life—going to college together, etc. But the Lord had other plans. He moved me by two significant traumas (at least to my teenage heart).

Trauma #1: Sometime during my Senior year, my father informed me that he had no money to send me to college. I had received recruiting letters from dozens of colleges, due to a very high ACT score and GPA, and graduating third in my class. I remember mt Dad telling me: "There is no way you can go to college unless you get a significant scholarship," as he encouraged me to enroll in the local community college. In my academic pride, I took that as an insult. All my friends were going to some great regional Christian universities: Calvin College, Hope, Dordt, Moody. There was no way I was going to some "junior" college. Besides, I wanted to go to a Christian college, as that was in my comfort zone.

Trauma #2: My parents' marriage had hit rock bottom. They were either fighting or avoiding each other most of my Senior year. Both worked long hours, leaving my sister and I to care for our two younger brothers (also known as the "post-divorce kids"). It was driving me crazy. There is no way I could stomach another year at home. I prayed regularly for a way out. Truthfully, I stayed angry at God as well as my parents. I was not filled with hope, to stay the least. I resolved in my heart to not only go to a "real" college, but one far, far away from home. The regional Christian schools would just not do. In my wrath, I pinned a United States map on my bedroom wall and drew a "twelve-hour radius" circle around it. Any university had to be outside that circle to be in competition for my services. I wanted to make it impossible for my parents to just drop in and visit. Take that, Mom and Dad!

But let me rewind for a moment. Before "trauma #1" hit, I had applied to several Christian colleges, including Oral Roberts University, in Tulsa Oklahoma—also known as ORU. Why this university? The summer before my Senior year, my cousin Whitney got married to Mark, and they were attending, you guessed it, Oral Roberts University. Our family made that thirteen-hour drive from our home to Tulsa for the wedding. I fell in love. Not with a bridesmaid, but with the campus. It was gorgeous. It was Christian. And I knew nothing else. It was love at first sight. So, just for fun, I applied. But, of course, I couldn't afford it.

Back to my after-trauma period. A letter arrived from ORU in late spring, 1984. I thought it would be another acceptance letter, but it was much more than that. It notified me that I had received one of twenty "Presidential Scholarships". Four years, full ride. Free tuition and room and board. I was stunned. And it was outside the "circle of death" as I called it. Thirteen hours away. Wow. This had to be from the Lord, even though I certainly didn't deserve it. But He knew I needed it.

From my first day at ORU until my last, I journaled my life at the Christian University. It wasn't just a record of my thoughts and feelings, but a full accounting of my day-to-day experiences. Thankfully, after forty years, my written journals still exist. That means all that is included in this story is true. I would have liked to put myself in a better light, but what's the fun in that? God is the one who gives us our lives and directs our steps. Our choices are certainly our responsibility, yet God is sovereign over all. He is the One who writes the stories of our lives.

So, off we go to August 1984, and the life of just an ordinary Freshman at Oral Roberts University.

Contents

Tulsa, Oklahoma

August, 1984

Sunday, August 12, 1984

I arrived in Tulsa, Oklahoma at Oral Roberts University at about 6:00 pm, after a long drive with my parents from the south suburbs of Chicago. ORU is located at 7777 Lewis Avenue, a perfect Christian address for those who are into Bible numerology. After making a pass through the campus, we dropped our overnight bags in the hotel and headed off to my cousin's apartment. This was the same cousin (Whitney) who was married the year before to Mark—the wedding that brought me to Tulsa for the first time. Whitney and Mark welcomed mom and me into their home, while dad stayed at the hotel feeling sick to his stomach. We promptly went out to dinner and then on to an arcade.

One of my cousin's friends, Jeff, joined us. He was very cool, and he has been newly hired as a P.E. professor at ORU. I hoped he would be one of my teachers this year. Not knowing a single other freshman, I needed all the help I could get. When we finished at the arcade, I returned to Whitney and Mark's apartment for a game of Time Trivia. Mom went back to the hotel. Trivia would play a big part of my college education, which wasn't very scholarly of me-I just love useless information.

"You know you are welcome any time in our home," Whitney said. This was extremely comforting to an introverted nearly eighteen-year-old. "And, we need to go to Arizona to visit Grandma and Grandpa over Fall Break!"

Arizona. My happy place. Even since I was a youngster, we made a yearly pilgrimage to Scottsdale to visit my grandparents. Little did I know then that it would continue to play a significant role in my college life as well.

"I would love that. Maybe we could convince Wes to come along." Wes was Whitney's brother and my closest cousin. We were born ten days apart. Wes was supposed to come to ORU with me but changed his mind at the very last minute. As much as that disappointed me, it was probably a good thing.

Upon arrival back at the hotel, I learned that my mom and dad were at the hospital that was on the campus. Dad had become violently ill due to food poisoning.

"You won't believe what happened!" exclaimed Mom when she and dad walked into the hotel room. "Dad was miserable, totally nauseated and in pain. A doctor entered the room, checked him over, then laid hands on him and prayed. Dad immediately went into the bathroom, vomited several times, and felt so much better. Can you believe it?"

What kind of university hospital had doctors who prayed for you? I had a lot to learn about this place. But, so far, I loved everything about it.

Monday, August 13, 1984

First stop this morning: The Mabee Center, ORU's multi-purpose athletic facility. I would watch my fair share of basketball games here, as well as attend weekly chapel services, Sunday worship services, and Christian concerts. But today, it was a two and a half hour wait to register for classes. Yes, decades before the internet, we had to wait in line to physically register for classes. The one benefit of waiting in line was meeting people, especially freshmen girls. Lisa from Chicago and Kay from Texas were my favorites.

After registration, it was off to unpack my first dorm room, on the seventh floor of "The Towers". Our Tower was known as "Ed Hughes," named for a significant donor named Ed Hughes, I guess. I was very fortunate to be in a traditionally upperclassman dorm, and so was my freshman roommate, Gregg, from Colorado. Gregg and I got along great, right from the start. As an extreme extrovert, he was a great match for my more introverted nature.

It was finally time to say goodbye to my parents. Was it dishonoring to be happy they were leaving; and that it would be a long time until I saw them again? Probably. But I was ready to make my own way in a new state, new place, new setting, with all new people. And, besides, my parents needed to work on their marriage without me being in the middle of it.

Gregg and I immediately went to a picnic where we probably met nearly a hundred new students (the benefit of an extroverted roommate). Of course, both of us were most interested in the girls. And the best news of the day was that Gregg had a car, unlike me. That would come in handy.

After a stop off at the video game arcade on campus, it was back to the room to fix it up. A trio of upperclassmen stopped by: "Hi, my name is Chuck," said the very tall Junior. "I'm your R.A. This is our Academic Advisor, Darrel, and our Chaplain, Skip." This was my first introduction to student leaders. I hadn't ever heard of an R.A., and the thought of a student chaplain was intriguing to me. Skip actually seemed cool, rather than just a holy guy.

As we were winding down for the evening, Greg and I were invited down to Skip the Chaplain's room to play a game of Trivial Pursuit. Two days on campus, two games of trivia. This allowed me to meet three other freshmen on the floor: Steve, Joe, and Kerry. We played and talked and got to know each other long into the night. At this point, no one knew my real name—they all called me John. I'm "The Kwas!"

Tuesday, August 14, 1984

Picture this: Sixteen rooms in a circular floor layout. Two male students per room. So, our "wing" of the Ed Tower was made up of thirty-two college guys. And there was one large bathroom and showers in the center. It may sound like a recipe for disaster, but it seemed to work out pretty well. At least the dorm rooms themselves were very spacious. Like I said, these were not dorms typically inhabited by freshmen. I didn't know how fortunate I was until I visited other freshmen!

Before breakfast, Gregg and I signed up for flag football intramurals. Intramurals were a big part of dorm life at ORU. Being my first meal in the cafeteria, also known as Saga, meant the first time to adhere to the ORU dress code: button-down shirts and ties for the males, skirts for the females. We'll get back to that later. I was thankful that breakfast was rather tasty, since you always hear bad reports about cafeteria food. Being well-fed allowed me to make it through my very first chapel service which lasted over two hours. After much singing and preaching, all of us first year students were introduced to President Richard Roberts and all the department heads.

There was still much to be done to settle into my new life at ORU. We had to get our phone service set up (landlines, of course), post office box opened (this was way before email), and other logistical matters. I ran into Kay from Texas three different times, which was a pleasure. Yes, I was starting to get hooked. But, alas, having only been on two dates with two different girls in high school, I was not well-prepared to do anything about it.

The time after lunch afforded the opportunity to start writing letters to friends back home. I wrote a lot of letters that first year! Kerry from Arizona popped in for a visit.

"Hey, I wanted to come by and get to know you better. Most of all, I want to know about your relationship with the Lord."

Well, that was a first for me. I don't think any peer, even my best friends, ever started a conversation like that! Or, for that matter, ever asked about the "state of my soul." From that moment on, I made a heart commitment to strive to become more like Christ. And, as a corollary, a commitment to spend time with guys like Kerry, and his roommate, Joe. Up until this point, I had never met teenagers who were this serious about Jesus. I thought their sort of devotion was just for adults. Boy, was I wrong.

Kerry and I talked the afternoon away, continuing through dinner in the cafeteria. After a stopover at the arcade, I took a required reading comprehension test. Thankfully, it was very easy. Kay was there, so Kerry and I sat with her. She was so nice, which in my mental calculation would make her difficult to date. There

would be guys lining up to ask her out! I resolved to pray about it.
See, I was already becoming much more spiritual!

Later that night, I joined a bunch of guys for my first trip to "The Depot." This was our student center—a great place to hang out, eat, and get to know people. I met another girl from Texas named Gena. She was the first person whom I ever heard say: "mash the button" when telling me to push the elevator button. So much fun for this Chicago boy! But I had to learn not to stay up so late with my roommate because...

Wednesday, August 15, 1984.

We overslept. We way overslept. We missed wing devotions. We missed breakfast. And we almost missed academic registration. The long line of registration three days prior was only the preliminary stuff. Gregg and I had to rush over to the Mabee Center to get all our first semester classes. And, this was the day I had to declare a major. Declare a major? I wasn't ready for that. I had no idea! I landed on Computer Science. Why, Computer Science?

1. I loved playing video games.
2. I loved my Apple II computer.
3. I was really good at math.

Sounds reasonable, right?

After bumping into Gena and wondering if she were the real Texan I should pursue, it was back to the cafeteria and then the arcade. Boy, I needed to have actual classes begin soon! I was still lacking my required meeting with a Computer Science professor to sign off on my classes, so back and forth I went to find him. Thankfully, he finally became available and I was squared away in time for dinner. This was the day that the upperclassmen were all moving in, making campus much, much busier. All told, we would have nearly 5,000 students this year!

The evening began with an English placement test, allowing me to meet even more new freshmen. From there, it was my first visit to Howard Auditorium, a multipurpose building for smaller worship services, concerts, and performances. That night was my first movie night: *The Hiding Place.* I was familiar with the story, but glad to watch the movie. This was my first chance to sit with members of our sister wing. ORU in 1984 didn't have sororities or fraternities. In its place, we had brother and sister wings. So, our seventh floor Ed Tower wing was matched with a ladies seventh floor Evelyn Tower wing. Thirty-two guys and thirty-two girls.

The night ended with a meeting of a half dozen of us in Room 714 to discuss our wing name. Each year, every wing had to come up with their own name. Many dorm wings on campus had legacy names that were used year after year. Not ours. Ideas flew around for what seemed hours, with none landing. Off to bed, only to be awakened by Gregg, coming in very late after a date. He skipped half the movie and went dancing with a girl. Oh, and at ORU, dancing was strictly prohibited.

Thursday, August 16, 1984

Thankfully, I got up on time today, no thanks to Gregg who snored away. I made it on time to breakfast and then wing devotions, led by Skip the Chaplain. Afterwards, all freshmen went to a study skills seminar. You would think that first year college students would already have study skills. But I guess college is different. The one tip that stood out to me: If you are a good student, you can get all of your classes and studies into an 8:00 to 5:00 time slot. That sounded good to me! But, was it realistic?

After Kerry, Joe, and I walked a couple of girls back to their dorm (quite the gentlemen), it was time for my first trip to the campus bookstore. There is nothing quite like getting new textbooks (said the book nerd). Rather than talking about books, however, our topic of conversation always seemed to return to girls. Unfortunately, the three of us liked the same ones already.

"Why don't you ask her out?" I asked Kerry.

"Why don't you?" asked Joe.

"Really, why don't you?" I asked.

"Maybe I will," we all thought while shaking our heads. Riveting boy-talk, don't you think?

Later that afternoon, I made my first trip to the Athletic Center. I was scheduled to take my first yearly college physical.

Now, why would that be a university requirement? Well, ORU's motto was: "Educating the whole person: Spirit, Soul, and Body." In order to "educate" our bodies, we were required to have a benchmark of physical health each year. We were weighed, our body fat was measured, and blood tests were taken. The best part was: if it was deemed that you were overweight, you were put on a special diet and exercise program. At least that's what I heard; I was always underweight! Should I have been bothered by this intrusion into the privacy of my physical body? Or, should I have understood that having a healthy body connects to a healthy mind and soul?

Since I had to wait for almost three hours to finish at the Athletic Center, I missed dinner. This was a cardinal sin in my book. Famished, Gregg the roommate and I went to a mandatory meeting with the Dean of Men. All new male students were told all the rules for life on a Christian university campus. And there were a lot of them. Most were okay, but I wasn't too fond of "No R-rated movies" or the midnight curfew. But, being a law-keeper, I dedicated myself to obedience. I was also scared of the punishments.

I met the guys at the Depot for a little talk about the more oppressive ORU rules, followed by a wing meeting with Chuck the R.A. After meeting all the upperclassman, I still think the Arizona guys, Kerry and Joe, are the coolest of the group. A trip back to the Depot meant more time to talk about important things—this time:

religion. Joe and I had the best conversation, even though we came from decidedly different Christian backgrounds. He was serious about his faith. I wasn't quite sure what to make of the more "Charismatic" Christianity it seemed most people practiced here. What would "educating the whole person" look like when it comes to our faith?

At this point I was satisfied to play Trivial Pursuit long into the night (I should say, to the early morning).

Oh, by the way, I did get my hair cut today. Believe it or not, that was very important act in the eyes of the ORU administration.

Friday, August 17, 1984

Last week day before classes begin! So, how did it start for me? Sleeping in until 11:00 am and a late, late breakfast with the brothers (guys from the wing). I loved thinking of thirty-one other guys as brothers in the Lord. What to do on my last weekday before classes commenced? Relax, of course. And ask my roommate to run me to the store for laundry detergent. That might come in handy. After a game of tennis with Joe, it was off to dinner with Kerry. It's amazing how fast your first friend group appears in college. Would it hold together for four years (and beyond)?

One of the fun things of Saga for me happened at the end of this week. Almost every dorm wing took time to clump several tables together to form their own "reserved" dining area. You weren't required to eat with your wing brothers and sisters, but it was sure handy to have a place to belong. It also allowed you to get to know one another throughout the year. I resolved to be at our table clump like clockwork, three times a day!

Friday night movie night was also a regular aspect of ORU campus life. Tonight's feature: "The Cross and the Switchblade". Would we only watch Christian movies on campus? If not, I knew that an R-rated feature was not in the cards. A couple of tenth floor girls "adopted" Joe, Kerry, and I for this first year. They introduced us to the Prayer Gardens. And, while you may be understandably suspicious that something more physical went on here, we actually went there to talk and pray! We even sang same some songs together. On a Friday night!

"You need to find your life verse, " shared one of the Junior girls. "You will be amazed how God will use it to form the calling in your life. Just pray and pray, asking Him to show it to you."

Life verse? Weren't all the verses in the Bible important for your life? It wouldn't be long until the Lord directed me to mine. But, before that, there was something more important for Gregg to show me. He had bought three fish for our room: Doug, Bob, and Fred. No female fish allowed. And, Skip the Chaplain had even bigger news for us. He proposed that our wing name be "Club Hawaiian". Coolest name ever. So much more vital for our lives than finding a life verse, right? All I knew after this time in the prayer gardens was: I needed to recommit my life to Christ. Nothing else mattered.

Saturday, August 18, 1984

Today was my first opportunity to hear from our founder, Oral Roberts. He was no longer the president of the university, but this famous evangelist was still actively involved in campus life. He preached for almost an hour, and I hung on every word. The main message was: Be hot or cold, but never lukewarm. This resonated with where I was just a few days before my eighteenth birthday. I wanted to be filled with the Spirit like Oral was. But what did I need to do to get there?

After lunch, we headed back to the Mabee Center for a second message from Dr. Roberts. This time, our large group of wing brothers scored third row seats! It was better than a rock concert. Great singing by the ORU praise team, and another convicting message by our founder. It seemed to me that some great things were coming in the life of this university.

Tennis and the arcade were on tap for the late afternoon. Then a trip to the Depot for more late-evening food and fellowship. I was still meeting new people, while keeping my eye on the girls that we all seem to like. Gena, the tall girl from Texas, did just happen to sit next to me. Of course, that meant something to me (which she probably didn't intend). Upon return to my room, Gregg the roommate could only talk about Angie, now on their fourth date already. Would I have one date after four months here? God only knows...

Sunday, August 19, 1984

One of the many rules of life at this Christian university was to honor the Sabbath day by keeping it holy (Exodus 20:8). In practicality, this meant a requirement to attend a church of your choice every Sunday morning. How could an academic institution make sure that over five thousand students went to church every Sunday? Simple. By locking down all the dorms at 10:00 a.m. and reopening them at noon. The R.A.s had the tasking of clearing everyone out of their rooms. But how does that actually ensure that I will go to church?

Several of us met in the Fishbowl (the glassed enclosed space between boy's and girl's Tower dorms). We piled into Gena's car and headed to Grace Fellowship Church. It was a great service, even though I was not used to it running just over two hours. That was a lot of singing! After a quick pre-lunch nap, Kerry and I headed over to the cafeteria for lunch, followed by a phone call from Dad. I didn't call home much, since I didn't want to hear about the regular conflict between my parents. I was enjoying my thirteen-hour drive buffer.

A beautiful, but hot, August afternoon in Tulsa called for another game of tennis with Joe and Kerry, followed by the weekly washing of the clothes ritual. About 4:00, a girl from our sister wing called Gregg and me asking to move a bunk bed up to her room. Did I mention already that boys were not allowed in the girl's dorms? Well, we weren't—which meant we had to get special permission. It felt sort of naughty being in the sister wing, even though it wasn't like what you see in movies about college dorms.

After our usual trek to Saga, followed by the arcade at the Depot, a few of us headed back to the dorm. This was the first time I met Cheryl from Illinois, my home state. She and Todd (another wing brother) and I went back to the Depot and visited for a while, joined shortly afterwards by Gena and her roommate, Joanna.

"What's your name?" Cheryl asked.

"John Kwasny. What's yours?"

"I'm Cheryl. Has anyone every called you Kwas?"

Yes! Maybe she is the one! Just kidding. Was I going to fall for a girl that quickly, just because she called me by my real name? We will have to see—but, at least, Cheryl said she would meet me for breakfast tomorrow!

Monday, August 20, 1984

First day of classes! I bounced out of bed at 6:30, making it to breakfast at 7:15, only to learn that Cheryl had eaten and run to an early class. This was not a good start to my true first week of Freshman year. But, putting my game face on, I hustled on to my 7:50 class: Introduction to Computing. Scanning the faces of my fellow students, this already looked like a boring group. What was especially discouraging was that I didn't know a single soul—no one from my new circle of friends or my dorm brothers or sisters.

But my day quickly improved in my 8:50 class: Humanities. I sat next to the "Georgia girls" Michelle and Jenny, from my sister wing. They are so funny. I wasn't quite sure what Humanities was all about, but it looked pretty interesting. After a discussion class, Jenny and I walked back to the Towers dorm. After killing some time watching my small color television, it was already time for lunch.

When I had free time in the afternoons, I made a regular habit of writing letters (as well as checking my post office box for mail). I received a letter today from one of my two best friends from high school: Bryan. Bryan had decided to work after high school, not sure if he wanted to go to college. It was good to hear from him. I wrote a letter to Randy, another long-time childhood friend who was still in high school. I also dropped notes to Kay and Cheryl (there was a note box in each dorm lobby for intra-dorm communication).

As I discovered a few days earlier, physical fitness was a requirement at Oral Roberts University. One system designed to ensure physical health was the accumulation of "aerobic points." Each semester, every student had to earn a certain amount of these activity points. You received points for running, working out, playing a sport, etc. One sport that netted a bunch of aerobic points was tennis. So, I played tennis with two different groups of guys before dinner and after dinner today. We all were given cards to keep track of our points, on the Christian honor system, of course.

My regular evening at the Depot was uneventful until 10:00, when Cheryl walked in with another guy. They sat down in a booth across from my group. At first, I tried to ignore her, but then I gave an awkward wave. Fighting back depressed feelings, I kept peeking over there. It didn't seem like she was having a good time, but who knew? Trudging back to the dorm, I took a look into the note box, and to my amazement, there was a note from Cheryl! To my nearly teenage eyes, it seemed as though she sort of likes me. With a bounce in my step, I arrived at our 11:00 wing meeting. I didn't hear a word that was said. A good first real day of college!

Tuesday, August 21, 1984

My Tuesday classes began at 7:50 with English Comp 1 and 8:50 with Old Testament Survey. How could a professor make the Bible anymore boring? At 9:50, I had my first Oral Communication class. As an introvert, I was not looking forward to this required class. I steadfastly avoided speech class in high school for a reason! I barely made it to class anyway, since the campus was a challenge to learn. I should have searched for my classrooms last week.

My first chapel of the week was our yearly responsibility to sign the Honor Code. The ORU chaplain read through it page by page, emphasizing the things that would get us expelled from the university. It may have been intimidating to many, but to a rule-keeper, I wasn't really worried. Much of it just seemed sort of nit-picky and hard to enforce. But I appreciated the high standard being set. After chapel, the entire student body emptied out into the Mabee Center parking lot for a group picture. I think I had my eyes closed.

The afternoon was my first opportunity to begin studying and doing homework. While some students made the library their study destination, I found it too quiet to concentrate. I always thrived among distractions—other people, television, or music. After attempting to study in my room, I headed to the Fishbowl. There, I could people-watch as well as read. But that proved to be a disastrous mistake. Kay from Texas came up to me and acted like we were the best of friends. She really was just using me to do a favor for her—to go upstairs and get a message to the guy she really liked named Bill. And, of course, like her pet sheep, I did it. That's it for me and Kay—we're finished.

After dinner, Kerry, Kyle and I ran into Cheryl. Thankfully, Kerry and Kyle had decided to go a different way back to the dorm, leaving Cheryl and me to walk alone to the post office. We both found out we passed our English Placement Test (Yay, no remedial English). I have no idea where the courage came from, but I used the opportunity to ask Cheryl out. My first college date! The conversation went something like this:

"Since we both passed out tests, why don't we celebrate?"

"Sounds great! What do you want to do?"

"How about we go to the Depot to hang out? And then get married."

Alright, so I didn't say that last part, but I probably thought it. So, we met at the Depot and had a long, get-to-know-you conversation. I learned three very important things about Cheryl from Illinois that night:

1. She didn't go to R-rated movies. Ever.

2. She didn't listen to secular rock music. Ever.

3. She didn't really do anything wrong. Ever.

I felt both amazement by her level of Christianity and condemnation regarding the status of my own. I saw R-rated movies all the time. I loved rock music. But I saw myself so much holier than most of my peers from my Christian high school. Another remarkable characteristic was that she prayed all the time. All the time! I tried my best to keep a good game face on as I walked her back to her dorm just before curfew. How could I like someone who is also way too Christian for me? How terrible am I?

Wednesday, August 22, 1984

This was a mind-boggling day (probably a spiritual hangover from the night before). After my morning classes and breakfast, I got a very nice note from Kay. Kay? Why would I care, after what she had done to me! But I did care. What hurt my head more was a huge argument I got into that morning with Todd, my wing brother from Illinois. No, it wasn't about a girl—it was about secular rock music and Christianity. Just like Cheryl, he claimed you can't be a good Christian and listen to rock music. Music was designed for worship, and we should use it to worship Jesus, not the world. While he had good points, I was not ready to give up my 70s and 80s rock music collection. I had brought a huge box of cassettes with me to ORU and I wasn't about to be disloyal to them!

The afternoon was a mixture of letter writing to friends back home and studying. A visit to the post office rendered four birthday cards from the family (my birthday is tomorrow)! After a quick phone call from Cheryl, I went to dinner with Kerry. Kay sat with us at our wing table. I just don't know what to think anymore. What is God doing to my mind? Time at the Depot should have cleared up my boggled thoughts, but it didn't really help at all. Even talking to Tina and Michelle, some of our Junior wing sisters, didn't provide any relief from my torment.

At 8:30, I met Cheryl to go to Vespers for our second date. I had no idea what this was. I came to discover that Wednesday evening vespers was a time of prayer, singing, and worship led by students in the chapel. Truthfully, it was a real struggle for me to sit through it. I resolved to never go back. The way they did communion was weird too. I felt so out of place, like everyone knew I was some sort of pseudo-Christian imposter. I was really getting scared, so I cut the date off early and walked Cheryl back to her dorm.

"I'll pray for you!" Cheryl said as I turned and walked away. Pray for me? That hurt my pride. But I guess I needed her to. Could I be lost when I thought I was already found?

Thursday, August 23, 1984

My eighteenth birthday! But I did not wake up in a birthday-ing mood. Thursday morning classes meant more English Comp. 1, O.T. Survey, and Oral Comm. Chapel didn't help my mood, as I continued to wrestle with God about the state of my soul. It was a small solace that most everyone I bumped into wished me happy birthday. And I received a birthday package from home, as well as a phone call from my mom. Cheryl also called and said we needed to talk. So we planned a third date after dinner.

We went back to the Depot again (don't forget: I don't have a car). Cheryl gave me a birthday card and we talked for a couple of hours. Her words really started to convict me. She challenged me to give up worldly things. At one level, it was really depressing; but at another, I was feeling God move on my stubborn heart. I had heard about a girl practicing "missionary" dating, but I never thought it would happen to me. After all, I was a Christian at a Christian university—not some drug addict member of a biker gang! But for the first time, I was praying about the things Cheryl shared with me about the Christian life. I even thanked God for sending her to me. But at this point, it seemed that Cheryl was just meant to be a good friend—a very godly sister to me. Thankfully, I think she is actually glad to know me too.

After walking Cheryl back to her dorm, I went to mine. It was time for nightly devotions with Skip the Chaplain. For the first time, I got something out of it. I was even asked to close in prayer, which was a first for me. The guys hung out and celebrated my birthday with me late into the evening, giving me a card signed by all thirty-one of them. Maybe the Lord was redeeming my birthday—or even beginning something new in my heart and soul. I went to bed at 1:00 am, hoping and praying for a new life.

Friday, August 24, 1984

Last day of my first week of college, as well as my first look at Pascal in "Intro to Computing." Pascal? This was a pretty popular computer language system in the 1980's. I was lost from the beginning. And, it didn't help that it was a 7:50 a.m. class. At 8:50, I had my first Health-Fitness class with Jeff—yes, the same Jeff whom I first met at my cousin's apartment. It was nice to have a professor that knew my name. Joanna, one of my sister wingmates, was in the class, so we walked back to our dorm together afterwards. We had a great conversation about Christianity. It was beginning to be easier for me to talk about.

That afternoon, our wing, now named "Lifeguard" played our first pre-season intramural flag football game. I was learning very quickly how intramural sports were such a big part of dorm life. We beat one of the EMR dorms 12-0. We were awesome. A non-athlete like myself still dreams about being a real athlete once in a while. On the way back to the dorms, I ran into Cheryl and had a nice, but short conversation.

Friday nights would become a challenge for me. Many of the guys on our wing had dates on Fridays. Some others went out dancing or drinking, against ORU policies. It got really quiet on the floor those nights. I tried to find someone to go to the movie on campus, but it didn't work out. Somehow, I ended up getting into a big argument with a brother named Steve. This time, the argument was about Oral Roberts, the big man himself! Steve seemed to know things about him that I didn't—but I defended Chancellor Roberts like he was a member of my family. I just saw him as an amazing man of God!

Thankfully, at 10:30, Tina from the sister wing called to invite me and a few other lonely guys to go out for pie. Nothing can make a boring Friday night better than pie. I tried to talk with Tina and Cindy (her roommate) all I could. They were fun Junior girls who were nice enough to be true big sisters.

Saturday, August 25, 1984

Saturday morning in college means sleeping in. At least it did for me. The first event of the day began at noon in the Fishbowl, with my (official) fourth date with Cheryl. We joined Gregg (the roommate) and his new girlfriend (also named Cheryl) for a trip to the local shopping mall. Thankfully, we separated as couples once we got there, making the afternoon much better in my book. But, sadly, I was already starting to lose interest in Cheryl. Why? I have no idea. My fickle young heart didn't know what it wanted—and it certainly was yet to be decidedly focused on what God wanted for me.

After some late afternoon study, a large group of brothers and sisters loaded up in cars and went to see the movie, "Romancing the Stone." I was fortunate enough to sit next to Cindy, one of the two Junior girls from our sister wing. Cindy was silly, a music major, and just easy to talk to. After the movie, a bunch of us went to a surprise birthday party for another sister. When you have thirty-two guys and thirty-two girls, you are always celebrating something!

At 10:00, Kerry and I met Gena and Joanna at the Depot. We talked for a while, then took a long walk around campus. ORU is really a beautiful place, especially at night. We returned to the Depot and shared a pizza. Like college students of all recent generations, we ate a lot of late-night pizza at ORU.

The night ended back in the dorms, chatting with several brothers. Right before bed, I was elected to be this year's social chairman of the wing. Me? Shouldn't that job be reserved for someone way more extroverted than me? I guess nobody else wanted it. I took the job, not quite knowing what I was in for. It was the first of many times I agreed to do something that inwardly scared me to death.

Sunday, August 26, 1984

When you don't have a car in college, your options are very limited when it comes to church on Sunday. Today, Joe, Kerry, and I went to something called "wing church" with members of the Towers Tenth Floor. It was an outdoor praise and prayer service combined with frisbee and hot dogs. My kind of church! But was this really best for my young spiritual life?

Sunday afternoon was time for more doubles tennis, already doing a great job keeping up with our aerobics points. After a short time of study, it was off to dinner at Saga. Cheryl called and we talked a bit, and my dad checked in as well. One of the most interesting conversations of the day was with Tina, who was a social work major, and the Social Director for our sister wing. She had to do some research for a project that made me think that her major was much cooler than computer science.

Later that night, Tina and Cindy and a few of us ended up at Burger King, another popular light night spot for us college students. It was amazing how many hamburgers you could get for a couple of bucks!

Monday, August 27, 1984

The alarm always rang early on Monday mornings. I was already becoming less interested in my Intro to Computing class, which is a bad sign for a computer science major. Even Humanities was more interesting at this point. My first semester meal routine was starting to crystalize: breakfast at 7:30, lunch at noon, and dinner at 5:30. My fellow wingmates claimed they were beginning to set their watches by my eating habits.

After lunch, it was post office time, where I was greeted by letters from Dad and my grandma, with money in the envelopes from both of them (belated birthday cash). Since I had yet to find (or even seek) a job, the gift of money was always a welcome sight. After some necessary studying, Gregg agreed to cut my hair. Every month at ORU, the men had to go to "hair check." According to the rules, our hair could not touch our collars (with a tie on). This was a challenge to those of us with short necks! So, I was glad Gregg was willing to give me a trim once in a while (for no charge).

Tina gave me a call that afternoon. As respective Social Chairmen of our wings, we had regular planning to do! Another walk to the post office gave me even more late birthday cards—this time from my best buddies from high school, Bry and Peck. They even sent me a Sammy Hagar cassette, which was so great; but, it also struck a bit at my conscience.

Back in my room, there was a knock at my door. It was Skip the Chaplain.

"Hey, I've got a question for you. Would you be one of my small group leaders?" Skip asked.

Small group leader? Wasn't being Social Chairman enough?

"Sure, I guess so."

Here again, I agreed to do something that scared me to death on the inside. What was God doing?

"Thanks! You'll be great."

So, that night at our wing meeting, I made my first official announcements as Social Chairman. And, I was announced as a small group leader, even though I didn't know what that entailed either. I closed the day watching Late Night with David Letterman, when I should have been reading my Bible. And spending time in prayer. I have a long way to go.

Tuesday, August 28, 1984

English Comp. 1. O.T. Survey. Oral Comm. Nothing new to see here—except in Oral Comm class. I had to give my first speech! No wonder I didn't sleep well last night. Sure, it was only a three-minute speech, but I was as nervous as I have ever been. At this point, I could never see myself as having any future in the public speaking arena. Sitting in chapel afterwards just confirmed my lack of desire to stand up and talk to any group, large or small.

But one thing I didn't mind doing was planning our first big social event for our brother and sister wings: Big Splash Waterpark. I wasn't the best at making posters, but mine would do for a bunch of guys. It was actually nice to have a "job" (non-paying) in my dorm, even if I wasn't the most social of social directors. The rest of the afternoon was a mingling of study, letter writing, a phone call with Cheryl, and relaxation. I was beginning to master the art of the fifteen-minute power nap too.

Later that evening, I enjoyed yet another visit with Tina and her roommate, Cindy. Tina and I mapped out our wing social plans for the semester. At 9:00, I attended my first small group leader's meeting. I have to say, it was pretty exciting. I sat with Cheryl, which made me feel much more secure about this new role. The question rolling around in my mind was, "Would I be spiritual enough to lead a small group Bible study?"

Wednesday, August 29, 1984

At this point, I was settling into a good routine. Even though I was still staying up too late, I was glad to have to get up each morning. Many of my wingmates were happy to stay away from morning classes in order to sleep in. This morning, I had a gap in my schedule to do some laundry. Unfortunately, I washed my meal ticket! Always check your pockets, right? Your meal ticket was necessary to eat in the cafeteria. You had three punches each day, every day, each semester. How would I eat now? Chuck the R.A. was no help.

Before I talked my way into the cafeteria for dinner with my sad story of a washed ticket, it was time for our first official flag football game. We were blanked, 14-0. So much for thinking we were great! After dinner, Kyle and I made our regular trip to the Depot. It was always the best place to see people, and by that I mean: girls. Back to the dorm for a phone call, then a return trip to the Depot. Kerry, Gena, Joanna and I had yet another great conversation about school and life.

I finally landed on my life verse! After regular attempts of flipping through my Bible, one passage just stuck out to me like it was highlighted with a bright yellow marker. I'm not sure what it will mean for me, but here it is...

Galatians 6:9–10

9 And let us not grow weary of doing good, for in due season we will reap, if we do not give up. 10 So then, as we have opportunity, let us do good to everyone, and especially to those who are of the household of faith.

Thursday, August 30, 1984

After English Comp. 1, I obtained my new, crisp, meal ticket. What a relief! I had already become quite dependent on the cafeteria. That was pretty much the highlight of my day. Every day can't be earthshattering and life altering, right? As I was getting into the meat of my semester, I was becoming more serious about studying. Kerry and I studied together most of the afternoon. Michelle and I studied Spanish together later that night. Have I mentioned Spanish class yet? It was quickly becoming my favorite class. I really liked learning languages.

Friday, August 31, 1984

My body had become programmed to wake up at 7:00 am every weekday morning. Today was no exception. Intro to Computing (Pascal) at 7:50 was still a class I didn't enjoy so early. So, after a conversation with Joanna, I walked over to the registrar office and dropped the class. Boy, was that liberating! So, what would I do about the fact that I was a Computer Science major? No time to worry about that, as I had an important tennis match with Kyle to make sure I had enough aerobic points this week.

After dinner, it was time for our first big social event: Big Splash! The water slides and the lazy river were fun and relaxing. It was great to have social time with our brothers and sisters (especially Tina and Cindy).

From there, it was late night pizza at Mazzio's, one of the most popular pizza joint for ORU students. But the fun didn't end there, as many of us ended up back at the Depot. The only frustrating thing about this first social event was my roommate, Gregg. He didn't even attempt to show up for any of it. He is starting to get on my nerves. But what could I do about it (I was not the confrontational type of guy.)

September, 1984

Saturday, September 1, 1984

Hello September! Saturday mornings were definitely for sleeping in (sorry, Mom—I know you raised me better than that). Waking up at 11:30 meant eating breakfast for lunch at Saga. I appreciated the extensive cafeteria cereal bar on days like this, that's for sure. I also enjoyed a quiet afternoon in the dorm which allowed me to catch up on my studies.

The Saturday night movie showing on campus was "The Wiz." Kerry and I double-dated with Gena and her roommate, Joanna. To clarify, it wasn't technically a double date, since we were all just good friends. But I enjoyed thinking that one of the girls may enjoy my company. Since Gena had a car, we ended up at Taco Bueno after the movie. Nothing better than late night tacos. The evening ended with a brief stroll around the City of Faith, our campus medical center. It was a pretty romantic site at night. But no romance happened for us.

Sunday, September 2, 1984

The third Sunday morning on campus for me meant a third different church experience. This morning, I went to Asbury Methodist Church with Kyle, Scott, and Joe. This was my first time at a United Methodist worship service. It was pretty dull, with a lightweight sermon. Crossed that one off my potential church home list.

While the university administration preached the necessity of Sunday morning worship, it was fairly mute about honoring the rest of the Sabbath day. So, that meant a guilt-free afternoon of watching NFL football.

After dinner, I spent an hour and a half on the phone with Cheryl. Even though I don't know what I think about her (yet), this was one of our better conversations as of late. Later in the evening, it was time for a wing brother-sister Trivial Pursuit game in the Towers Fishbowl. My team won! The night ended with a trip to Burger King followed by small group meeting at 11:45 pm. I'm just not sure how effective small group time is so late at night!

Monday, September 3, 1984
The highlight to this Monday was our first victory in intramural flag football! That mindless fun was followed by an evening at the Depot with Cheryl. As much as I tried again to avoid it, she loved pulling me into yet another deep, Christian conversation. I still couldn't keep up with her. Did the Christian life have to be this hard? Did I really have to figure out what I believed? Did she have to analyze everything we were supposed to (or not supposed to) do? As I walked around the wing early into the

next morning getting information on my wing mates (official Social Director duty), my thoughts kept on racing.

Tuesday, September 4, 1984

Chapel at ORU was quickly becoming a highlight for me during Freshman year. We had assigned seating with our sister wing, which was enjoyable. But more than the social aspect, the speakers were pretty interesting. Today, it was time to hear again from our Chancellor himself, the one and only, Oral Roberts. His topic was anger; specifically, anger with God. But one thing he said didn't sit well with me:

"When you find yourself angry at God, the solution is that you need to forgive God. He's a big boy...He can handle your anger. Forgiving God is the only way to overcome your anger towards Him," Dr. Roberts said

Forgive God? That just sounded sort of blasphemous to me. But what were you supposed to do when you were angry at God? Personally, I just pouted.

That afternoon, Tina and I met in the fishbowl and worked on posters for our next social event. Yes, posters are what we Social Directors do. After that, it was time to clean my room. No, I wasn't a clean freak—it was our dorm's first open house at 6:30! Every so often, our dorm rooms were open to anyone, most notably girls (since they were not allowed in the boys' dorm—and vice versa). Cheryl, Jennifer, Tina, Cindy, Gena, and Joanna all came by for a visit. I'm not quite sure what the theory was behind open house, but it may have simply been to motivate us to clean our rooms every so often.

At 8:30, it was time for the girls' dorms open house. Our usual group of guys visited all the girls who visited us, along with extra stops to see Kay, Michelle, and Jamie. I'm not entirely sure why, but it was all sort of depressing. A late-night visit to the Depot cheered me up, including a good visit with Gena. It appears that my best bud Kerry and Gena are getting closer and closer. They make a good pair. When would I find my better half?

Wednesday, September 5, 1984

I made my first return trip to Vespers tonight. This time, I went with a group of brothers and sisters, which made it more tolerable. It just seems like a time to sing emotional songs, raise your hands, and act like everything is wonderful. I wasn't feeling it. I couldn't quite shake my depression.

Thursday, September 6, 1984

Little did I know this would be such a monumental day when I awoke at 7:00 a.m. I received an A on my first English Comp paper (no, that isn't what I am referring to). It happened at small group meeting. In this Christian college culture, our small groups were light on Bible study and heavy on singing and prayer. This particular meeting was more emotionally moving than the others.

Then it happened. "Do you want to speak in tongues?' Scott asked.

"I guess so...I've never done it before," I responded.

"Just open your mouth and start making noises. It's like priming a pump. Then the angelic tongues will come."

I began speaking in tongues! As it was explained to me later, I had received my "prayer language." Up until this point, I thought my prayer language was English. But real prayer was done in an angelic language, straight from the Holy Spirit. This was totally new to me. Whatever was really going on, it certainly made me feel much less depressed! I wanted to tell Cheryl about it, but she was unavailable. On a separate note, I was becoming more and more irritated with Gregg, the roommate. Hopefully, I was praying for him in my new tongue.

Friday, September 7, 1984

After a morning of PE class, a long nap (speaking in tongues must be exhausting) and some studying, I finally had a long phone conversation with Cheryl. She was thrilled about my new spiritual experience. So was I. Sadly, the afternoon ended with another flag football loss. I know, it shouldn't matter. But it does.

At 9:00 that night Joe and I went with Tina and Cindy to the movie "Dreamscape." Those girls seem to be all about fun all the time. We went out for nachos and turtle pie afterwards.

Back at the dorm, I was forced to listen to Gregg and Kyle talk all about the "big dance" that they went to....the big against-the-rules, underground dance. Yet another reason to be irritated with him. As I put my head on the pillow, I had the following thoughts:

1. I am very angry with Greg's moral standards.
2. I am sort of angry with my own moral standards.
3. What do I do with Cheryl?
4. How great are Tina and Cindy—all good clean fun, all the time.
5. What about Kay? Never.
6. What about Gena? If Kerry wasn't my best friend...
7. What does it mean to be filled with the Spirit?
8. What a mess I am!

Saturday, September 8, 1984

The only thing that got me up early on a Saturday was a 10:00 flag football game. We lost again. Our wing is not full of athletes, to say the least. Missing the chance to sleep all morning just meant sleeping most of the afternoon. Was I sleeping just to avoid the big questions of my life?

When I woke up (again), I called Laura, one of our sister wing Juniors, and asked her out. Unfortunately, she had plans. I called Mechelle (just realized that she spelled her name with an "e") but she couldn't go out either. Third try: Cheryl (my safety valve). But, she had a date! Three strikes and I was a lonely college student for Saturday night.

I guess the Lord had better plans for my evening. One of the benefits of a Christian university is the free Christian concerts that were scheduled throughout the school year. I knew nothing about Christian Contemporary Music (CCM), since all my love and devotion was given to secular rock and pop music. On this night, Mylon LeFevre and Broken Heart plus Scott Wesley Brown were on campus. Todd, Cindy and I went together, getting in free thanks to wingmates who oversaw security. The concert went from 8:00 to midnight! It was awesome! I never knew Christian music could be so cool. My favorite Mylon song was "Trains up in the Sky" from his new album. This was the catchiest part:

Get up, try and find a way

We will find a way today

You, try and find a way

Get up, trains up in the sky

Sit down, listen to the sound

Fill up, stand on holy ground

Look up, the trains up in the sky

Maybe I should let God direct my plans more often...

Sunday, September 9, 1984

Fourth Sunday morning; fourth different church experience. Since so many students didn't have cars, the university allowed a church to meet on campus at the Mabee Center (our athletic center). It was interesting going to Victory Church that met on the floor of our basketball auditorium. The pastor was a former

ORU student. It felt like a chapel service and a basketball game at the same time. But it was certainly nice to get to walk to church and then to lunch.

My Sunday afternoon was given to NFL football and multiple calls back home to family and friends. I was glad to re-connect with folks in my pre-college life. It's so easy to make college life your entire life, disconnecting from all else. Or at least it was for me. In the evening, it was time for another meeting with Tina about social events. Study time and fellowship at the Depot ended the day.

Monday, September 10, 1984

Another day, another flag football loss. News of the day: Laura and Jennifer are my secret sisters. I'm not sure what that means.

Tuesday, September 11, 1984

Another English Comp paper, another A. I wonder what I could do with an English major? After some afternoon homework, I went with Stacy and Todd to shop for our secret sisters. I guess it was a good tradition to give gifts to one another secretly. On the schedule for this evening was another open house at another dorm on the other side of campus. Steve (another wingmate) and I went to visit Joanna and Amy. It was uneventful.

I found out today that my job as social director entailed helping the guys deliver their secret sister gifts to the sister wing. Another one of the duties not in my original job description was helping struggling students with their homework. This was a skill I brought from high school, as The Kwas was well-known for helping students (mainly athletes) pass their exams. At my high school graduation, there were several parents who thanked me for enabling their child to graduate. So, my legacy as "unpaid tutor" continued at ORU. I really didn't mind.

At 10:00, I called Laura (one of my secret sisters) and asked her to the upcoming Sandi Patti concert. Amazingly, she said YES! But, the tone of her voice made me feel like she was reluctantly acquiescing. A hesitant date is better than no date, right? Just past midnight, I delivered secret sister gifts to my counterpart, Tina. Unfortunately, I had not yet bought my own gifts.

Wednesday, September 12, 1984

After morning classes, Kerry and I went to the store to take care of gifts for our secret sisters. I bought $20 worth of posters, teddy bears, and books. Afterwards, Gregg went out and bought my tickets for the Sandi Patty concert—reluctantly (I was sensing a trend here). In the evening, I spent an hour on the phone catching up with Cheryl. I'm still unsure about how I feel about her.

More importantly, I engaged in the first prank of my college career. It was on Steve, one of the more annoying brothers on our wing. Kyle and I wrote a note to a girl he liked and put it in the dorm note box. Steve asked her to marry him. Classic, right? After gleefully dropping off the note, we headed to Vespers. Yes, I know, that seems incongruous. I did confess and repent, though. The night ended with doing my job of gathering more secret sister gifts and delivering them to Tina.

Thursday, September 13, 1984

It's the one-month anniversary of my life at ORU! Time flies when you're having fun! Unfortunately, Amy (the girl Steve likes) found out that I sent the prank note. She officially hates me. So, off to chapel and more repentance. It's really hard to know if I was more of a child or becoming an adult.

The evening started with helping Scott with his homework, followed by yet another girls' dorm open house. This is the dorm where Cheryl, Jennifer, Gena, and Joanna lived—so visited all of them. I don't know what it is about these open houses, but they bum me out.

After a trip back to the dorm, Kyle and I went to the Depot until 10:30. We met Gena and Joanna there. Then, it was time to gather more secret sister gifts and drop them off with Tina. When would this whole secret sister thing be over? One thing I was ready to get over with was watching Gregg the roommate "smooth-talk" women. He was such a fake. What was my responsibility as his brother in Christ?

Friday, September 14, 1984

My phone rang. "What are you doing right now?" asked Tina. "Well, as usual, my social calendar is absolutely booked. After all, I am the social chairman." I replied, trying to be humorous.

"I'm sure you could squeeze a fellow social director in! We're going to the mall. Are you in?"

As you may have already guessed, I had nothing to do. It had been a very routine college Friday for me. When the phone rang at 4:30, all I had to look forward to was dinner and an evening of studying! Instead, Tina, Cindy and I headed for Woodland Hills Mall—and got, how do I put this, crazy! Now, you've already learned that my Junior sisters, Tina and Cindy, were all about fun all the time. And it was always good, clean, fun—usually on the silly side.

So, we weren't at the mall to do shopping. Instead, Tina and Cindy dressed up in silly costumes and wanted me to be their "glamour" photographer. I took pictures of them with stuffed animals, with Barbies in a toy store, and dressed in various outfits in several clothing stores. I'm not sure why they chose me for this task, but it's probably because I was the safest choice of the brothers. We went to dinner at Taco Bueno and back to the dorms.

I had hoped to go to the movie on campus tonight, but Gena didn't want to go with me. So after the entertainment of the afternoon, I literally sat in my bed all night, until midnight. On a Friday night. This was starting to be a bad trend. I finally got some more gifts ready for our secret sisters and delivered them to Tina and Cindy at 1:20 a.m. The social chairman with no social life!

Saturday, September 15, 1984

Another Saturday morning intramural flag football game, another loss. Boy, we are really bad. After lunch it was an afternoon of watching college football on my own, punctuated with a phone conversation with Cheryl.

After dinner, Scott and I went to see "Ninja III" at the movies. Yes, it was an R-rated movie, which was against the honor code. I felt very guilty about it, but I didn't care for the alternative: another weekend night alone in my room. Wasn't it okay with the Lord to disobey a silly rule?

The night ended in usual fashion these days, with gifts for secret sisters being gathered and delivered, followed by chats with brothers into the early morning. My mind is stuck on Laura now. I'm looking forward to our first date.

Sunday, September 16, 1984

After getting up and out of the dorm, it was my second Sunday morning at Victory Christian Church. I'm still not getting much out of the church services here in Tulsa. Full disclosure: I was not too invested in my church at home either. The sermons were just not challenging to my mind. Was it the preacher's problem or mine? I mulled that question over lunch, but checked out of that deep heart work to watch my favorite Chicago Bears play football. Why did I enjoy Sunday football more than Sunday church?

After checking in with my dad and resting away the afternoon, it was time for dinner and homework. That evening, I met with Tina and both our R.A.s to discuss our next wing church and picnic. Now, that's something I can look forward to! After some more study, it was time for Sunday night devotions (Devos) with the brothers. I am getting a bit more out of these each passing week. A late-night Burger King run and hang out with Tina, Cindy, Joe, and Kyle ended the day. Maybe I did have a social life after all.

Monday, September 17, 1984

One of the penalties for getting up late on Monday morning was a very cold shower. I guess the hot water heaters couldn't handle all these guys! Dropping Intro to Computing allowed a later wake up time, but I didn't count on the miserable shower experience. After Humanities class and discussion, it was a pretty relaxing Monday. The only challenge was waiting in line for hair check. It was close this time, producing a warning. Guess it's time for a haircut.

That night, it was the annual Rush Night picnic. Since ORU doesn't have fraternities and sororities, this was a time to learn about campus organizations. Hung out for a while, then went back to the dorm to study. Had a nice, friendly phone call with Gena.

Called Cheryl, but she wasn't in her room. Tina called, and we talked more social director stuff. Monday Night Football and pizza took up the rest of my evening, followed by a wing meeting. I tried to collect money for the upcoming picnic, but you know college guys: they have no money. At least not for wing church and picnic.

Tuesday, September 18, 1984

For the first time in my short college history, I fell asleep in class. I slept through my entire Old Testament class. The theater style seats were just way too comfortable. What does it say about me that I slept through a Bible class? I vowed to start going to bed earlier. Thankfully, I was well-rested to give my next speech in Oral Comm class. Come to think about it, maybe I fell asleep due to anxiety! I was glad to make it through the speech without fainting--or vomiting.

At chapel, Jennifer thanked me for all her secret sister gifts. Laura, my other secret sister, sent me a very sweet note thanking me for her gifts too. I became instantly optimistic about our date this coming Thursday. Maybe she was interested in me after all!

Kerry and I ran some errands that afternoon, and bought birthday cards for a couple of sisters. After dinner, it was time for serious study for Humanities in the Fishbowl. I continue to study better while I can do some important people watching. Who knows who (what girl) I'll run into?

When I had studied enough, it was time for another late-night trip to the Depot, followed by picking up gifts for the brothers from our secret sisters. It was our turn to receive rather than give. Mine gave me a note and hot dog erasers. Not a bad start. Called Cindy and wished her a happy birthday. Studied until 1:30 am. So much for going to bed early.

Wednesday, September 19, 1984

I'm happy to report that I made it to Old Testament Survey and stayed awake through it all. But I did take a morning nap after that. I had to be rested to study for my all-important Humanities test. I took the exam at 4:30, and it went great. I think I'm getting the hang of college. Being the expert student that I was, I lent my help to Gena for her English test until 7:00. Then, I picked up more aerobic points on the tennis court until 9:00.

Back to the books. Took a study break to write a letter to Laura. I'm really hooked on her. Picked up another round of secret sister gifts for the brothers. Went room by room, delivering to everyone, like a severely underweight Santa Claus. I received another sweet note, two big cookies, and a bath towel. A pretty good haul for a poor college student. I have no idea of the identity of my secret sister. I did get two phone calls that night, from one girl who claimed to be my secret sister, and the other checking if I enjoyed my gifts. Went to bed thinking about Laura.

Thursday, September 20, 1984

If there was a universal rating system for days in your life, today would get five stars (out of five). It didn't start that way (in my experience, great days rarely start out great). I slept through my alarm and missed English Comp. After chapel, I went to get Slurpees with Tina and Cindy (a great day always seems to include them), then headed for lunch. At 4:45, it was time for me to support Tina's flag football team. Kerry, Cindy and I rooted her on to a big win.

Then came the reason for the five stars: The Sandi Patty concert. At that point, I had never heard a Sandi Patti song in my life. Her song, "The Via Delarosa" brought me to tears. As much as I would like to think it was my growing spirituality that made this day so great, it was more about my date: the fabulous Laura. I was totally smitten with her now. We walked to the Mabee Center for the concert and then back to her dorm at 11:00 afterwards. She really is an awesome girl. Cheryl was no longer in the picture, even though she had done the most for my growth as a Christian (however slight it was at the time). Laura and I just really connected.

The night ended with the next round of picking up secret sister gifts and delivering them to the brothers. I got a Garfield door hanger, but no note. I collected money for the picnic, watched TV and, yet again, went to bed much too late.

Friday, September 21, 1984

What do you do after an amazing first date? In 1984, you wrote a hand-written note to your love interest. At least that's what I did after lunch today. It was really hard to concentrate on a class like P.E.

That night, I went with some of the guys to see "Karate Kid" at the theater. At least I didn't break the honor code with this one! Picked up more gifts from our secret sisters at 12:30 a.m. All I got this time was a bag of cookies. As I munched on them into the wee hours of the morning, my mind was only on Laura. Would liking a girl always keep me from focusing on the Lord?

Saturday, September 22, 1984

It was really hard to make the most of Saturdays in college, especially when you don't wake up until after lunch. But since it was the fall, there was always college football on my small color television. And there was usually a phone call from Cheryl, who was becoming more and more just a faithful friend. I ran into Laura at dinner, which made my day. It was so easy to talk to her.

I rented some movies to watch (alone on Saturday night, of course), and ordered a large pizza from Crusty's, which I finished all on my own. Ironically, later that night, I received another pizza from my secret sister. That one would have to wait until tomorrow. At the end of the night, I faithfully delivered the other secret sister gifts to the brothers, visiting with several of them. Most of them had wonderful date stories which made me jealous. Lord, what is my future with Laura?

Sunday, September 23, 1984

Met Tina at 9:00 a.m. to go shopping for today's picnic. She actually let me drive her car, which was my first time driving in Tulsa. Today was our second wing church and picnic! We met the brothers and sisters at Chandler Park at 10:00. It was very disorganized—more picnic than church. I spent most of my time talking to Laura and Jennifer. Our secret sisters were revealed, and mine was Korrine. Sorry to say, she is not my favorite sister. Oh well. Back to the dorm at 2:00 for a little afternoon football and phone calls to my parents and my grandma. I am still not sure where I will go for fall break.

After dinner, Kyle, Scott, and I went to see "Conan the Destroyer". From 10:00 on, it was time to buckle down and study for the rest of the night—with a brief Burger King run at 11:00. I currently have three big questions on my mind:

1. Where do I go for Fall Break? Arizona (to the grandparents) or home?

2. What major should I pursue now that I have ditched computer science?

3. And of course, what about Laura? Or, is it Cheryl? Or someone else?

Monday, September 24, 1984

Went to my Humanities class at 8:50, followed by discussion class at 9:50. Got an 88 on my first major exam. Not bad, but not up to my standards. In high school, I would have cried over it—so I guess I'm maturing. Sent another card to Laura. Was I moving too fast? Came back to the dorm, did my laundry, and took it easy. After lunch, took a good power nap. Stacy invited me to go to the mall, so we walked around and window shopped for a couple of hours.

After dinner, I went to the Fishbowl to study from 7:00-8:30. The people watching was too distracting for me this time. Made a few phone calls to various sisters and went to a wing meeting at 11:00. Carla and Jenny (more sisters) needed help with Old Testament, so I tutored them by phone for an hour after that. Finished with my own studies at 2:00 a.m. and went to bed. Oh, by the way, I got accepted into the ORU Honor Society today! How was that possible after just six weeks in school? Must be based on my fine high school academic work. Unfortunately, I didn't see Laura all day.

Tuesday, September 25, 1984

First really cold day in Tulsa, especially at 7:00 a.m. After English Comp, I went to Christ's Chapel to take my Old Testament exam (think it went pretty well). This was followed by Oral Comm and chapel. Finally, I got to talk to Laura for a while. We ate lunch, and then went our separate ways. I dedicated all afternoon to Oral Comm—with a big test after dinner. It wasn't that bad.

That evening, I had my usual phone calls with Gena and Cheryl. When you aren't allowed to hang out in the dorms of the opposite sex, you still rely on the old-fashioned phone call. Gena talked me into meeting to study until 8:00. We did more talking than studying. I still like this tall beauty from Texas, even though my good friend Kerry is interested in her.

Later that night, all of us small group leaders met with Skip the Chaplain. We had a very frank discussion about the spiritual and political state of ORU. I didn't realize that there were some serious leadership issues here, as well as things going on behind the scenes that most students had no knowledge of. We spent a lot of time praying for our university. The night ended with a phone call with my grandmother, confirming that I would stay with them in Arizona for Fall Break!

Wednesday, September 26, 1984

Old Testament Survey class at 9:50. Got a 90 on that difficult first exam. I need to figure out how to get higher test scores in college. Went to lunch with Stacy, who had quietly become one of my better guy friends so far. We went to the post office, where I received a letter from Laura! But as I devoured it, I quickly realized it was Kyle in disguise. He got me good. I deserved it for what I did to Steve. Went to the LRC and got my Oral Comm exam score—an 88. Boy, I was stuck in that high B, low A territory.

After a brief workout at the A.C. with Kerry, we met Gena for dinner. Kerry and I then went to Tina's flag football game at 6:00. Went back to my dorm and talked with Cheryl on the phone while trying to focus on my homework assignments. Kyle and I went to the Depot at 9:00, followed by a trip to Mazzio's Pizza with Tina and Joe at 10:30. I was eating way too much pizza, but it was all so good. Came back to the dorm at midnight, and wrote a paper until 2:30 a.m.

Thursday, September 27, 1984

English Comp, Oral Comm, and chapel this morning. I have to say, the chapel speaker was pretty good. Little by little, I was trying to tune more into God's Word. Full disclosure: I saw Laura at chapel, which also put me in a good mood. My daily visit to the post office was disappointing, as my letters from friends and family at home had all but dried up. I was feeling more and more distant from people who had been my closest friends for so long. Later that afternoon, my beloved roommate actually did me a big favor and called Laura for me—setting us up on a blind date. That seemed like a good idea at the time.

After dinner and a brief conversation with Cheryl, some of the guys went to see "Purple Rain." The movie was really bad, but the company of Kyle, Scott, and Joe was great. Returned to the dorm at midnight and set a new bedtime record: 12:30 a.m. That was more like it!

Friday, September 28, 1984

Today was my second date with Laura, so I woke up with pep in my step. But I still needed my beauty sleep, so I took a morning nap after my P.E. class. After lunch, I met Lisa at the LRC and we studied together for our Oral Comm test. Kyle, Scott, and I drove Stacy's Firebird around town just to get off campus for a bit. When you don't have a car in college, it is refreshing to just go on a joy ride once in a while. Picked up my movie tickets and headed back to the dorm. After a brief phone call, it was time to get ready for my big date!

I met Laura at 6:30. Remember, this was a "blind date" set up by my roommate, so she was surprised to see me. Was it the good kind of surprise, or the disappointing sort of surprise? I had secured Stacy's Firebird for the evening, so this was a real, off-campus date. I took her to the Italian Inn for dinner, which turned out to be a great, romantic choice. Then, we went to the theater to see "All of Me". Can't beat a Steve Martin movie, at least not in my book. If I had to grade this date, I would have given it an A+. But I did not dare to ask Laura. As I settled in to bed, my only thought was: It is going to be hard work to win over Laura. But it was worth the effort.

Saturday, September 29, 1984

Slept in too long, so I had to run to my Oral Comm study meeting at 8:00. My mornings are still too undisciplined. After the meeting, I went back to bed until 12:30 p.m. See what I mean? Went to a late lunch with Gena and studied together until 2:30. Later that afternoon, had nice phone conversations with Cheryl and Gena again. Met Gena for dinner in the cafeteria. We were really becoming like a true brother and sister.

Tonight was my first trip to the Tulsa State Fair—with Gena, Skip the Chaplain, Pam, and Korrine. As more of a city slicker, this was still a good time. Nothing like expensive fair food to boot! The best part was that Gena and I broke off from the group for most of the time.

When we got back to campus, I walked Gena back to her dorm, as a good gentleman. Back to my dorm I went for a late-night game of Trivial Pursuit with some of the sisters until 1:00 a.m. For some reason, a wave of depression swept over me when I returned to my room. Maybe it was because I saw Laura from a distance and was teased by one of the sisters. Did they know something I didn't? What I do know right now is:

1. Gena and Cheryl are my best (girl) friends (especially Gena).
2. Kerry and Kyle are my best (guy) friends.

Sunday, September 30, 1984

For the first time my Freshman year, I skipped Sunday church. Just because you have to leave the dorm and can't return until lunch doesn't automatically equate to church attendance. After driving around, Kyle, Scott, and I ended up at Mr. Gatti's pizza this morning. And, other than a prayer over our food, there wasn't anything spiritual about it.

The afternoon was filled with napping, NFL football watching, and a call to my two best high school friends: Bry and Peck. One thing I learned today: Some of my friends back home are starting to dislike me due to my new-found spirituality. I had been challenging them in their faith (mostly by letter). Was I really more spiritual than I had been in high school? I must have been more confident on the outside than I felt on the inside. Unfortunately, the Lord sees the heart!

Before dinner, I called Cheryl and then Gena to complain about my new, strange reputation back home.

"Weren't we all supposed to be Christians?" I asked. "How was I coming off as some 'holy roller'?"

They were very sympathetic. Gena and I went to dinner and then we talked to Kerry about it. Kerry totally understood—he was the sort of true Christian friend I needed.

"You've got to understand. There are nominal Christians and there are spirit-filled Christians. Don't worry about your reputation. Worry about what God thinks about you." Wise words from Kerry.

Later that night, I spilled my guts to Kyle and Scott about it as well. It was so refreshing to be with peers who weren't afraid to talk about spiritual things (even though we did miss church this morning). By God's providence, Devos at 11:00 was all about witnessing to others. It really convicted me. After sharing my own struggles, Skip the Chaplain anointed me with oil and the brothers prayed over me. That was quite the new religious experience for me!

October, 1984

Monday, October 1, 1984

Awoke today with the feeling that October was going to be a great month! The first day of the month began pretty ordinary: Humanities and discussion at 8:50 and 9:50, followed by lunch at noon. I saw Laura, but only from a distance. After a two-hour nap, I met Stacy and Kyle to run some errands. I finally got mail after this long drought! It's amazing how some mail changes your day at college. I received my plane ticket for Arizona, as well as letters from my Peck and Bry. They were very encouraging to my heart. The night ended with a hall meeting until midnight and a fairly early bedtime for me: 1:00 a.m. So, why did I think October was going to be so awesome?

Tuesday, October 2, 1984

After English Comp at 7:50, I went to my first airing of the "Richard Roberts Show". Richard Roberts, son of Oral Roberts, was ORU president. Not only did he inherit the university from his father, but also his television show. The best way I can describe it is that it felt like a Christian variety show (think: a Christian Sonny and Cher Variety Hour). There were "Richard Roberts Singers", interviews with Christian celebrities, and a sort-of sermon by Richard. It was more funny to me than a serious Christian experience. As part of the studio audience, I did get to shake hands with Richard (and his sweet life Lindsey) for the first time.

Providentially, I had to go from the show to the chapel. Our chapel speaker today was Arthur Blessed (not sure that was his real name). He gave an incredible message! His claim to fame was that he walked around the world with a huge cross on his shoulder. He really challenged me (much more than President Roberts). Yet again, I saw Laura at chapel, with no real conversation. Went to lunch with Cindy. Enjoyed a late birthday gift from my great grandmother after a visit to the post office.

Later in the evening, I got together with Skip the Chaplain and Stacy for a time of prayer before our small group leader's meeting with Kerry. I was getting much more comfortable praying with the guys and interacting with group leaders. This was my first time to notice a friend of Cheryl's named Kendra. She was a girl's small group leader who had caught Kerry's eye.

After some time studying, I had my own small group meeting. It did not go well at all. Nobody wanted to share, or get involved doing spiritual things together—like witnessing or praying. All these guys are set in their ways. They remind me of—me! At least the me who came to ORU back in August. I need to pray for these guys to get more spiritual—Kyle, Gregg, Scott, Stacy. I aired my frustration to Kerry. He totally gets it. He is such a blessing to me, and only inspires me to be a better Christian every day. I also talked and prayed about it with Scott (a different Scott), a junior who is deeply spiritual. Sadly, the day ended with a long argument about worldliness vs. godliness with Gregg the roommate. He just doesn't get it either.

Wednesday, October 3, 1984

Walked over to the production center for my second viewing of the "Richard Roberts Show". It is sort of cool being in the studio audience. It took me back to when I was eight years old, being in the audience of the "Bozo the Clown Show" in Chicago. At least at that show I got to play the throw-the-ball-in-the-bucket game with Bozo! No, I'm not comparing Richard to Bozo, but it does seem that many in the student body don't respect him. After lunch and some homework, Kerry and I went to the LRC to run some errands. We conveniently saw Gena there (you're welcome, Kerry).

After dinner, I called Gena and talked for a while (yes, Kerry did come up in the conversation). My next call to Cheryl was even better. Once again, we got into a great theological conversation. She really knew just how to encourage me in my Christian walk! My evening ended with a three-hour Oral Comm meeting with my study group. Our assignment was to put on a series of skits as a group. This should be interesting.

Thursday, October 4, 1984

Met my Oral Comm group at 9:00 am to put some finishing touches on our skits. During our 9:50 class, we put them on for the whole class. It wasn't terrific. Maybe I should switch my major to Communication (said the introvert). Went to chapel at 10:50. Rev. David Wilkerson was the guest preacher. I had read his autobiography in high school, but hearing his stories again was captivating. And I didn't know anything about all the Teen Challenges he had opened over the years. I needed him to challenge my faith this morning. It needs action!

Had the pleasure of having lunch with Laura. She really is an awesome girl. But she wasn't very talkative today. I went to student accounts and settled my account. It was a blessing to be on full scholarship, but there were still incidental charges I had to pay on my bill. I need a job! I stopped by the bookstore and bought a card for Cheryl. Returned to my dorm, studied, and slept, studied, and slept. Went to dinner with Kerry at my cousin Whitney's house. It was always great to be with Whitney and Mark—they totally understood all my strange family dynamics.

Gena called when I got back to the dorm. We went to the Fishbowl and studied and talked until 9:00. Then, I met my newly assigned sister prayer partner for the first time in the prayer gardens. Her name is Tammy. We were just right for each other as prayer partners. We shared our struggles, prayed for each other, and hugged (in a good, Christian way) as we ended. It was so uplifting. Returned to my dorm and called Laura. We had a better conversation this time. Hung out with the guys until midnight.

Studied for my P.E. test until 1:30 a.m.   Ate a bunch of cheeseburgers before I fell asleep.   Probably not the best idea.

Scottsdale, Arizona

October 5, 1984

Friday, October 5, 1984

Took my P.E. test at 9:00 a.m. That marked my last official school act before heading out on Fall Break! I joyfully packed my bags and cleaned my room. Called Cheryl and met her for any early lunch at 11:30. I gave her a birthday card and we said our goodbyes. Loaded my luggage into Gena's car, and off we went to the airport. The fun part was that Kerry was on the same plane, since Phoenix was his hometown. My grandparents lived in Scottsdale. We saw Gena off to Texas at 2:30 and boarded our flight at 4:30. As I listened to music on some headphones, I thought that my college experience was going way too fast.

Kerry and I arrived in Phoenix at 7:00 p.m. Gram and Gramps picked me up. I met Kerry's very cool mom too. My grandparents took me out for a burger at Red Robin, ending up at their home at 8:30. So many memories came flooding back. Our family took a spring vacation to Scottsdale just about every year during my elementary and high school years. My grandparents lived in a beautiful home, with a huge pool surrounded by an astroturf putting green. I had loved the desert my entire life! In many ways, this was as much as my home as Chicago was. I had a very special bond with my grandparents.

Gram and Gramps indulged me as I went on and on about my newfound love for Christ that I found at ORU. They left at 10:30 to pick up my father from the airport. Unbeknownst to me, my dad had decided to fly in and spend some time with me. Why just my dad? After all, these are my mom's parents! When they all returned, my father shared some terrible news with me.

"I wanted you to be the first to know that our marriage is almost over. I believe your mom will divorce me any day now." Dad announced in a tearful whisper.

"Why do you say that? Why don't you go to counseling?" I said angrily.

"It's too late for that. Mom has been cold and distant for years. She keeps telling me that she wants to meet new guys."

Was my mom in high school? I abruptly got up and went to my bedroom to pray. I resolved to put my trust in the LORD, since there was nothing I could do to fix this. I had known about their marriage troubles for a while, but this was still a shock to my system. I went to sleep confident that the LORD would not let them break apart. But, boy, was my heart heavy with grief! What a way to start a school break...

Saturday, October 6, 1984

I went to brunch at El Charro's with my grandparents and my Uncle John and Aunt Char this morning. They made the best huevos rancheros. Aunt Char was my mom's older sister. She and Uncle John had moved out to Arizona long before my grandparents became "snowbirds" and eventually moved from Chicago themselves. It was good to spend some time with them. On the way home, we stopped by the florist so I could wire some flowers to Cheryl's house in southern Illinois. Caught up on some much-needed sleep that afternoon and watched TV.

For dinner, we went to Pacific Fish Co. I had the teriyaki shark. It was so good. My grandparents knew the best restaurants in Phoenix! Afterwards, I got a call from Kerry inviting me to hang out with him tomorrow. I spent the rest of the evening trying to drown my sorrows in mindless television shows. It didn't work. My parents were ruining my vacation! Choosing to avoid home for break didn't help.

Sunday, October 7, 1984

Went to church with my grandparents at Valley Cathedral. I had never gone to a church with the pulpit and platform in the center of the sanctuary. It was pretty cool. We went to brunch at Oscar Taylors with Uncle John and Aunt Char (brunch is my new favorite meal of the day). Back at the house, I called Bry and Peck, my best high school buds. It was a beautiful sunny day, so I laid out and swam for a while. For some reason, my grandparents' pool was the only place I enjoyed swimming.

At 4:30, I went over to Kerry's house. Gramps gave me his brand-new Mercedes to drive, which was very generous of him. Kerry and I ate dinner with his mother. We spent time talking, praying, and reading the Bible. Kerry's mom is a very godly woman. His father left her a few years ago, so they could relate to my current family drama.

Later that evening, Kerry and I cruised around Phoenix in the Mercedes. We ended up at his church, First Assembly of God, for evening worship. Pastor Tommy's sermon was very convicting. Afterwards, Kerry's mom prayed with me again (I obviously needed the prayer), and we went to Swenson's for some ice cream with his former youth group. They were very cool. His youth pastor just so happened to know Cheryl (was this a sign from the LORD?). The Mercedes and I made it home by 11:00 p.m., both safe and sound.

Monday, October 8, 1984

Dad flew back to Chicago this morning. I avoided him most of this trip. I guess I should have appreciated that he would travel across the country to give me this traumatic news, but I wasn't. All I wanted to do was enjoy my fall break in my favorite place in the world. I guess that was a selfish desire when my parent's marriage was falling apart!

With dad gone, I tried to re-focus on much-needed relaxation. After all, college was a grind, right? After lunch, I wrote letters, watched television, and took it easy. Grandma and I left at 4:30 to pick up my Uncle John and Aunt Char for dinner. Still nothing better than driving in Grandpa's black Mercedes. We picked up Gramps from the airport (he was on a quick trip to a racetrack in Vegas). It was good to just be the three of us again.

Tuesday, October 9, 1984

Ever since I was old enough to pay attention to such things, my grandmother got her hair done on Tuesdays. Her hairdresser in Scottsdale had become one of her closest friends. Grandpa and I dropped her off for her morning appointment and waited in the car for her. We read the newspaper, with very few words exchanged. We never talked about much, but I always felt a very close bond with Grandpa Charlie. I wanted to be him when I grew up in just about every way—especially the millionaire part. After Grandma returned with a fresh hairdo, we enjoyed brunch and a trip to Target for some shopping. Then, they waited for me to get my haircut too. I needed to be ready for hair check when I returned to ORU.

I wasted the rest of the day like a good college student on break. Even though I had some studying to do, I slept through most of it. Grandpa and I watched the World Series together. Of all the things we agreed on, baseball wasn't one of them. He was a long-suffering Chicago Cubs fan and I was a Chicago White Sox fan. Even though he worked hard to convert me to the dark side, I stayed true to my South Siders. Good pizza and a non-Chicago World Series game allowed us to get along well.

Wednesday, October 10, 1984

My morning was my own, so it was filled with television and letter writing. Writing letters to my friends in Chicago was the best way of staying connected to them.

At 2:30, I went over to Kerry's house. Yes, we cruised the town in my grandfather's Mercedes again. Not having a car in college made driving on break so much more enjoyable. Kerry and I talked about everything as usual, especially our family lives. We could relate to one another so well.

When I returned home, my grandparents and I went out to dinner. Even though my grandmother was a great cook, they loved to eat out—especially at cafeteria-style restaurants. Tonight, it was the King's Table, followed by World Series baseball. Being a White Sox fan, I was rooting hard against the Detroit Tigers. I studied a bit so I could get ready for some upcoming exams, then caught up on some much-needed sleep.

Thursday, October 11, 1984

After a quiet morning, my Aunt Char came over to pick me and Gram up. We went to my favorite Arizona shopping experience: Fiesta Mall. Grandma always loved to build up my wardrobe, and I was always extremely grateful. She also bought me a Sheena Easton cassette (even though she had no idea who that was).

After a quick stop at home, Aunt Char and I popped over to Los Arcos Mall, which was also a fun place to visit. We met Uncle John and my grandparents for dinner at CoCo's, our family's favorite restaurant. I think my grandparents ate there at least three times a week. Our evening activity was a trip to see "All of Me" at the theatre. Steve Martin came through for me again.

Friday, October 12, 1984

I made a return trip to Kerry's house for a bit in the afternoon. I brought him back to my grandparent's house to enjoy a swim and some Arizona sun. Did you know a "dry heat" was actually pretty cool? With the artificial turf putting green around the pool, we made it into an 18-hole putt-putt challenge. I won by two strokes, protecting my home turf (literally).

After dropping Kerry back at his house, the grandparents and my aunt and uncle all went to dinner at the Brown Derby. I had one of the best t-bone steaks of my life! Enjoyed another game of the World Series and went to be at 10:00, the earliest in a long time.

Saturday, October 13, 1984

I guess the Lord knew that I needed a good night's sleep. I awoke to a phone call from my dad, followed by one from my mom. As much as I tried to be the voice of reason with my mother, she didn't change her attitude about the state of the marriage. She was probably right, but I didn't want to believe divorce was an option.

I tried to get my mind off it by spending time on the phone with various friends from home. At 10:30, it was time for brunch at the Quilted Bear. I leaned that brunch was not only my favorite meal of the day, but most senior citizens'. What does that say about me? Topped off the morning with a swim.

Began the afternoon by watching a World Series game by myself, punctuated with a few phone calls to more friends. Made arrangements for Gregg the roommate to pick Kerry and me up from the airport tomorrow. This was my last full day in amazing Arizona! After a dinner at home, I spent all evening studying. It was time to get re-focused on my classes. I really wanted to get straight A's to start my college career.

As I drifted off to sleep, my mind went through a thorough evaluation of all the girls that the Lord had brought into my life at ORU. If I could only combine the best traits of each one into my future spouse. I'm sure the critical state of my parent's marriage had something to do with this very self-centered, fear-based analysis of mine. If you are interested, here's my current thinking:

Cheryl: Deep spirituality, pleasant personality

Laura: Great laugh, beautiful eyes, fun personality

Tammy: Genuine spirit, loving disposition

Cindy: Silly personality

Tina: Silly personality, free-spirited, mature

Gena: Solid spirituality, easy to talk to, great sense of humor, Texan accent

Alyson: Solid spirituality, beautiful figure

Mechelle: Pleasant personality, good height, fun accent

Jennifer: Beautiful face, charming personality

Kendra: Deep spirituality, fun personality, beautiful face, good height

Kay: Texan accent, mature woman

I wonder if any of them had me on their list? Probably not.

Tulsa, Oklahoma

October 14, 1984

Sunday, October 14, 1984

The morning worship service at Valley Cathedral with my grandparents started my day of departure. Grandpa always called it "L-Day" for "Leaving Day". He seemed to always have more pep in his step on L-Day—I didn't take it personally. We went to breakfast at the Ramada and went home.

At 1:00 we headed to Sky Harbor airport. Kerry met me there and we said a slightly tearful goodbye to his mom and my grandparents. We were in the air at 2:45 and touched down in Tulsa at 7:30 pm CST. Gregg met us at the gate and we headed back to school. Fall break was officially over!

After freshening up, Kerry and I went to the Claudius girls dorm to hang out, for our post-break catch-up time. We saw Cheryl, which was a welcome sight. She thanked me for the flowers. The three of us walked over to the Depot, where we parted ways. Kerry and I went back to the Fishbowl and sat around looking for returning friends. Gradually most of our brothers and sisters filed back, with luggage in tow. Skip the Chaplain, Paul, Stacy, Joe, Tina, and Cindy popped their heads in to greet us. Kerry and I exchanged hugs with Tina and Cindy. Cindy thanked me for the postcard. It was so good to be back home.

Later that night, a bunch of us went to QT for Slurpees. We returned to campus and walked to the Mabee Center. It was the night of the pep rally for our men's basketball team. Even though it was sort of boring, I was so glad to be with "my people".

When I returned to my room, Kyle was there, wanting to talk. I guess Skip the Chaplain was unavailable. He partied way too much with old friends back in Detroit. But he wanted to change his ways, which was good news to my ears. We stayed up until 2:00 a.m, talking about what Biblical change looked like. Who was I to help him? My mind was more on girls than the Lord. I think it is time to cool it for a while with Laura, and maybe everyone else on my list.

Monday, October 15, 1984

After morning classes, I went to the bookstore to buy a birthday card for Joe. Stopped by the post office, then loaned Stacy $60 so he could pay his phone bill. Good thing I still had some birthday cash! Ate lunch with Cindy, and talked about my mom and dad. She was very sympathetic. Back at the dorm, I listened to a talk by Tony Campolo on my cassette player. It was entitled: "You Can Make a Difference". Here is one of my favorite quotes:

"I don't know how your theology works, but if Jesus has a choice between stained glass windows and feeding starving kids in Haiti, I have a feeling he'd choose the starving kids in Haiti."

It was really inspiring and uplifting. Maybe I should go to the mission field? Gena called at 2:00 and we talked for over an hour. Again, it was great to be back.

I ate dinner with Tammy, followed by a phone conversation from a friend from Calvin College. Most of my high school classmates went there. I met Tina and Tammy at 7:15 to plan our upcoming wing retreat. Then, Kerry and I studied from 9:00 until 10:30. We all had wing meeting at 11:00. I learned that we had to register for next semester's classes in a week. I better decide on a new major soon! Lord, give me strength!

Tuesday, October 16, 1984

Went to English Comp, O.T. Survey, and Oral Comm. It felt good to be back in my regular rhythm. Ate lunch with Kerry, then went back to the dorm to study. I called Cheryl and we talked for a while. Maybe it was time to pursue her again?

After dinner, it was time for our first intramural volleyball game. Even though this was just c-league intramurals, this was one of my better sports. We won—by forfeit. After showering, I went with some brothers to the sisters' open house, from 6:30-8:30. Sadly, I didn't see Laura or Alyson. We had our open house from 8:30-10:30. It's a good thing my roommate cleaned his side of the room for once! Open house was actually exhausting, with no good visits at all.

It was good to get out at 10:45 with Tammy, even if it was only to the grocery store. Since she was my prayer partner, we did talk and pray in her car. She even prayed about Laura for me. I needed the Lord's help, that's for sure.

Wednesday, October 17, 1984

I slept in until 9:00, then headed off to Old Testament Survey. Went to an early lunch at 9:45 so I could catch up on homework. Freshman year was filled with what we called DAIR videos, which were required videos on all sorts of theological subjects, to round out our education. DAIRs were pretty boring.

An early lunch meant an early dinner at 4:45. Back to the homework grind after that. Broke up the drudgery with calls from Gena and Joanna, which was very helpful. Cindy invited me to go with her to evening Vespers, and I was only too happy to accept. We had a very good talk which God used to reveal some important things to me. For one thing, I was convicted that I had mishandled my relationship with Laura. It was really selfish of me. I needed to resolve that soon. Upon returning to the dorm, I shared some of my new insights with Kerry and Kyle. I wrote a very apologetic letter to

Laura and committed it (and her) to the Lord. Can you tell I would rather communicate by letter than face-to-face?

Thursday, October 18, 1984

I overslept and missed my 7:50 English Comp class. I'm going to try my best not to have early classes next semester! After lunch, I spent time putting together said schedule, praying that I would get the classes I wanted. Got back into my regular letter writing to high school friends and relaxed the afternoon away. At 3:30, a bunch of brothers and sisters went bowling and out to eat.

That night, I attended the initial day of my first "Healing Seminar". Oral Roberts became world famous for his miracle crusades during the 1950s and 60s. Our university even had "School of Signs and Wonders" which put on regular healing seminars. It was quite eye-opening. I have to say that it was pretty awesome to see people get physical healing from the Lord. I sat with Cindy, who claimed to get healed from her allergies! I'm not sure how she could tell.

Tammy drove me back to the dorm, giving us prayer partners some good time to talk. Skip the Chaplain and I went to Burger King with some sisters, which turned out to be a good time. Ended my night in Kerry's room, talking about the truth (and myths) of divine healing. I had a lot to learn.

Friday, October 19, 1984

Kerry and I went to breakfast at 8:30. He had become a true brother in the Lord. I wished he could be my roommate for the next three years! We returned to the healing seminar at 9:30 with some of our sisters. Students claimed to be healed of a variety of ailments—many much more severe than seasonal allergies.

We joined Tina, Cindy, and Korinne for lunch at Taco Bueno. The seminar continued at 2:00. To this freshman's eyes, it was awesome to see all these real miracles. I would have scoffed at them in high school, since our Christian school said that miracles didn't happen like that today.

After a dinner break, it was back for more healings until 10:00 p.m. Several of the brothers sat up into the early hours of the morning talking about what we witnessed.

Saturday, October 20, 1984

Another morning, another healing seminar session. Kerry and I got there early, and saved seats for Tina, Cindy, and Tammy. I am amazed by the healing power of God! The speakers preached passionately about Jesus and His mission to heal people.

"The same Jesus who healed people in the Bible can heal you today!" exclaimed one preacher.

"The only thing keeping you from a healing is your lack of faith," said another.

After lunch, I slept the afternoon away, resting up for the evening session. Tina and Cindy joined me after dinner. The keynote speaker was the famous Kenneth Copeland. I had never heard his preaching before, and it was awesome. He also brought several students on stage and healed them of their maladies. I wonder how many other universities had a seminar like this!

Tina and I walked back to the dorm after it was over. We rounded up a bunch of brothers and sisters to go to Ken's Pizza (doing our social director duty). It was an excellent event—and I beat Tina 13-12 (the brothers I recruited to her sisters). Returned to my room at 1:00 a.m. Talked with some brothers about the healing seminar, turning in at 2:30. Even though this was an exciting day, I was down in the dumps for some reason. My flesh was weaker than my spirit. I need some healing power for my emotions!

Sunday, October 21, 1984

Slept in until nearly Noon. Kerry and I went to the last healing seminar event. Sat with Tammy and was extremely inspired by the message. Did I mention we got all these days off from regular classes? Shows the priority of this university was on the spirit, not just the intellect.

After dinner, Kerry and I went to Claudius girls' dorm. He wrote a note to Kendra and I wrote one to Cheryl. They lived in the same wing. Being in the note-writing mood, I also wrote ones to Tammy, Alyson, and Cindy. The written word was a much better way to express my feelings. Maybe I should parlay that skill into a career?

Since the typical school schedule started back up tomorrow, I spent the night studying (with a football game as a distraction). Called Gena and had a nice talk. Also heard from Bry from back home. Sadly, he is having family problems just like me. Finished off the evening hanging out and talking with some brothers. I went to bed, praying for my next semester schedule.

Monday, October 22, 1984

Got up at 8:00 a.m. Had Humanities at 8:50 and 9:50. Very thankful to get a 10/10 on my Aeneid test! After a bit of a hassle, I finished registering for my next semester's classes.

After lunch, it was my least favorite time of the month: hair check. On the way, I saw Laura—but I effectively ignored her.

Back in my room, I was convicted of my sin. I have to stop acting so selfishly out of my hurt. I called Cheryl and we talked for over an hour. It was an awesome conversation. She helped me put together a "sermon" on relationships for my small group. She is so insightful and encouraging.

I walked over to the Saga for dinner, then bought Cinderella tickets for a Saturday night performance. The big question was: Who should I ask to join me? I got a letter from Laura which allowed me to write one in response. I fell asleep since I was developing a little cold. But I believe the Lord will heal me! Gena called at 8:30 and we talked for nearly an hour. Studied until late in the evening and went to bed without my healing.

Tuesday, October 23, 1984

Had my usual Tuesday regimen of English Comp, O.T Survey, and Oral Comm. Kerry and I went shopping for Halloween costumes. I picked out a Shakespeare one (appropriate for all my self-generated girl drama). After lunch I went to bed, sick as a dog. Even though I trusted God to heal me, this cold had grabbed hold of me!

Woke up to drowsily write another note to Laura. I got a great note from Cindy! I called and thanked her for being such an encouraging sister. Dragged myself to dinner at 5:00, followed by three hours of studying. I sat around in the Fishbowl for an hour, doing some people watching.

Back in my room, I called Gena and Cheryl for just a few minutes. I ended up asking Gena to Cinderella on Saturday night, and she said YES! Got some hot tea for my cold and went on to bed. I have to talk to Laura and clear the air. No more game playing!

Wednesday, October 24, 1984

Took it slow this morning. Was glad I only had O.T. Survey to attend today. After an early lunch, I studied for my Humanities exam for three hours. Ran some errands with Kerry, then took my exam at 4:30. Feeling so puny, I slept for almost three hours after dinner. I got a great note from Gena. Spent the rest of the night watching TV in bed. Still so sick. Even though I wanted to write a note to Laura, I was not up to it.

Thursday, October 25, 1984

My sickness forced me to sleep through English Comp. So much for God's healing power in my life! It was tough to be sick at a university that preached divine healing was the right of every believer. Me of little faith. I went to Oral Comm and then to chapel. The preacher was very challenging. Had lunch at noon with everyone, giving me enough strength to study the rest of the afternoon.

I went to dinner and 5:00 and had a real nice conversation with Scott. He was such a solid Christian.

"Do you pray without ceasing, like the Bible says?" he asked.
"What does that mean? I don't know how to do that!" I responded.
"It is first about the attitude of your heart. Is your focus on doing everything yourself, or depending on God?"
I think Scott knew my answer. I had a long way to go.

Back in my room, I had a nice call from Gena. Finished my note to Laura, which I tried to start the night before. Watched one of my favorite Steve Martin movies (The Jerk), then visited with Tina. Skip the Chaplain and I had another heart-to-heart conversation about the spiritual state of several of the brothers on our wing. He is really concerned. Should he be concerned about me too?

Called Tammy and invited her to the "Toymaker and Son" production on Sunday. She said YES! I was really trying to stay focused on being a good friend to a variety of girls instead of just pursuing one. Ended the night watching our volleyball team win their first game. Overdid it—feeling really run down.

Friday, October 26. 1984

Slept through my PE class, still wracked with sickness. Went to lunch with Gregg the roommate (for the first time in a long time). He's been a better friend lately. Invited Cheryl to eat with us at our wing table. Unfortunately, Laura showed up to eat at the same time. We ignored each other. What a mess!

Went back to the room and relaxed until 3:30. Cheryl called for a quick chat. At 4:30, Tina, Tammy and I left for some social director errands. We rented a VCR (not too many students owned one) and picked up my altered Shakespeare Halloween costume. We returned at 7:00 and got all the brothers and sisters moving to prepare for our party.

Twenty-three of us left at 8:45 and headed to Mazzio's for pizza. We had rented the movie, "Stripes" for the entertainment of the evening. As funny as it was, it was very off-color (and R-rated for a reason). Many of our wingmates were offended, which was very convicting to me. Not a wise choice. Other than that, the party went well. It's a challenge to be a social director at a truly Christian university!

Drove home with Tammy and Cathy. Was disappointed watching Tammy flirt with some guys, but she's still a great girl and prayer partner. Returned to my room at 10:30 and hung out with the guys for a few hours. Looking forward to hanging out with Gena tomorrow night!

Saturday, October 27, 1984

Slept in until 11:00. With great fear and trepidation, I gave Mom and Dad a call. It was past time to check in. They actually seem to be in a good place. But for how long?

I went to lunch with Kerry at 12:15, then returned my rented costume. Back in my room, I relaxed and gave Gena a call. I talked with some of the brothers, giving them my relationships "sermon." Even though I hadn't figured relationships out yet myself, it seemed like I inspired my brothers with my Biblical understanding of them.

We had an especially large group for dinner at our Saga table tonight. Laura was there, and I tried not to ignore her. I returned to my room to get ready for my date. Met Gena at 7:30 and headed for the performing arts center. Cinderella was actually very good! Our theater department is strong.

Afterwards, met a group of friends for a late-night movie (the Hitchcock movie, "Psycho"). Gena and I left a bit early and went to the Depot to have some time by ourselves. I gave her the outline of my relationship sermon—applying it to her and Kerry's relationship. Back to the Fishbowl at 12:45 for a visit with Tina and Kerry. Kerry and I talked alone about Gena from 12:00-1:00 a.m. (clocks turned back tonight!). I think I helped him get his relationship with Gena settled in his mind. As I closed my eyes to sleep, I gave all my dating relationships to the Lord too.

Sunday, October 28, 1984

Kerry and I went to Victory Church at 9:00 a.m. I'm still not convinced of where I need to go to church. It's just so easy to sleep in and walk to church. After lunch, I gave my newly minted relationship sermon to another group of guys. I was really getting this down pat! Went to an early dinner at 4:30, visiting with Tina and Cindy.

I met a group of brothers and sisters in the Fishbowl at 5:30 (including Tammy, whom I had asked specifically to this event). We walked to the Mabee Center to watch the production of "Toymaker and Son". It was an international mission group that used this drama to share Jesus. It was amazing!

Afterwards, Tammy and I went to the prayer gardens to pray together. She shared a lot of problems that really turned me off. I came back to my room with some pretty hurt feelings. Why do I take other people's problems so personally? To make myself feel better, I called Cheryl and then talked to Kerry about it.

At 11:00 it was time for wing devotions. It lasted until 1:30 a.m.! The anointing of the Spirit was clearly upon us. I personally felt the glory of God for the first time. Some brothers prayed over me and told me the Lord was calling me into ministry leadership. Was this the turning point of my life that I had been longing for? The brotherly love was amazing, as we cried and hugged—in a very masculine way.

I went back to my room and immediately threw all my secular rock music cassettes down the trash chute (over fifty of them). It was time for a pure life. I wrote a note to Tammy and went to bed at 3:00 a.m., refreshed in the Spirit.

Monday, October 29, 1984

I think I experienced every emotion today (which should have been expected after last night). I got up and went to Humanities. Got a 94 on my exam, which I praised God for!

After lunch, I called Gena, then studied until dinner. Then came the crushing blow: a letter from Laura.

"I am not interested in you at all...other than as a friend," it began. This ended any hope of a good relationship. I tried to give it to the Lord, but it really hurt. I guess I deserved it. I had not treated her well.

Gena and I went to an evening O.T. Survey class from 7:00-9:00. Then came the second crushing blow: a note from Tammy.

"You are supposed to be my friend and prayer partner. But you showed absolutely no compassion for my problems. That hurt more than what I'm going through!"

Hurt, hurt, and more hurt. So much for the guy who preached Biblical relationships! I called Tammy's answering machine and apologized to it. Thankfully, Skip the Chaplain was available for a relationship conversation. He gave me some great counsel and really encouraged me. He prayed with me before the hall meeting, where more brothers also reached out and prayed for me. With a cleansed heart, I wrote an honest and respectful letter to Laura. Lord, I need your strength and wisdom!

Tuesday, October 30, 1984

After English Comp, I went to breakfast. Unfortunately, Laura was at the table, and I couldn't even greet her! But, after O.T. Survey, I was able to make things right with Tammy. One out of two isn't bad, right? Hopefully, we can build back some sort of godly friendship.

After Oral Comm, I went to chapel and then to the cafeteria for lunch. The afternoon raced by with some study and conversation. I met Korrine in the Fishbowl for some exam study until dinner.

Immediately after dinner, it was time for my Oral Comm exam. It went okay, but it wasn't easy. Back to the Fishbowl at 6:15 to help Kay with Spanish. It had been a while since I spent any time with her. After returning to my room, I called Gena and studied O.T. with Kerry.

We joined Tina, Skip the Chaplain, Tammy, and Korrine for a study break snack at Q.T. Back to exam study until midnight. A group of eight of us joined together for a prayer meeting until 12:45. It was such a blessing to be able to pray together with a group of brothers!

Here's my current state of relationships with girls:

Cheryl: Awesome

Gena: Awesome

Cindy: We are really close (in the Lord)

Tina: Ditto

Tammy: Slowly repairing our friendship

Laura: Irreparable, unless the Lord does a miracle.

One big takeaway: Grow closer to God first! Listen to my own sermon and make God-honoring friendships!

Wednesday, October 31, 1984

O.T. Survey class at 9:50. Relaxed away the rest of the morning. After lunch, it was study time until dinner. Got an 82 on Oral Comm exam, which was extremely disappointing. Read a letter from my mother, which was encouraging.

The evening was for more studying. I talked to Tina for a while, and saw Laura from a distance. Best part of this pretty average day was the Cheryl called and said I was great! Me, great? On to November the Lord and I go!

November, 1984

Thursday, November 1, 1984

It's a good feeling to start the day (and a new month) with a fairly easy exam. Old Testament Survey afforded me that opportunity. Going to a Christian elementary and high school certainly helped me ace my required Bible classes.

At chapel, the entire ORU student body had the chance to see the "Toymaker and Son" drama. It was just as enjoyable the second time. After lunch, it was an afternoon of mostly relaxation. Our intramural volleyball team played from 6:00-7:00. We lost again. Caught up with Tina afterwards. Then, talked to Cheryl for over an hour! Watched TV until 12:30. For some reason, had Cindy on my mind tonight. Stopped and prayed for her.

Friday, November 2, 1984

In my 9:00 P.E. class, it was time for our Freshman swimming test. I guess our motto "educating the whole man" included the ability to swim. Thankfully, I passed. I wasn't the greatest of swimmers—even with all those lessons at the YWCA as a child.

After lunch, I did laundry and relaxed. Talked to Gena for a while. The better news of the day was that Cindy called and asked me to a concert! No, it wasn't a date—since Tina and Kim were also going. But I was thankful to be included. Maybe that's why Cindy was on my mind last night.

At 7:00, we all walked over to Cardone Hall for the "Souls Afire" choir concert. This gospel music group was awesome. It was excellent praise and worship music and a fabulously spiritual way to spend a Friday night! I returned to the dorm just in time for a prayer meeting from 11:15 until 12:30. I'm really learning to love God more! Talked with some brothers into the early hours of Saturday morning. Went to bed more content with my relationships—trying to trust the LORD.

Saturday, November 3, 1984

Woke up to a call from my friend Bry from back home. Went to a late lunch, and had a nice visit with Cheryl. Skip the Chaplain and I went to the mall for the afternoon. Then Kerry, Tina, Skip, Steve, and I picked out some movies and rented a VCR. That night, we all watched "Mr. Mom" and "Blade Runner" in the dorms. Stayed up until 2:00 am, ate pizza, and went to bed.

For some reason, this was a depressing day. And when I get down, I show it. Tammy and I are still at odds, which means I may have lost my prayer partner. Cindy is dating someone else, and I miss spending time with her. I feel like I'm giving much to a lot of different people but receiving little in return. Maybe I need to spend more time with Cheryl. Or, maybe I need to learn to be content in Jesus.

Sunday, November 4, 1984

I dragged myself out of bed late and went to Victory Christian Church with Kerry at 11:00 a.m. Depression was still hanging with me. I talked a little to Kerry about it.

"You know, depression is of the Devil. He is just trying to attack you, distracting you from the calling on your life." Kerry was so wise.

"Yeah, and he's winning big time." I said trying to smile.

After lunch, I tried to drown my sorrows in NFL football—to no avail. I gave Cheryl a call, and we had a good talk. She actually prayed for me over the phone! Who does that? Her prayers were powerful, as it felt like a dark cloud instantly lifted. I had enough joy to call my mother, my sister Amy, and my grandmother. It was good to hear their voices.

I went to dinner at 5:00. Visited some with Cindy, but ignored Tammy. Upon returning to my room, I called my dad and then studied for a while. Went running with Kerry, then met Korrine and Skip the Chaplain to talk about future wing plans. Had Devos from 10:00-11:45. What an awesome time! We spent most of it talking about relationships, which was really helpful. Again. Overall, I felt much better about my life today. I'm confident that Tammy and I will make-up and be friends again. Other relationships with girls will only get better as I keep my eyes on the Lord. This should be a great week!

Monday, November 5, 1984

Monday meant Humanities at 8:50 and discussion group at 9:50. Went to the LRC with Kerry to study a bit. We went to lunch at the wrong time, since both Tammy and Laura were at the table. I did my best to be civil. Not sure I was well-received.

Gena called me at 1:45. She sprained her ankle last night, so I drove her to the City of Faith Medical Center for some pain medication. Even though ORU preaches faith healing, it still dispenses medication. Interesting. We went from there to the bookstore and a return trip to her dorm.

I went to dinner at 5:30. Cindy was at the table. She thanked me for the kind note I had written her. Back to the dorm and my studies. At 8:00, Kerry and I went to the A.C. to play volleyball with Tina and some other girls. More studying afterword, interrupted by Monday Night Football, of course.

Skip the Chaplain and I made a late-night run to Burger King. Barely made it back for wing meeting at 11:00. Gregg, the roommate I hardly see, came back from a trip back to Colorado. He bought me a very cool comforter for my bed, which was very nice. Should help in the coming winter months. A group of us played Bible Trivia until 12:30 a.m. The highlight of the day was that I got my new schedule, and it looked great.

Tuesday, November 6, 1984

Remember the "easy" O.T. Survey exam? I got my grade back today, and it was 100. Another great way to start a day. Typical Tuesday morning schedule, ending with chapel at 10:50.

After lunch, Kerry and I ran some errands. Returned to my room and talked to Gena and Cheryl. After dinner, all of our eyes were glued to our televisions. Today was presidential election day. Ronald Reagan vs. Walter Mondale. And it was my first election to vote in as a new eighteen year-old! A group of us took a break from watching the results come in at 10:00 for an important trip to Taco Bueno. Still having trouble talking to Tammy. Reagan wiped the floor with Mondale—525-13 electoral votes. Wow! What a great day to be an American (and a Republican, of course).

The only down moment of the night occurred when Skip the Chaplain told me that Tammy thinks that I'm "playing with her feelings". What do I do with that? I have no idea what that means. Did she somehow like me as more than just a friend?

Wednesday, November 7, 1984

At lunch, I finally took the bull by the horns. I pulled Tammy aside and asked to talk...tomorrow. I had to figure out what to say! Maybe I just needed to learn to listen better to girls.

Kerry and I studied all afternoon, then went to dinner. From 7:45-9:15, I had a talk with Mitch, a wing brother I didn't know that well. He's really cool. Mitch asked me to pray for him about a challenging problem. About ten minutes after our time together, he popped his head in my room to tell me that the Lord had answered his (and my) prayer! Wow. Very cool to see God at work.

Went with Kerry to run another mile and a half. Aerobic points, remember? Talked to Cheryl and planned a date for Friday. She is so awesome. Talked to some brothers and went to bed filled with joy.

Thursday, November 8, 1984

After English Comp, I went for a late breakfast in the cafeteria. Laura was there. We don't even greet each other, which is so strange. I have to figure out how to navigate relationships better! Chapel was great again, which always helps. It gets my eyes back on Jesus—at least for an hour.

After lunch, I cleaned my half of our room and did some homework. I listened to a sermon on relationships, which is always appropriate for me. Got dressed for intramural volleyball and recruited people to watch (remember, I'm still our social director!). We finally had a good game, soundly defeating our much weaker opponent. After dinner, I went to our A-Team volleyball game, only to see us lose a close one. Tina was great though.

At 8:30, I met Tammy in the Fishbowl for the big talk. It took a while (until 9:45), but I think we got everything straightened out. It sure helps to take the time to talk things through. I feel like we finally regained our friendship! We even talked about my difficulties with Laura. I really had missed our friendship and how easy we could talk together.

At 10:00, it was time for co-ed Devos with our sister wing. Only ten of us showed up, which shows the state of our fellow brothers and sisters (in my mind at least). We used the time to listen to another talk on...wait for it...relationships. I think God is trying to tell me something! After a trip to QT, Skip the Chaplain and I stayed up late talking about Tammy mostly. I'm thankful to have such a good counselor in my life.

Friday, November 9, 1984

After P.E. class, I spent some time in the Fishbowl with Tina for some social director planning. That afternoon, I did my job running around the dorm, getting guys to sign up for wing t-shirts. It was a challenge.

After dinner, it was time to get ready for my double date. Kerry and I were taking out Kendra and Cheryl! We took them to Woodland Hills Mall and walked around (quite an 80s sort of date!). We saw the movie, "American Dreamer" at 9:30. It was a fun rom-com, which always works for date night, right? Ended the night at Pippin's for some excellent pie and conversation. I think this was the first time I had ever heard of (or seen) a "spork".

We got back on campus at 12:15. Cheryl and I walked around and had another awesome conversation about relationships. It is so gratifying to be like-minded with a girl about Christ-honoring relationships! After dropping her off, I stayed up and talked to Kerry and some other brothers.

Saturday, November 10, 1984

Slept in on a lazy Saturday morning. After lunch, I put some needed time into my studies. Gena called and we talked for a while, which was a welcomed interruption. I'm not sure if she is over Kerry.

Went to dinner and then back to the dorm, feeling kind of down. Don't know why. Am I just the kind of guy whose emotions stay on a roller coaster? My mom used to call me "melancholic" a lot, so it must be true. Called Cindy and she lifted my spirits. She is just a really great friend.

Keith (another wing brother) and I went out at 7:00 for a second dinner and to watch "American Dreamer" (again). I'm always up to see most movies over and over again. Back to the dorm at midnight. Gregg showed up drunk again. Did I mention he has a drinking problem? I don't know what to do about it.

Sunday, November 11, 1984

Kerry and I went to Victory Christian Church at 9:00 this morning. It was good to get going early for once on a Sunday. After hanging out for a while, we went to lunch when the cafeteria opened up.

From there, we went to the mall. It was time for me to start building up a cassette library of Contemporary Christian Music (since I destroyed all my secular music a few weeks ago). I bought Steve Taylor and Steve Camp cassette tapes. Tried to order our wing t-shirts, but was unsuccessful. After another errand, I returned to my room for my usual Sunday calls with Mom and Dad. It seems like they are still doing somewhat better.

After dinner, I talked with Mitch for a while. Watched some TV and did some homework. Hung out with some of the brothers. Talked with Korrine for a while, then talked to Skip the Chaplain about that conversation. I do a lot of talking! The worst part of the night was that Kerry and I had a big fight. It was not our first.

"You know, I sort of feel smothered by you some of the time!" Kerry yelled

"Well, excuse me for trying to be a good friend. You act as though I'm too dependent on you," I retorted.

"You are. You need to lower your expectations. You need to stop preaching about relationships all the time and just chill out."

I nodded. "You got it."

I think I expect too much out of our friendship.

Monday, November 12, 1984

Humanities at 8:50 and 9:50. After lunch, I received my official schedule for next semester. Somehow, it is looked totally different than I thought it would be. I need to get it fixed. Talked to Cheryl for an hour. Mostly about Kerry. Checked in with Tina, as well as Bry, my back home friend. His problems at home are getting much, much worse. He let me pray for him.

For the first time in a long time, I saw my cousin, Whitney. We had a good time catching up. I went to small group leaders meeting at 8:00, followed by another losing volleyball effort. Skip the Chaplain and I went to Taco Bueno for tacos and conversation. He counseled me to stop "prying" into Tammy and Korrine's business. Really? I thought we were friends! Now I have a problem with Korrine?

Wow, I really don't know what I'm doing. I guess I just care too much (and talk too much). I have to pace myself better. In all my relationships.

Tuesday, November 13, 1984

This morning's chapel speaker was Rev. James Robeson. I had never heard him before, but apparently he was pretty famous in the Charismatic Christian world. He was really practical and passionate, which I appreciated.

After lunch, I went to the bank and the mall with Skip and Paul. After some needed relaxation, I went to dinner. It was a special turkey dinner, since we are getting close to Thanksgiving. Didn't even feel like it was cafeteria food! Not that I ever hated cafeteria food.

Left at 6:30 with Tina, Tammy, and Skip to go attend James Robeson's "crusade". I don't know if I had ever been to a crusade. It was really exciting and convicting. Tina was especially fun to talk to during it.

We had our open house from 9:30 until 10:30. Saw Kendra and met some other girls for the first time. Got a late-night call from Kim (wing sister) who needed some help with Humanities. Went to bed thinking a lot about something James Robeson said: *"Fan your inner fire more each day"*.

Wednesday, November 14, 1984

An easy class morning, with only O.T. Survey on the schedule. After lunch, I stood in line to purchase Steve Taylor concert tickets. His music is really edgy and unique, for Christian music. Hung out with Tina for a while.

Had dinner at 5:15, followed by homework. Called Cheryl and talked for over an hour again. I took the opportunity to tell her how much I liked her. Yes, I know I should be wiser about relationships, but I couldn't help myself. I asked her to a banquet and the Steve Taylor concert. She said YES! I can't wait!

Late night pizza afterwards, followed by some letter writing to friends back home. My only concern tonight is that Tina and Cindy seem to be detaching more and more from me. What's wrong with me?

Thursday, November 15, 1984

English Comp. Breakfast. Oral Comm. Chapel. Rinse and repeat. After lunch, I caught up on both sleep and homework.

After dinner, it was intramural volleyball time again. It was close, but we lost again. We missed the playoffs by two points, so our season was over. The best part of this event was that so many sisters attended to cheer us on, even Laura.

I went to a required seminar at 7:30, followed by more studying. For some reason, I went to bed feeling sort of blah. I think Cindy's mad at me. Probably because I have been rude to her. Again, what's wrong with me?

Friday, November 16, 1984

PE class was dedicated solely to running this morning. Not my favorite thing. So, after a good long shower I went to lunch. The afternoon was dedicated to catching up on essential homework. As you probably guessed, I still made time to call Cheryl. And Gena. Saw Laura and Jennifer at dinner—and survived.

Afterwards, spent over an hour trying to get a date for Tomba. He's a wing brother from one of the Polynesian islands. No success. I guess I'm not the great social director I thought I was! Worked on homework until 9:00, then went to the movie, "The Elephant Man" with some sisters and brothers. Talk about a sad movie. Back at midnight for a late-night conversation with Kerry and Skip the Chaplain. Still feeling blah.

Saturday, November 17, 1984

Lunch at noon with Kerry. We went to the LRC to study all afternoon. Cheryl and I bumped into each other and we had a good talk.

After dinner, it was time for my first intramural basketball game. I was on the C team again. That's the sort of athlete I am. We won (but it was just an exhibition). Afterwards, a bunch of us went to Metro Diner for a snack. It was a lot of fun. But I went to bed discouraged again. So many questions about my life. Social events have become less and less attended, which means I'm not doing my job well. Or maybe people have developed their own social lives by now!

Sunday, November 18, 1984

Instead of staying on campus for church today, Kerry and I went to one of the hottest churches in Tulsa, Higher Dimensions. It was a three hour service (basically two hours of singing, followed by a one hour sermon). Rev. Carlton Pierson is something. I have never seen such a passionate preacher. We were some of the only white people there, which was fine by us.

Got out at 12:30 and went to the mall. I bought gifts for Tina and Cindy. Went to a late lunch at Saga. From 3:00-5:00, I went to the girls' open house. Visited Tina, Cindy, Korrine, Julie, etc. It was actually pretty boring. These open houses were losing their lustre for me.

Went to dinner with Kerry and Tina at 5:00. Studied humanities with Kim for most of the evening, then on my own. Called it quits and talked with Art (my next-door wing brother) until bedtime. About girls. Of course. I need a more positive attitude!

Monday, November 19, 1984

After Humanities and discussion, I went to the registrar's office and got my schedule fixed. Finally. Nothing more important in college than the academic schedule!

After lunch, Julie and I studied for Humanities in the Fishbowl. We left at 4:00 for the 4:30 exam. Went to dinner at 5:15. Called Julie and talked for an hour about the exam and other things. She is really cool and seems to like me a little.

Off to wing meeting at 11:00 and a fairly early bedtime. One of the sisters told me that Cindy thinks I'm mad at her. Why? What do I do with that? I'm realizing that no ORU girl matches up to Cheryl in my book. She is the most godly and consistent.

Tuesday, November 20, 1984

English Comp, O.T. Survey, and Oral Comm. Chapel was uninspiring for once. Lunchtime with the brothers and sisters was better. The afternoon was filled with studying.

After dinner, I had an Oral Comm exam. I think it went well. After a relaxing evening, I talked to Julie and Gena on the phone. Kerry and I caught up too. I'm not happy with the direction Gena is walking. She has become a bit to secular. Cindy has just disappeared from my life. Lord, help me focus on what's important!

Wednesday, November 21, 1984

After O.T. Survey, I went to the bookstore to pick out a Thanksgiving card for Cheryl. Then, I went to my Social Director's meeting to learn about the annual ORU Christmas banquet. It's going to be a lot of fun!

After lunch, I went to the LRC to study a bit. Called Cheryl to say goodbye for the Thanksgiving holiday. She is going home, but I'm not. Better news: She committed to going to the Christmas banquet with me! I got more good news later that afternoon—a 90 on my Oral Comm exam.

For the rest of the day, several of us brothers and sisters said our goodbyes to one another. It made me feel sort of sad. We are getting close—like brothers and sisters! I went to the mall with Skip the Chaplain and Darrell. We met Tina, Kerry, and Julie. Gregg the roommate gave me an early Christmas present: a new pair of shoes. Very nice. But I think he is trying to assuage his guilt. Yet, he is a very outgoing, giving guy.

After dinner, played Trivial Pursuit with Skip, Darrell, Tina, and Kerry until Midnight. Went to bed feeling thankful for Christian brothers and sisters.

Thursday, November 22, 1984

Thanksgiving Day, 1984! Slept in late and got a call from Bry. Good to hear from back home since I wasn't able to go home for the holiday. He's doing a lot better.

Mark (my cousin Whitney's husband) picked me up at noon, and I went to their house for Thanksgiving dinner. It was an awesome time. There were nine of us gathered. Mom and Dad called me there. We did the typical American Thanksgiving things: ate, watched football, ate some more, and talked all afternoon.

Mark brought me back to the dorm at 6:30. I called Tina and we had a nice talk. Watched TV and did some homework. Talked to Tina again. Skip the Chaplain and I went to get late night snacks. Returned to the dorm and talked with Kerry about his day. Was glad he had a good Thanksgiving too. Trying to navigate our new, slightly distant but close relationship. Found out that he's so in love with Tina, but he also likes Kendra.

As I turned in for the night, the people I am most thankful for here are Kerry and Cheryl. I pray that God would grow my gratitude and joy!

Friday, November 23, 1984

Got up early and had breakfast. Went to the Mabee Center at 8:00 and signed in. I had volunteered to help for our "college weekend." High school students from all over the country came to check out ORU. So cool! Rode the bus to the airport and worked all day, directing students and carrying luggage. Met some great guys and girls. Even though it was fun, it was exhausting welcoming all those students. Rode the bus back to campus at 7:00.

Mark picked me up at 8:30 to hang out with him and Whitney at their apartment. Watched "Uncommon Valor" and "Trading Places" with two other couples. It must be nice being a couple. Jealous much? Kerry came over later, and we left at 1:00 am to return to our dorm. Met Kerry's college weekend guest (mine was already asleep). I already miss Cheryl!

Saturday, November 24, 1984

Studied a little after sleeping in, then headed to lunch with Kerry. The cafeteria was packed with high schoolers. Met a high school junior named Angela and hung out with her in the Fishbowl.

Later. I went with Skip the Chaplain to shop and eat. We ran into Cindy (who hugged me and complained about my lack of spunkiness). What's up with that? Returned to the dorm and took some high schoolers to dinner in the cafeteria. Tried to convince them that ORU was the absolute best Christian university in the world. I should be an ambassador!

Afterward, went to the Mabee Center for a basketball game with Cindy and Tina. We won! Tina kept bugging me because I seemed "down". I guess I was. Maybe that's what people react to—

my moodiness. We went for pie at Pippin's with a bunch of girls and guys. Afterwards we came back to hang out some more in the Fishbowl. Tina continued her relentless questioning about what was troubling me. I didn't give in.

So, what's my problem? I'll tell you. I think I'm grieving the loss of so many girls as good friends (Tina, Cindy, Tammy, Gena, Laura, etc.). Yes, Cheryl was still my friend. But she didn't seem to like me as much as I liked her. Who can I talk to about all these things?

Sunday, November 25, 1984

Being the college weekend, it was important to spend some time with these potential new students before they left for home. Be an ambassador, they told us! So, Kerry and I had lunch with several of them. We had fun conversations.

Afterwards, I went to the mall with Tina, Tammy, Chris, and Kerry. Tina kept up her interrogation from yesterday. I refused to play that game. Returned to my room ay 4:00 for some study time. Called Mom and Dad after dinner. Studied the rest of the night.

Tina called and I finally agreed to write her a letter about it. I felt like this was some sort of hostage negotiation! So, I stayed up until 1:30, carefully crafting the letter. I do better with sharing my feelings by letter—but that was also often how I got into trouble. Such a conundrum. Kerry peeked his head in before I turned out to the lights to tell me all was good with him and Tina. I'm happy for him. Things seem to work out better for everyone else in my life. Lord, give me strength!

Monday, November 26, 1984

Went to Humanities. Got a 98 on my exam! Praise the Lord! After lunch, I devoted the afternoon to preparing my Oral Comm speech. This was the last thing I wanted to do. I hope I never go into a career that requires public speaking. After dinner, I studied my speech even more. My anxiety was still high, that's for sure.

At 9:00, I met Kendra at her dorm. She wanted to talk about Kerry. They are having relationship problems already. This didn't surprise me, since I feel like Kerry has trouble getting close to people. We walked and talked. We talked everything out. She is really an awesome girl. Came back to the dorm at about 11:00 and talked to Kerry about her. Counseled him until well past midnight. Went over my speech one more time. Helping others kept my mind off my own relationship problems (and my speech)!

Tuesday, November 27, 1984

I gave my speech on comics during Oral Comm class. It went great! I don't know what I was so worried about. But I did get this feedback from the professor:

"You use your hands too much when you speak," she said.

"It's probably my Italian side that's to blame," I replied. The class laughed.

"Let's try the last part of your speech with your hands tied behind your back."

It didn't go so well.

After chapel it was time for lunch. I lost my class notebook, so I stopped and prayed that it would be returned to me somehow. I needed it! Studied and relaxed all afternoon. Kerry and I talked a bunch about Tina and Kendra. At least he is confiding in me again as a friend.

After dinner, I went to the basketball game (ORU vs. Tulsa University). It was a lot of fun, even though we lost by four points. I sat next to Cheryl and we talked through most of it. Returned to my room depressed again. I think I am just one of several guys that Cheryl is interested in. Ended the day talking to Kerry about my struggles this time. He is still such a good friend.

Went to bed feeling sort of empty and without purpose. I think I have the gift of helping others. But do I want it?

Wednesday, November 28, 1984

After my morning classes, I went to lunch. Came back to the room and studied with Kerry. I found my notebook! Why do I doubt that the Lord is looking out for me?

I got some letters from my younger brothers, Josh and Matt—cute Christmas pictures (they are 8 and 6). Went to my Synthesis meeting, and it went well. Walked to dinner with Korrine. Made reservations for the Christmas banquet on Sunday. Kerry and I are going during the same time slot with Kendra and Cheryl.

In the evening, I did some studying and talked to Cheryl and Julie. I met Cheryl at 10:00 and told her ALL I felt about her. I laid it all on the line. I opened my heart to her. And...she told me she wanted to be "just friends". She said it would take time to feel more than that. I told her I understood, and I just wanted honesty in our relationship because I valued it so much.

I went back to my dorm feeling a little let down, but not totally depressed. I went into our dorm conference room and read my Bible until midnight. Talked to Skip the Chaplain and Kerry about it all too. My time in God's Word really encouraged me. I am still thankful for Cheryl even if she wants to be "just friends".

Thursday, November 29, 1984

Received a pleasant surprise in my Oral Comm class—an A on my speech! Even with my hands going all over the place.

Lunch at noon, then off to the LRC to study. Back to the dorm to catch up on necessary sleep. Dinner at 5:00 and more relaxation in the evening. I was caught up on my studies. Called

Cheryl and studied a little with Kerry. Krusty's Pizza. TV. Bed. Praising the Lord for my life.

Friday, November 30, 1984

At the end of each semester, every ORU student had to run a "field test." We had to run a certain distance by a set amount of time. Or else. Or else what? It was not my favorite thing to do. I ran the field test in 10 minutes, 36 seconds, which wasn't too bad. But I was dying.

Went to an early lunch, then met Kerry to run errands. We bought Christmas cards and ordered corsages for our dates. Got a haircut too. Mom called and checked in. I called Julie and we talked for a while.

After dinner, I went with Skip and Paul to rent two of my favorite movies: "The Pink Panther Strikes Again" and "Live and Let Die". We watched them until 1:30 a.m. Other brothers joined in. Had pizza and turned in at 2:00 a.m. Another month in the books here at ORU. God is Love! How can I learn to love Him and other people well?

December, 1984

Saturday, December 1, 1984

Slept in until 11:30. Went to lunch, then watched basketball in my room until 2:30. I love college basketball season! Kerry and I picked up our corsages and put them in Whitney's fridge. Chilled out in Skip the Chaplain's room the rest of the afternoon. Had a great spiritual talk. Took a few minutes to call Cheryl.

Went to dinner, then to the ORU vs. LSU basketball game at 6:30. It was an exciting game, but we lost by three. Returned to my dorm room and talked with the guys until midnight. Made a McDonald's run to put me to sleep. Yes, late night burgers had that effect on me. Thinking about Cheryl, but don't know what to do. Trusting God for us and my other "friend" relationships.

Sunday, December 2, 1984

Went to Higher Dimensions for church with Kerry. It was an awesome service. Pastor Carlton can preach the Word! Still not used to a three-hour worship service, though. Because of that, we don't mind showing up an hour late. Still an hour of singing left!

After lunch, I gave Bry a call, then Mom and Dad. They were all good conversations. Studied with Kerry until 3:30. Went over to Whitney's and picked up our corsages, then got dressed for the banquet.

Almost like giddy schoolboys, we picked up Cheryl and Kendra for the Christmas banquet. The night was awesome! Had appetizers and took pictures at 5:15, followed by a prime rib dinner. Sure, it was in the cafeteria, but it was still great. After dessert, we took some goofy pictures together, then listened to the band and choir perform in a candlelight concert.

For the "after party, we went to Claudius dorm and waited for the girls to change clothes. We drove them to Denny's, and sat around and talked. Big spenders, aren't we! Came back to campus at midnight and dropped them off. Cheryl was awesome! Kerry and I debriefed early into the morning. What a day!

Monday, December 3, 1984

Went to Humanities at 8:50, then had a late breakfast. Came home in time to watch Jeopardy with Gregg the roommate. This was becoming our morning tradition now—a little friendly competition. Have I said how much I like any form of trivia game? Relaxed, then went to lunch. Studied all afternoon.

Went to dinner at 5:15. Spent the evening talking and watching television with Mitch. Gave Tina a call. Went to a wing meeting at 11:00. Studied until 12:30 a.m., then talked to Kerry before bed. I'm actually looking forward to going home for Christmas break, which sort of surprises me. Maybe God is changing my heart.

Tuesday, December 4, 1984

I slept through my English class (which meant I missed a test!). I need to invest in a better alarm clock. Or put it further across the room. Went to Old Testament at 8:50, then took the test at 9:50 (which meant I missed Oral Comm). I either need to go to bed earlier or take later classes! Went to chapel at 10:50, then off to lunch. It started to snow! Three inches today!

Went back to my room and studied. Left at 1:45 for the mall with Korrine. Got the film from my camera developed (some great pictures with Cheryl from the Christmas banquet) and bought Christmas presents for Whitney, Kerry, Gregg the roommate, Tina, and Cindy. We shopped until 5:00, then back to the cafeteria for dinner.

Talked to Cheryl, then relaxed and studied the rest of the evening. It seemed like everyone on campus was out playing in the snow—major snowball fights! Cafeteria trays were great for sledding down the big hill! Drifted off to sleep at 12:45.

Wednesday, December 5, 1984

Went to Old Testament at 9:50, and came back in time to watch (and play) Jeopardy with Gregg. New drama on the floor: Ted (a brother I don't know very well) has been secretly taping conversations to give to the head R.A. of all R.A.s. I have no idea who is getting in trouble for what.

After lunch, relaxed and wrote Christmas cards. Started reading a new book: "The Romance Factor" by Alan Loy McGuinness. It's the sequel to "The Friendship Factor" which really helped me with my "relationship sermon". I was ready to move from friendship to romance!

Went to the mall with Kerry and Keith at 4:00 and got a special Christmas card for Cheryl. Ate dinner in the cafeteria, followed by a phone call from Gena! First conversation in over two weeks. We reconciled, so everything's cool again. I called Cheryl and had an awesome half-hour talk. Talked to Tina too. Studied, watched TV, and ate late-night Krusty's pizza. Another great day.

Thursday, December 6, 1984

Went to my last English Comp 1 class (yay!), followed by breakfast. Went to Oral Comm, then chapel in a packed Christ's Chapel. It was really good. Campus Chaplain B.J. taught on marriage and sex. Just what I wanted to hear.

Afterward, walked over to the City of Faith with Kerry to wait for his mom (who was having a medical check-up of some kind). We went to the mall for a late lunch and some shopping. Came back to the dorm, read, and then went to dinner.   Went to Claudius girls' dorm open house from 7:00-8:00. Hung out with Cheryl and met her actual brother who was visiting. Came back to my room and wrote Christmas cards all evening. Ended the night watching TV and talking to Kerry. Another great day.

Friday, December 7, 1984

Started my day in PE class, took my test, and got re-weighed. I gained two pounds this semester (for a total of 132 lbs). I'm massive! Thankfully, I don't have to worry about being forced on a special diet to lose weight. I would gain more, if it wasn't for my extremely fast metabolism. Got back to my room to read and play Jeopardy with Gregg.

After lunch, I sent out all my Christmas cards. Spent the afternoon in the bookstore and at the mall again. Kerry and I exchanged gifts—I got him a calendar, and he got me Sweet Comfort Band's "Perfect Timing" cassette. Awesome. The title song was so appropriate for me at this point in my life.

When I needed a shoulder to cry on

You dried all my tears

When I wanted someone to rely on

That's when you came near

And when it comes to loving me
You're the best of all
You're always in the right place at the right time
To catch me when I fall

Chorus: You've got perfect timing
You're not a minute too soon
Not a moment too late
You've got perfect timing
I can see when you move
I can feel when you wait

You hold tomorrow in the palm of your hand
Everything runs by your master plan
You've got perfect timing

When I had to have someone to count on
You were second to none
When I needed a friend that would hold on
You were the only one

And when it comes to loving me
You're the best of all
You're always in the right place at the right time
To catch me when I fall

After hanging out for a while, I went to dinner with Julie. We talked a lot, and I asked her out again. Rejected! She (and the other sisters) were too busy studying, so Skip, Darrell and I went to see "Beverly Hills Cop" at the mall. Funny movie, but I felt guilty watching it. Still, another pretty great day!

Saturday, December 8, 1984

Slept in. Went to lunch at 11:45 with Kerry and Tina. Returned to my room and called Cheryl, then Dad. Sadly, things are back to being tough at home. Divorce is on the horizon again, at least according to my father. So much for being excited about going home for Christmas break,

Spent some time cleaning my room, then left at 3:00 with Skip the Chaplain to get Christmas decorations for the hall. We put tissue paper on lights, and ribbons all around. We worked through dinner until 7:00. I got ready and picked up Cheryl to see Steve Taylor and Bryan Duncan (formerly of Sweet Comfort Band) in concert on campus. Both were awesome, but had way different styles. Steve Taylor's "Meltdown" was quite the political statement. The concert went until 11:00!

After the concert, Cheryl and I sat in the Prayer Gardens, looked at Christmas banquet photos, talked and prayed together. She is really so awesome. Was I moving from the friend zone to the romance zone yet?

Returned to the dorm and started decorating again—until 4:30 in the morning! Kerry helped for a while, but the last survivors were Skip the Chaplain, Randy, Keith, and me. Randy and I ordered pizza at 1:30. We put "snow" on all the doors, with various jolly Christmas quotes (from our favorite Christmas movies). Our Christmas tree was set up in our little chapel areas with bright flashing lights. We even made a fireplace with stockings and all our pictures on them. Even though this all sounds sort of nerdy, it was a lot of fun. A neon "Merry Christmas" sign was the last thing we put over the elevator doors. We were ready for the season!

Sunday, December 9, 1984

Got up at 10:30. After an early lunch, vacuumed and cleaned our room. Called Whitney, then went to the sister wing's open house at 1:30. Hung out with Julie a lot, as well as Tina and Cindy.

Our reciprocal open house was from 3:30 to 5:30. That's why we worked so hard to decorate the seventh floor! We served sparkling cider and cookies to the girls. Everyone loved it! (Not bad for social director). Even some of the cool ninth floor girls came for a visit (and Christmas hugs). Sadly, Cheryl couldn't come because she was sick. Gave Tina and Cindy their gifts, which they loved.

At 6:30, Kerry and I went over to Whitney and Mark's apartment for dinner and a gift exchange. I got an Uno game. We left there at 8:30. I relaxed and went to bed at 10:30 (new freshman year record).

Monday, December 10, 1984

Got up in time to play Jeopardy with Gregg. Went to a nearly empty cafeteria at 11:30 for lunch. Returned to study and relax. Got a call from Dad and a card from Julie. Even better, got a card with $200 from Gram and Gramps!

Went to dinner at 5:00, then studied more. Took my Oral Comm final exam from 7:00-8:00. It was rough. Called Cheryl. Talked to Becky, her roommate, for a half hour. She's cool. Finally caught up with Cheryl. She's a bit depressed, for some reason. Made some prank Christmas calls before bed. Fifteen Christmas cards sent, two received (Cousin Whitney and Julie).

Tuesday, December 11, 1984

Slept in. Went to the mall at 11:00 with Darrell and Kerry to pick up our wing t-shirts. They weren't done. Sad. Bought Amy Grant's "Straight Ahead" cassette and went to lunch. I was slowly building my Contemporary Christian Music collection. After lunch, studied for my Humanities final all afternoon with Kim and Kerry. Went to the LRC to check on my Oral Comm exam grade. I made a lowly 76, but made an A in the class. My first A of my college career! Went on to my Humanities final at 4:30.

After dinner, I went to an O.T. study group from 7:00 until 9:00. Afterwards, Kerry, Kendra and I went to the mall. Kendra is quickly become one of my favorite ORU girls. She thanked me for her Christmas card. We finally picked up the wing "Lifeguard" shirts. It was a total hassle. They tried to charge us a whopping $17/shirt. I got it down to $12. Returned to the dorm at 10:30 and handed out the shirts. Kendra called me to check on me, sympathizing with my frustration. She is so sweet. Studied a little, talked with Kerry, and went to bed at 1:00 a.m.

Reflections on the day:

- Didn't get to talk to Cheryl today which was a bummer. Don't know what to feel about her, since she clearly likes Sean too. A lot. I will be giving her a present tomorrow, so her reaction will be interesting.

- Laura and Gena still haven't acknowledged their cards (Laura is to be expected).

- Kendra is a very cool friend to have, so I must keep that friendship.

- Cheryl's roommate, Becky, is cool too.

- The t-shirt hassle really bottomed out my day! But the Lord is pumping me up with joy!

Wednesday, December 12, 1984.

Got up in time to play Jeopardy with Gregg. Beat him again (up 4-2). Went to lunch at 11:30. Got my plane tickets in the mail. Studied all afternoon for my Old Testament final. During one of my study breaks, got into an argument with Kerry about Christmas cards. He thinks I am making a subtle move on Kendra. We made up. But he may be right.

Went to dinner at 5:15. Talked to Cheryl on the phone. More study of O.T. until 9:00. Then, I met Cheryl and we exchanged Christmas gifts.

I gave Cheryl: a charm necklace with a key and a heart.

Cheryl gave me: a Lifesaver candy book, chocolate cars, and a very friendly card.

Well, I guess I know where I stand! Still friendship factor territory. Went back to my studies until 12:45. Went to bed with Cheryl on my mind. She seems to be afraid to show any feelings towards me (if she has any at all).

Thursday, December 13, 1984.

Got up about as early as possible for me—7:00! Went to my English Comp exam at 8:00. Came back to my room to watch TV, including the all-important Jeopardy competition.

After lunch, studied Old Testament all afternoon. Talked to Julie, saying our goodbyes. She may not return to school next semester. Took my exam from 5:00-6:00. It was the worst exam ever (but I think I aced it).

After dinner, packed, cleaned my room, and relaxed all evening. Called Cindy and said goodbye. Tried to call Cheryl, but no answer. Got pretty depressed talking late into the night with Stacy, then Mitch, then Kerry—all about "my friend" Cheryl. Went to bed at 2:00 a.m. Sad that I never got to tell Cheryl goodbye, and she doesn't seem to care.

The big question: Why am I such a good counselor but lousy in my own relationships? Praying for answers. Praying for my upcoming counseling job at home.

Crete, Illinois (Home)

December 14, 1984

Friday, December 14, 1984.

Got up and finished packing. Said goodbyes to all my wingmates. Went to the Fishbowl at 10:00 and hugged Tina goodbye. Got my money from Stacy, then left with Kerry at 10:30 for the airport. Said goodbye to Kerry and gave him a good bro hug. My plane took off at 11:30. Landed first in St. Louis. Changed planes, and arrived at Chicago O-Hare at 3:15. Mom and Dad met me at the airport and we drove home together.

Went to dinner at The Charley Horse at 5:15 with the whole family. After dinner, came home and relaxed. Peck, one of my best high school friends, came over to catch up. We talked a long time about our "love interests" (Darcy and Cheryl). Looks like we are in the same boat! It was great talking to him again. We even had a decent theological conversation. After he left, I talked to Mom. Stayed up late, contemplating everything. Talked to Amy, my 11th grade sister, when she got home at midnight. I need serenity for the next three weeks!

Saturday, December 15, 1984.

Got up late. Baked Christmas cookies with Mom and the boys. Watched some college basketball and relaxed away the afternoon. Had dinner. Bry, my other best high school friend, came over at 7:30. We talked until 10:30. Then visited with Chris and Rachel, two other friends. We talked a lot about spirituality and the things we hope to accomplish in the future. It was great. Went to bed at 3:00 a.m. Still on the college sleep schedule!

Sunday, December 16, 1984.

Sunday late service at my home church! Bry, Amy (my sister) and I sat with my little brothers Josh and Matt. It was a really good service. Marcy, a girl I took out once in high school, sat with us. We didn't talk much. It was not a good date. She was more interested in Kevin Bacon (the actor) than me. Bry went home, and the four of us went home for Sunday dinner. Afterwards, watched some NFL football, then the movie "The Natural." Great baseball movie.

Went back to evening worship at 6:00. Picked up Rachel (Amy's friend) on the way. We had a great talk. She said she has really noticed my spiritual transformation! Our family had to greet at church, so I had the chance to talk to some people about ORU. Ambassador again! The service went until 7:30, since it was a Christmas concert. Amy and I drove home, dropping off Rachel on the way. We spent some time discussing the "gift of tongues" which was interesting. They don't believe in it.

Ate dinner with Amy, then called Peck. Watched "Moscow on the Hudson" until midnight, then off to bed. Drifted off to sleep thinking about leading a small Bible study while I'm home. Will talk to the pastor about. Cheryl is still on my mind!

Monday, December 17, 1984

Got up and jogged on Mom's mini-trampoline, the hippest exercise method of the mid-eighties. Have to stay fit! Gram and Gramps called me from Scottsdale and we talked for a while. After breakfast, relaxed, read the newspaper, and watched TV. Found some old teaching cassette tapes, to pass the time.

Mom and the boys came home from school at 4:00, and the four of us left at 5:00. I drove the family van and picked up Amy and Dad. We got to Uncle Charlie's and Aunt Karen's at 6:00 for a family Christmas celebration. I got a desk set from them. We ate Chinese food for dinner and left at 8:00.

When we got home, I set up the boys' racetracks. Watched TV and called Peck and Bry. Bed.

Tuesday, December 18, 1984

Got up, exercised, showered, and ate breakfast. At 11:15, left the house and picked up Peck. We went to lunch at Denny's and talked. It was very uncomfortable. We weren't on the same page spiritually anymore.

"You know, a lot of our classmates think you have joined some kind of cult at that college of yours," Peck said with a scowl.

"So, what do you think?" I asked.

"Well...I'm not sure. The speaking in tongues thing seems crazy to me. And you are much more serious than you used to be."

We went to his house and talked, until 3:00. I'm not sure if we can ever be close again, at this rate.

I picked up Amy at the bus stop at 3:30, came home and addressed envelopes. Dad came home soon afterwards. He broke down and cried with me. He told me that the marriage is all but over. Mom doesn't love him anymore! Here we go again. This is getting old, and more desperate with each passing day. I spent some time alone in prayer after that.

The little brothers and I had dinner alone. Bry called and we talked about it. Mom and Dad left. I watched TV alone all evening, punctuated by the writing of a letter to Cheryl. I told her that I would wait for her and apologized for putting any pressure on her. I'm sure the crumbling of my parents' marriage fueled that sentiment. Went to bed distraught, but trying to trust in the LORD.

Wednesday, December 19, 1984

Got up early and drove the boys to their school, Calvary Academy. Came home and wrapped Christmas gifts. Exercised and showered, then ate a late breakfast. Pretty much relaxed all morning and early afternoon. Left at 2:30 to pick up the boys from school.

Came home and read some of my old high school journals, and looked at pictures of Cheryl. I miss Tulsa! Peck called. He apologized for coming on too strong. Ate dinner with the family then watched some TV. Played Scrabble with Dad until 9:00. Talked with Amy about our parents late into the night. We share hopelessness.

Thursday, December 20, 1984

Relaxed the morning away. Read the newspaper, listened to cassette tapes, and read old letters. Left at 3:30 with Amy. We ran errands and then ended up at Lincoln Mall. I bought four cards and two books of poems. Do you think I'm becoming too emotional about my life?

Ate at McDonald's and got home at 7:30. Relaxed and watched TV all night. Talked to Bry before bed. Feeling a bit down, with no support from the family. Amy is just waiting for me to slip up—she doesn't think I've really changed. I get it. I have not been the best brother to her. I desperately want to be God's instrument of change!

Friday, December 21, 1984

Almost Christmas, and still no snow on the south side of Chicago. Sad. Ate breakfast, and talked to Peck on the phone. I'm just trying to stay connected. Left at 12:30 for Bry's house. We went to lunch at Wendy's, had a great talk, and picked up Peck at 2:00. Went out to Southlake Mall. Finished buying all my Christmas gifts.

Got back to Peck's house at 7:00, had dinner, and watched the TV show "V." Jeff, another friend from high school, came over. Leanne, Lisa, Michelle, Sue, Sandy, and Jeannine also stopped by. After the girls left, we played Trivial Pursuit until 10:00. After Jeff left, Sharon and Donna came over. It was like a mini-high school reunion! Darcy, Peck's girlfriend, came by for a minute. We sat around talking until 1:30 am. Even though it was nice to see everyone, I miss my college friends. Is my three weeks here up yet?

Saturday, December 22, 1984.

Watched sports all afternoon. No mail yet! At dinner, got into a huge conversation about Charismatic Christianity. It didn't go very well—my family doesn't understand me either. I thought we all claimed to be Christians!

Went to Peck's house, then to Bry's. Peck and Sharon came over and we all played pool and watched "This is Spinal Tap." It was hilarious. Lisa came over at 9:30. The five of us went to see the movie "Starman" in the theater at 10:00. Solid movie. Peck went home; the four of us went back to Bry's house. I went home at 12:30. Bry and I had another great chat about the Christian life. I'm surprised Bry is growing more in the faith than Peck.

Sunday, December 23, 1984

Got up and went to Sunday morning church. It was a good service. We picked up Grandma and returned home at 11:45. Had lunch, then talked to Peck on the phone.

At 3:30, Laura and Rachel came over (first time I've seen my old friend Laura since I've been home). We left at 4:00 to go to downtown Chicago for the Christmas lights and decorations (our annual family event). Had Chicago deep-dish pizza, of course! Got home at 8:15. Went over to some of Amy's friends for a couple of hours. Watched TV until after midnight. Still feel so out of place. Fell asleep telling myself that I need to bring Cheryl to Chicago this summer.

Monday, December 24, 1984

Christmas Eve! Got up late, then the whole family went back to downtown Chicago. We dropped off a gift at a friend of my dad's. Had lunch in the city, and came home. I tried to do my part by cleaning the house. Talked to Bry. He let me know that people continue to talk about how I have changed—especially my Charismatic beliefs. Sigh. Was I being a good or bad witness?

At 3:30, Amy and I picked up movies, then some family friends came over. We exchanged gifts (I got underwear). They left at 9:00. I complained to my parents about Chris (Amy's boyfriend) coming over on Christmas Eve. In my view, this should be a family

night! As usual, Amy won. She has always been the golden child."
I was pretty upset.

Chris and Amy stayed downstairs until 12:30 (away from the family) doing what exactly? I watched "It's a Wonderful Life." The best movie ever! It got me back into the spirit of Christmas. Finally got a couple of cards in the mail—from Tina and Cindy! I went to bed praying for Amy, and that I could be a witness to her. I don't want to alienate her. I really am very blessed.

Tuesday, December 25, 1984

Christmas! Woke up bright and early at 6:30, like I was a kid. The family opened presents until 9:00. Mom and Dad always got us way too many gifts. I got a Bible, a cassette tape, a calendar, Bible Trivia, a pocket trivia game, cologne, underwear (of course), a tie, two shirts, a sweater, and a jogging suit. As usual, a huge haul.

Watched "The Return of the Pink Panther" with Dad. The two of us were big Pink Panther fans. We all ate Christmas dinner at 2:30. Slept and relaxed, talked to Peck and Bry, and wrote letters.

Bry came over at 8:00 and we played Bible Trivia and talked until 1:15. Great talk yet again. At least I have one ally back home! Wrote a letter to Cheryl before falling asleep. Happy Birthday, Jesus! I need sleep!

Wednesday, December 26, 1984

Got up late, talked to Peck, and wrote a letter to Kendra. Peck came over for lunch. We went back to his house, then stopped at River Oaks Mall for some after-Christmas shopping (bought nothing).

We went to Bry's house, watched TV and played pool. Then, the three of us went to Denny's for dinner, then to Peck's house. Musical houses. At Peck's house, we played foosball. When the three of us were together, it was smarter to not talk about Christian stuff too much. It was like we were back in high school again.

Later, we went to the movies to see "2010." It was really good. From there we went to Sharon's house and played Trivial Pursuit until 11:30. Went back to Peck's, then he brought me home late. Exhausted. Sadly, Bry will be gone for five days on a family vacation. What will I do now?

Thursday, December 27, 1984

Morning babysitting duty of the little brothers. I think they see me more as an uncle than a true brother. Ate breakfast together, then wrote letters while they played. Talked to Peck. Made lunch for the boys.

We (and Amy) met Mom and Dad at River Oaks Mall at 3:00 to watch "Micki and Maude." Funny movie. Called some old high school friends, then ate dinner.

Afterwards, left my family and picked up Lynda, one of my best friend-girls at 7:30 and went to Baker's Square for some pie. We talked a lot...about everything. Dropped her off at 11:30 and came home. It was really a great talk. She gets me. Found out that I missed a call from Cheryl! Huge bummer! Went to bed after watching David Letterman.

Friday, December 28, 1984

Got up early and called Cheryl right away. We talked for a half hour. It was so good to hear her voice! Went back to bed. Got up again at 10:30 and talked to Peck. Left at 11:15 with Mom, Amy, and the boys (I drove separately). We went out to lunch, then to my Great Grandma Georgia's house. We had a great time (and I got $50 from her). It's so nice to still have one living great grandparent.

I got home at 3:30, but was locked out of the house. Napped in the van. The neighbor finally left me in. Nice to have trusted neighbors who shared house keys! Got dressed and went with Mom and Dad to a friend's wedding reception. It was weird being in my childhood Baptist church. Sat with Randy and Don, some old friends from elementary school. Got home late and talked with Kerry on the phone for the first time during Christmas break. I really miss him. Missing Cheryl, and still depressed about my parents' marriage.

Saturday, December 29, 1984

Slept in, then went to Peck's house. Watched some football and had lunch. Left at 2:30 and went to Randy's house. Randy, Don, and I hung out the rest of the afternoon. We had dinner, then a couple other friends came over. We rented the movie "Best Friends." I could really relate to it. Had a nice talk with Sandra, a cute Dutch girl from Canada. I'll probably write her when I get back to ORU. Went home at midnight.

Sunday, December 30, 1984

Got up at 10:30. We skipped church this morning, which is sort of sad. Watched the Bears games with Dad. They won! The Chicago Bears are now one game away from the Super Bowl! I talked to Peck afterwards, relaxed, and slept the rest of the afternoon. Had dinner, and played Bible Trivia with Mom and Dad. Spent the rest of the evening watching TV. Went to bed missing Cheryl. Again.

Monday, December 31, 1984

New Year's Eve! Pretty much did nothing all day, with a couple of phone calls to Peck and Randy. Had a late dinner at 6:15.

Lowlight of the day: a big argument with Amy about Illiana, our Christian high school.

"You know, most of the students aren't true Christians. They would rather party and goof off than serve the Lord," I said judgmentally,

"You don't know that. Maybe some in your class, but I have some good Christian friends!" Amy exclaimed.

"Like who... Rachel maybe. Even most of my friends are more secular than spiritual," I retorted,

"This is the brother I know...How is pride and arrogance spiritual? I knew you hadn't changed!"

That one really hurt.

I really blew it with her, and apologized later, but I don't think she really accepted it.

I left at 7:45 and went to Peck's house. Saw Leanne for a few minutes. Hung out and played cards until midnight. I was sad that Bry never called—who knows where he is. I left at 12:45 since it was storming terribly. Got home and watched TV until 2:00. Can't wait to get back to Tulsa. I won't be able to stand a whole summer here!

January, 1985

Tuesday, January 1, 1985

Woke to a basement flood! What a way to start 1985. This was a typical occurrence for houses with basements in Chicago. Too many cold pipes for one not to burst once in a while! The whole family was deployed for clean-up duty.

After lunch, I went over to Randy's house. We talked a lot until 5:00—about college, life, Charismatics, and music. We listened to some of my cassette tapes (my new Christian music). Had dinner with his family at 6:00. Love Randy's very normal parents. Rented the movie, "Sudden Impact."

I left at 9:15 and went over to Bry's house. Peck, Bry and I talked until 10:45 and then made a Burger King run. Returned to Bry's house and watched David Letterman until midnight. Peck left. Bry and I talked for a while, about missions, what he learned at the Urbana Missions Conference, etc. We prayed together for the first time ever. What a way to start 1985!

Five days left until Tulsa! Can't wait to see everyone! I am committed to making 1985 a year of service to the LORD. Bry has

really come around, and is growing big-time. We make a good pair.
Kerry and I also make a good pair. Cheryl is still awesome. Life is
really good, if you let it be.

Wednesday, January 2, 1985

Got up at 9:30 to a phone call from the police station. Not a
phone call you want to get first thing in the morning. Thankfully, it
was just about Amy having a flat tire. I called Dad and sent him to
help, since I had to babysit the boys.

Mom came home at 1:30, and I left for Peck's house. We
went to Southlake Mall. I bought a picture, a jacket, and a sweater.
We went back to Peck's house at 6:30. We ate dinner, then went to
Marshall Field's at 7:00. As we left the mall, I realized I had a flat
tire too! How weird! Peck and I changed it, and we got back to his
house at 9:00. We played cards with his mom and dad until 11:45.
Got home at 12:15, exhausted.

Leave for Tulsa at 10:00 am on Sunday. Can't wait to see
Cheryl, Kerry, Kendra, Tina, Cindy, Julie, Joe, Kyle, Brandon, Todd,
Walter, Mitch, Skip the Chaplain, Gena, Kim, Alyson, Kay, Becky,
Jennifer, Tammy, Laura, Kandy, Art, Gregg, Chuck, Paul, Darell,
Korinne,   Daphne,   Cheryl,   Cheryl,   Cheryl,   Cheryl,
Cheryl...EVERYONE! Even Oral!

Thursday, January 3, 1985

Amy and I went to the hairdresser's to get my hair permed (yes, men got perms in the 80s). From there, we went to lunch together. Most of our conversations are still at the surface, which keeps us out of trouble. I went to Randy's at 12:15 and stayed for a while. We had a great talk and said our goodbyes for the semester. I picked up Amy at 2:00 and went home. Relaxed until dinner. Went over to Bry's house, talked for a while, then went to another friend's house until 11:00. Dropped Bry off and went home. I'm looking forward to having a Bible study with some of my friends this summer, but I can't wait to get back to college! I was also glad to have wavy hair again.

Friday, January 4, 1985

Hung out all morning at home. Peck came over at 2:30 and we ran some errands. Went over to his house. We played cards with his sister until 5:30, then had some dinner. Bry came over at 7:15, and the three of us went to our high school "Physics Class Party." The party bombed—just us and three girls showed up (and Mr. Van Eck, our Physics teacher). We did an experiment and watched a science movie. Are we boring nerds or what?

Returned to Peck's house and played Trivial Pursuit, followed by a late snack at McDonald's. Peck took me home at 12:30. On the way home, we actually had our first great spiritual talk about a lot of things. He really seemed to understand. He told me that people had seen the change for good in me (even though it was pretty radical), which was gratifying. I hope this will lead to future talks. Went to bed at 1:30, satisfied.

Saturday, January 5, 1985

Last Day home for Christmas break! Got up late, showered, and went to see Grandma. She gave me quarters for laundry, and we said goodbye. Went home for lunch. Peck came over and watched me pack for school. Called Kerry and we talked for a while. Called Lynda and said goodbye. Peck and I ate dinner with my family, including my favorites of my dad's cousins, Carm and Ron. They are the funniest old-man twins ever.

Peck and I left at 7:00. We met Bry at Peck's house. We talked, played cards, and watched TV until midnight. Said my final goodbye to Peck. Bry drove me home and broke down emotionally; he is really suffering, losing everyone important in his life. I prayed with him, for the LORD to give him strength. Got home and finished packing. Hopefully, Bry can make it to the summer, where I can be there for him. I wish I could help him more! I wish he was at ORU with me!

Tulsa, Oklahoma

January 6, 1985

Sunday, January 6, 1985

Left for the airport at 8:00 with the whole family, stopping for breakfast on the way. Said my goodbyes and got on the plane at 10:00. It was sort of sad, but I was ready to go. Stopped over in St. Louis, arriving in Tulsa at 1:30. Waited for Kerry until his plane landed, and we caught the shuttle back to campus together. Unpacked and watched my beloved Chicago Bears lose! 23-0! It stunk! No Super Bowl for us.

We all got our first semester grades in our post office boxes when we arrived back at school. Kerry got a 4.0 and I got a 3.8. I was actually very thankful! It could have been much worse. We ate dinner in the cafeteria with Lisa and Joanna. Went back to the dorm and played Bible Trivia with Kerry and Skip the Chaplain. Hung out, and talked to Mitch and Skip. I called Tina at 11:30 and we talked for a while. Finally went to bed at 12:20, very tired. But it was so great to be back! Everyone else should arrive tomorrow!

Monday, January 7, 1985

First thing in the morning, I went to the Mabee Center with Paul and Skip. Kerry met us there, and we waited in line for four hours for various sports tickets! Saw a lot of people: Tina, Cindy, Jennifer, Mechelle, etc. It was a long morning, but fun. At 1:30, Skip the Chaplain, Paul and I went to Arby's for lunch. Went back to the dorm and chatted with Kyle and Joe for a while. Got five new cassette tapes in the mail. My Christian music library was starting to take shape. Welcomed back everyone to school for a new semester!

Went to dinner at 5:15. Met Tina, Cindy, Tammy, and Daphne at 7:00 and walked back to the Mabee Center. We watched our basketball team win! Saw Kendra. It was great to talk with her. Came back to my room and called Dad. Watched TV and went to bed. Still haven't seen Cheryl. It's great to be back.

Tuesday, January 8, 1985

First day of my new spring classes! Had New Testament Survey at 8:50. Afterwards went to the bookstore with Julie and bought all my new textbooks. They were expensive, as usual. Went to the first chapel of the semester in Christ's Chapel at 10:45. It was cool. Saw Laura and Gena. Then went on to Calculus at 12:30. Talked with Cheryl (finally) and Becky. Sean cut into our time. Upsetting! He was definitely making moves on Cheryl.

Went to a late lunch at 1:15. Back to the room and did my Calculus homework. Went to Media Writing at 5:00. What a great class! I made a good choice becoming a Communication/Journalism major. Went to dinner at 6:15. Saw Alyson, Cathy, and Jennifer! Back for a relaxing evening and good conversation with the guys.

Went to bed with a lot of peace about Cheryl. God continues to answer my prayers. I just need to sit back and let things cool down for a while. I'll see her every day in Calculus, but I don't plan on calling her too much. I really like her. I wish she would give me the chance to love her.

Wednesday, January 9, 1985

Went to New Testament Discussion class at 8:50, and English at 9:50. Played Jeopardy with Greg at 11:00. Went to lunch, mailed a letter to Sandra, then off to Calculus. Talked to Cheryl a little, but Sean is in the class too. Bummer.

After doing some homework later in the afternoon, I went to dinner with Todd, Tina, and Cindy. Afterwards, did more homework, watched TV, and ate pizza. Bed. About as normal of a college day as you could ask for.

Thursday, January 10, 1985

I woke up believing it would be a great day for some reason. Went to NT Survey at 8:50 with Kerry, followed by breakfast. Went to chapel at 10:50. The 1980 Miss America, Cheryl Pruitt spoke! She was awesome. What a great thing to be beautiful inside and out! Went to lunch at 12:30 with Kerry and Cindy. Back to the dorm at 1:00 for homework and a nap. Went to Media Writing at 5:00, followed by dinner at 6:15. Had a great talk with Tompa, Robin, and Richard (a new brother on our floor).

After dinner, Todd, Kerry and I met Tina and Pam at 7:15 at Christ's Chapel. We saw "Soul's Afire" sing (an all-black choir), followed by Carlton Pearson preaching. It was awesome. What a great time of praise, worship, and rededication. My favorite quote of Carlton's was:

"Sometimes God doesn't tell us His plan because we wouldn't believe it anyway."

That is so true! Returned to my room at 10:30. Read my Bible for a while and went to bed. This was a great day!

Friday, January 11, 1985

Got up and went to English Comp at 9:50 with Kendra. Back to the dorm for another Jeopardy match with Gregg. After lunch, went to Calculus (Cheryl wasn't there, for some reason). Returned home and slept and relaxed the afternoon away.

Went to dinner at 5:15. Found out that Jennifer is finally returning to school tomorrow. Went to see "Terminator" at 9:00 with Kerry, Ted, Pam, Tammy, Kathy, Daphne, and Reena. It was a cool movie, but very violent! Returned home and talked to Tina. Worried about Joe and Kyle—they seem to be moving away from the Lord. Kerry is almost giving up on Kendra, but I still like her!

Saturday, January 12, 1985

Met Tina, Tammy, Paul, and Mary Lynn (new sister) at 9:30. Stood in line for Petra concert tickets! I had fallen in love with this Christian rock band. We froze until 11:30, but got tenth row seats, so it was worth it. Went to Denny's afterward and had a great breakfast. Came back at 1:00 and called Bry. He's doing well. Our Bible study that I'm planning on leading this summer is growing! Spent the afternoon playing Skip the Chaplain's new computer game and talking.

Went to dinner at 6:15, then to a basketball game. We won! Saw Cheryl there with Sean. Depressing. Home at 9:30. Talked with Skip the Chaplain until 1:00 am. Also talked to Kerry about Cheryl until 2:15.

Lord, this has been an awesome week in many respects, but... I don't understand your will or your timing! What's to become of me and Cheryl? I think it's over. My first day of accepting this fact. Too many friendships, with no potential for a future with anyone!

Sunday, January 13, 1985

Went to Higher Dimensions with Kerry at 9:30. Awesome service. This is my church now, for sure. The singing and preaching pulled me out of my depression. Came home at 12:30 and had lunch. Helped Kerry change the oil in his car. Went over to cousin Whitney's apartment and talked with her. Returned to my room and did some homework. Called Dad at 3:00. Talked to Mom too. Called Peck. Went to dinner at 5:30. Played Skip the Chaplain's computer game, and watched TV. Ate pizza and talked.

Still need to know God's will on my relationships!

Monday, January 14, 1985

Went to Humanities at 8:50, then to breakfast with Kerry afterwards. Played Jeopardy with Greg at 11:00. Lunch at 11:30, then Calculus.

"Hi! How's life?" asked Cheryl.

"Great, how are you?" I said.

She smiled and gave me a thumbs up. That was it. Confirmation.

Went to the bookstore and then off to PE class at 2:30. Back at the dorm, talked with Todd until 5:00. Called Kendra, but no answer. Went to dinner, and talked to Tina. Back to the dorm for homework. Had a nice talk with Walter. He is quickly becoming my favorite African-American friend. He's from New York and is very spiritually minded.

Had a wing meeting at 11:30, with leader's meeting afterwards. We discussed our small groups. Skip the Chaplain talked to me about Tammy. Still. Went to bed at 12:30, wanting to at least salvage a friendship with Cheryl.

Tuesday, January 15, 1985

Went to NT Survey at 8:50. Saw Cindy. Went to breakfast with Kerry. Went to chapel at 10:45, followed by Calculus. Saw Cheryl. Went back to the room, then to Humanities at 2:20. It's just as boring as last year. Had Media Writing at 5:00. Got a 90 on my first paper!

Talked with Cindy at dinner. Came back to my room and studied all evening. The highlight was an hour-long phone call with Kendra! She gave me great help with Cheryl, and I counseled her about Kerry. Ate pizza and hung out with the guys. Our R.A. was cracking down on Gregg, Kyle, and Joe tonight. They need to stop their rebellious ways. They need Jesus! I need new girls in my life (and Jesus too, of course).

Wednesday, January 16, 1985

New Testament Discussion at 8:50, followed by English Comp. Gregg and I had our traditional game of Jeopardy at 11:00.

Wish I could talk with him about his choices in life. Went to lunch, then off to Calculus. Wrote a note to Alyson and picked out a card for Cindy. Came back to the room, slept, and watched a Dair video.

Dinner at 5:30. Ran into Cheryl for a brief moment. After some TV watching, called Cheryl at 10:00. We actually talked until 11:30.

"I really like Sean...a lot," Cheryl finally blurted out.

Just what I figured. "Well, I hope you know that I want the best for you," I replied.

"I do know that. I really admire you. You have matured so much since we first met."

Sigh. Just what I wanted. Maturity. Admiration.

"Whoever marries you would be one lucky girl," she continued.

Well, at least I got my wish that we will stay good friends. All in all, it turned out good, I guess. I talked to Kerry about it afterwards, as well as Skip the Chaplain. Went to bed very relaxed for the first time in a while. Thankful for some closure.

Thursday, January 17, 1985

New Testament Survey at 8:50. Went to breakfast then back to the room. Chapel at 10:45. Met Tina at 12:30 for social director business and went to lunch. Afterwards, hung out and talked with Skip the Chaplain and Kerry. Did homework. Went to dinner, then returned to study all evening. Talked to Tina again. Solidly normal day with peace in my heart. A no drama.

Friday, January 18, 1985

Got up at 7:00 and had a prayer meeting with some of the brothers until 7:30. Studied a little and relaxed. Went to a late breakfast at 9:15, then to English Comp at 9:50. Came back and played Jeopardy with Gregg. Mailed Cheryl a poem I had written. I just can't help myself. Went to Calculus at 12:20 and took a very rough test. Drove around with Kerry until 5:30, then to dinner.

After dinner, went with Randy, Art, and Skip to babysit for a local family. At 9:30, met Todd, Walter, Mitch, Robin, Tammy, and Mary Lynn. Went to see "The Muppet Movie." It was fun. Went to the Depot at 11:20 and saw Kerry and Brandon. Bed at 1:30 am. Time to continue strengthening my friendships!

Saturday, January 19, 1985

Slept in until 11:00. Went to lunch. Saw Cheryl and talked for a bit. Came home and did homework until 4:30. Called Tina. Went to an early dinner with Kerry, then to the shopping mall. Saw Kay, Carla, and Darlena! Kerry and I came back to the dorm and watched TV together all evening. Did nothing on a Saturday night! (It was cold and windy; hitting zero degrees). Talked to Skip the Chaplain about relationships again. Glad the chaplain was always available. Went to bed early in the morning. Happy.

Sunday, January 20, 1985

Super Bowl Sunday! Went to Higher Dimensions for church at 9:30 with Kerry, Walter, and Todd. It was awesome as usual. Went to lunch at 12:30. Back to the dorm. Called Mom and Dad, Peck and Bry. Everything is cool at home, on all fronts. Talked to Tina and got a note from Cindy. Left at 4:30 with Skip the Chaplain and Art for the grocery store. Bought food and went over to Randy's (he's housesitting for another local family). Watched the 1985 Super Bowl! Sadly, the Miami Dolphins lost. Back to the dorm at 10:30. Called Cheryl and talked until 11:30. Great talk. Another happy day.

Two words the Lord has given me for 1985:
SUCCESS in all things, relationships, etc.
CONSISTENCY always. No fluctuations, continual growth.

Monday, January 21, 1985

Humanities at 8:50, followed by breakfast. Back to the room to watch the Presidential Inauguration. It's President Ronald Reagan again, thankfully! Went to lunch at 11:30, then to Calculus. Surprisingly, got a 96 on my test! Talked to Cheryl. Back to the dorm at 1:15. Went to HPE at 2:30. Ran a mile afterwards.

Dinner at 5:15. Talked to Tina and Cindy. We planned our wing retreat for March 2-3. Did homework all evening. Called Cheryl at 9:30. We are talking more now as friends. Wing meeting at 11:00. Bed at 12:30. Happy.

Tuesday, January 22, 1985

New Testament Survey, breakfast, and chapel. Meadowlark Lemon of the Globetrotters spoke! He's actually attending ORU as a student—at the age of 52—to become a preacher. How cool is that?

Went to Calculus at 12:20, then lunch. Studied and relaxed. Boring Humanities at 2:20. Went to Media Writing at 5:00. After dinner, I studied and relaxed. All of a sudden, I started feeling terrible. Ate pizza, but remarkably it didn't cure my oncoming winter cold! Heal me Lord. Give me a date Lord! (In no particular order)

Wednesday, January 23. 1985

Went to breakfast. Had a great talk with Reena, another cool sister. Went to NT Survey, followed by English Comp and Jeopardy with the roommate. Lunch and Calculus at 12:20. It is starting to become more and more difficult to see Cheryl all the time! Maybe that's the head cold talking. After class, wrote letters to friends back home: Randy, Julie, Rachel, and Lynda. Studied.

Went to dinner at 5:15. Still felt very under the weather, so got in bed at 6:30. Watched TV and tried to rest. Got some Excedrin from Tina and finally fell asleep. I want a date for Friday night, but probably don't need one!

Thursday, January 24, 1985

Went to NT Survey at 8:50 followed by breakfast. Went to chapel at 10:30. It was very good. At 1:00, went to lunch and to the bank with Skip the Chaplain. Returned to the dorm and called Dad. Studied. Went to Media Writing at 5:00. Left at 5:20, since the teacher didn't show (he's probably sick too).

Went to dinner, then studied, and slept the evening away. Talked to Mom and Tina. Had a huge argument with Mitch about salvation. Faith alone? Or faith plus good works? Eternal security? Can we lose our salvation? Followed up with good talks with Kerry and Todd. Bed. Still trying to let go of Cheryl!

Friday, January 25, 1985

Up at 7:00. Had prayer meeting until 7:30. Read my Bible and prayed. Went to breakfast with Skip the Chaplain at 9:15. Went to English Comp at 9:50 (saw Kendra). Played Jeopardy with Greg. Went to lunch, then Calculus. Greeted Cheryl cordially.

After doing some homework, went to the AC with Todd and ran two miles. Each semester, our aerobics points started over. It was time to get exercising! Saw Cheryl again. At 4:30, went to the mall with Skip, Walter, Art, and Randy. Ate dinner in the food court. Back at the dorm at 6:30, just in time to see Kerry off on a date with Kay to see Randy Stonehill in concert. I decided to sit this concert out, since I didn't have a date myself

I spent the evening playing computer games. Called Tina. Thankfully, she had another option for us single people. Met Tina, Art, Walter, Skip the Chaplain, and Korrinne at the movies to see "The Flamingo Kid" at 9:45. Good dessert and conversation afterwards.

Saturday, January 26, 1985

Slept in. Early lunch with Kerry at 11:30. Afterwards, we went to the LRC to study until 2:30. I bought the newest Petra cassette: "Beat the System"! I need to find a way to beat the system. Back to the dorm to relax. Talked to Tina.

At 7:00, went to the basketball game with Mitch, Skip, Tina and Mary Lynn. We lost! Back at the Fishbowl, twelve of us played Trivial Pursuit until 11:15. Tina was my partner. We were good. We all went to Mazzio's Pizza at 11:30.

Fun day, even though Cheryl is always in the back of my mind. Kerry confided in me that he is still in love with Tina. Tina and Cindy are just great sisters to me!

Sunday, January 27, 1985

Cleaned my room, then off to Higher Dimensions with Kerry at 9:30. It snowed while we were in worship! Home at 12:15 for lunch. The girls' open house started at 1:00. Saw some sisters and some other good acquaintances. Stayed until 2:30. We had our open house from 3:00-5:00. Cheryl never visited.

Went to dinner at 5:00. Had a great talk with Cindy. Talked to Mitch for an hour. Wrote a paper. Bed at 12:15.

Monday, January 28, 1985

Humanities at 8:50, followed by breakfast. Played Jeopardy with Gregg at 11:00. Went to lunch, then to Calculus. Actually had a nice talk with Cheryl. Got a package from home. Called my cousin Whitney. Went to HPE at 2:30. Ran two miles again. Home and showered because it was hair check day. Passed.

Ate dinner at 5:15. Came back to the room and called Mom and Dad. Went to the basketball game. We lost again. Spent the rest of the evening doing homework and talking. Got my plane tickets to Arizona for Spring Break! Called Grams and told her I was coming with Whitney. Talked to Whitney about Cheryl. Went to bed at 1:00 am.

Tuesday, January 29, 1985

Went to New Testament Survey at 8:50. Talked with Tina at breakfast. Went to chapel at 10:45, then to Calculus. Not a word from Cheryl. Went to lunch, followed by boring Humanities at 2:20 and Media Writing at 5:00.

After dinner, did my social director job (collected money), studied, and took a poll for homecoming queen. Called Tina. Watched TV and went to bed.

Wednesday, January 30, 1985

Got up and went to NT Survey at 8:50, followed by English Comp at 9:50. Had a nice talk with Kendra. Played Jeopardy with the roommate at 11:00. Went to lunch and Calculus. Back to the dorm, feeling a bit down. Talked to Todd about it.

Studied, then went to dinner at 5:00. Returned to the dorm, walking with Tina. Tina and I went to Vespers at 9:00. It was freezing outside! But Vespers helped me to get some peace with the LORD. Went back to my room, watched TV, ate hamburgers, and went to bed. Talked to Kerry about Kendra. He gave me the go-ahead to pursue her! This was a very surprising turn of events.

Thursday, January 31, 1985

Went to NT Survey at 8:50 with Kerry. Still freezing outside. Talked to Kendra on the way to breakfast. After I ate, talked with Tammy until 10:30. It was a good talk, for us. Went to chapel at 10:45. It was awesome! Had a report on summer missions. The ORU student mission teams were introduced. It was convicting.

Maybe I should have signed up. As our Missions Director finished his report, I prayed this prayer in my heart:

"Lord, you know I would love to go on a missions trip this summer. But, alas, the teams are full and set for this summer. I guess you don't want me to go this year. I'll be ready next summer, maybe! Your will be done."

Back to the dorm and then to lunch at 12:30. After lunch, typed up a paper all afternoon. Talked to Whitney and Grams. Went to Media Writing at 5:00. My teacher really liked my paper! After dinner, called Tina and had a good, fun talk. Studied. Talked to Kendra briefly. Talked to and prayed with Scott the "Spiritual One" on the hall. Talked with Skip the Chaplain and Todd. Watched TV. Waited up for a call from Kendra, but it never came. Finally went to bed at 1:00 am. I love you LORD! You are number one!

February, 1985

Friday, February 1, 1985

Got up at 7:00. Prayed until 7:30. Went to breakfast and then English Comp at 9:50. I talked to Kendra; she is busy tonight—may see her tomorrow. Won my fourth straight Jeopardy match against Gregg, followed by an early lunch.

Went to Calculus at 12:20. Talked to Cheryl a little. Went running with Todd at 2:30, then lifted weights. Back to the dorm at 3:45 for relaxation and laundry. After dinner, I picked up my banquet photos with Tina, Skip, and Todd. They were so good that they were depressing. Watched TV all evening. At pizza with Mitch, Rob, and Todd. Bed!

$20 worth of quarters stolen from me for a second time! Strangely, I am overflowing with joy, for no earthly reason.

Saturday, February 2, 1985

Saturday morning sleep-in. Went to lunch at 11:30. Did homework and watched TV. Talked to Cindy and Tina. Called Kendra.

Went to dinner at 5:00. Kerry and I picked up Art from work, then back to the dorm. Kerry and I went to the AC, ran, and worked out until 8:00. Talked to Walter and Todd. Met Kendra at 9:30 at the Depot and talked until midnight! Unbelievable! Awesome! Weird! I can't hardly describe it. We have absolutely everything in common. We are the same person! That must be why I like her so much. We even hugged goodnight.

Went back to the dorm and talked to Todd and Mitch, on a bit of a high. Then this happened:

"Our summer missions team lost our sound technician today," Todd said. I had forgotten that Todd was on the Southeast Asia music missions team. He was a great singer.

"That's too bad. I'll pray that you find a replacement quickly," I replied.

"Well...here's the thing. I already prayed. And God told me that you are the one to replace our lost team member. God wants you to be our sound guy!"

My head exploded. I didn't know what to say. I got up and went back to my room in utter torment. Was I really serious when I told God I would go to the mission field? Kerry popped his head in to say goodnight. I talked with him about this shocker. He prayed with me into the wee hours of the morning. My head is still spinning.

Sunday, February 3, 1985

I'm glad it's Sunday, especially in light of the crazy roller coaster of emotions I was on yesterday. Went to Higher Dimensions at 9:30 with Kerry and Todd. Awesome sermon by a guest speaker. Kerry and I had lunch with Cousin Whitney and Mark. It was great to be with them. They are so stable and mature.

Back to the room at 2:30. Called Mom and Dad, Bry and Peck. Went to dinner at 5:00 with Todd. Talked to Daphne and Reena. Came back to the room but did absolutely no homework; my head was still filled with questions about the summer. Talked to Tammy, Kendra, Tina, and Cindy. Sat around and talked with the guys until bedtime. Maybe I should go? Is God sending me? Do I have a choice in the matter? What about all my summer plans with my friends back home? Maybe that's my mission field. After all, when you walk out of Higher Dimension Evangelical Center, the big words on the wall say:

"You are now entering your mission field."

Monday, February 4, 1985

Three inches of snowfall as my eyes opened this morning. Went to Humanities at 8:50, then breakfast, then Jeopardy with Gregg at 11:00. Went to lunch, then Calculus at 12:20. Did see Kendra at lunch for a moment. Back to the dorm at 1:15. Went to PE at 2:30. Ran two miles and worked out.

Kerry and I went to dinner, and hung out with Tammy, Tina, and Cindy. Got a letter and $25 from Grandma. Studied for the rest of the night. Had a wing meeting at 11:00. The Head R.A. spoke— he was great. Just after midnight, Todd's summer music mission team director came and interviewed me in my room. He seems to really like me. There's a good possibility I'll be going to Southeast Asia this summer! Too wild. Went to bed, joyful and anxious at the same time. Lord, help me follow your lead.

Tuesday, February 5, 1985

Went to NT Survey at 8:50, then breakfast. Went to chapel at 10:45, then Calculus at 12:20. Calculus is so boring, which makes no sense for someone who loves math. I don't understand this stuff (and I'm not sure it's really math)!

Went to lunch, then Humanities at 2:20. Also boring. Studied. Media Writing at 5:00. Got a 95 on my paper and 100 on my quiz! My teacher loved my news story! Went to dinner at 6:15. Studied Humanities all evening. Bed at 12:45, overflowing with joy and peace.

Wednesday, February 6, 1985

Got up at 8:00. Went to NT Discussion at 8:50, and English Comp at 9:50 (but it was cancelled). Went back to the dorm and studied. Played Jeopardy with the roommate at 11:00, like clockwork. Lunch at 11:30 and Calculus at 12:20. Back to the dorm and more studying. Called Kendra and talked. Took my Humanities exam at 4:15.

Afterward, I went to dinner, then relaxed and watched TV. Talked with Walter and Kerry. Kendra called and we took a walk through the beautiful snow at 10:00. I asked her out for next weekend. She said YES! Stayed up late talking to Todd and Kerry. So weird how Kendra and I have become best friends so quickly!

Thursday, February 7, 1985

Went to NT Survey at 8:50, then breakfast, then dropped off a note to Kendra at her dorm. Went to chapel—the sermon was great. Lunch at noon with Cindy and Todd. Relaxed and napped all afternoon. Went to Media Writing at 5:00. The teacher didn't show, so went to dinner at 5:30. Talked to Tina. Started my paper. Typed until 10:45, and ate a pizza. Early bedtime; average day.

Friday, February 8, 1985

Had a prayer meeting from 7:00-7:30. Late breakfast at 9:15 with Kerry. Bumped into Kendra in the cafeteria and talked. Jeopardy with Gregg at 11:00. I love routine college mornings.

After lunch, went out on a limb and bought six carnations for Kendra. Carnations are for friendship, right? Went to Calculus at 12:20. Relaxed the afternoon away. Went to dinner at 5:15 with Kerry. Went bowling with Cheryl (sister), Skip, Art, and Randy. So much fun. Came home at 8:15 and played Trivial Pursuit well past midnight.

Saturday, February 9, 1985

A lazy Saturday. Got up at 11:15 and went to lunch. Went back to my room and did a little homework. Called Tina. Talked to Cheryl for a while. Relaxed. Went to dinner at 5:30, then to the mall with Kerry, Todd, and Walter. Bought some Valentine's cards. Home at 8:00, TV, and pizza. Tomorrow night is the first performance of our summer music missions team! Can I handle being their sound man?

Sunday, February 10, 1985

Went to Victory Church with Kerry. It's really a boring church. We need to stick with Higher Dimensions. Went to lunch with Todd at 11:30. It's great that Todd is now my wing brother AND my summer missions brother. We went to our missions team meeting at 1:00. Met everyone for the first time. It was so cool! I'm going to love spending the summer with this group!

Back to the dorm at 2:30. Called Mom and Dad, Peck and Bry. Got dressed for our first performance. We need the practice before we leave the country. I certainly need to figure out how to properly run a sound board. We loaded a van, and went to a small church of about fifty people. Took us two hours to set up, which was quite the hassle. The musicians did great! They are some gifted men and women.

When I returned to campus, I called Kendra and told her all about it. Ate hamburgers. Helped Walter with his homework. Studied a little. Left at 11:15 and went with Kendra and her friend Clancy to the Directory Hotel, right next to campus. We hung out with Kendra's parents! Awesome time. I really like them. I hope they like me—at least made a good first impression. Back to my dorm at 1:30 am. Crazy long day, with a hectic week ahead!

Monday, February 11, 1985

Woke up at 8:00, exhausted. Went to Humanities at 8:50 with Kerry, then to the cafeteria for breakfast. Played Jeopardy with Gregg at 11:00. Met Todd to make our appointments for passport pictures. Went to Calculus at 12:20 and took a very hard test. This may be the toughest class I've ever had!

Went to lunch at 1:00. At 1:30, got my picture taken for my passport. Went to PE at 2:30. Ran two miles, worked out, and chatted with Cheryl. Dinner at 5:15. Talked to Cindy. Back to the dorm at 6:00. Talked to Tina, did homework, and watched TV with the guys. Went to wing meeting at 11:00. Bed.

Tuesday, February 12, 1985

NT Survey at 8:50, followed by breakfast. Went to chapel at 10:45. Gregg the roommate went on stage and actually got healed by the guest preacher! Maybe that will change Gregg's behavior.

Talked to Kendra on the way out. She is awesome as usual. Went to Calculus at 12:20.

Went to lunch at 1:15 all by myself! It was sort of fun. Humanities at 2:20. Got a 96 on my test! Went to Media Writing at 5:00, then to dinner. Back to the room at 7:00. Studied and talked to the guys until bed.

Wednesday, February 13, 1985

Got up at 8:00. Went to NT Discussion at 8:50, followed by English Comp. I was distracted—watched Kendra the whole class! I am really infatuated. Back to the dorm. Kendra called and we talked. She thought something was wrong with me. Wow. I guess I telegraph my emotions too much. Need to work on that. Played Jeopardy at 11:00, followed by lunch at 11:30. Talked to Tammy.

Went to Calculus at 12:20. Picked up a package from Mom and Dad. Food for Valentine's Day! Love a good college care package. Went to the business office with Todd to cash checks and pick up passport photos. Studied, then dinner at 5:15. Saw Tina and Cindy.

Returned home at 6:00 and studied. Went to NT review class at 7:00. Walked back to the dorms with Kendra and her roommate Meri. Called Mom and Dad. Went to missions team music rehearsal from 9:30-11:30. Good practice. Back to the dorm, and had all the guys sign a Valentine's Card for the entire sister wing. Studied until 1:15, and wrote Kendra's card. Went to bed, really scared about being rejected by Kendra. It seems to always go that way for me. Friends...then, that's it!

Thursday, February 14, 1985

Valentine's Day! Went to NT Survey at 8:50, then to breakfast. Studied. Went to Chapel at 10:45. Good one. Got Valentine's cards from Cindy, Tina, and Alyson. Ran into Kendra, and she hugged me in thanks for the carnations! Kerry, Todd, and I went to Christ Chapel and studied Bible until 1:30. I met with the Summer Missions Coordinator for my final interview. I was "officially" accepted to the team! What a satisfying Valentine's gift. Saw Aaron, a teammate, and told him.

Back to the dorm for more studying. Gave Tina the sister wing's Valentine's card. Went to Christ's Chapel at 4:30 and took my NT test. Met a bunch of brothers and sisters at 6:00 and went to Casa Bonita's for some awesome Tex-Mex food. Then we all went to see Petra and Leslie Phillips at 8:00. Beyond awesome. What a spiritual blessing.   Petra's "Beat the System" lead song really hits home, especially the chorus:

> *You can be more than a conqueror, you will never face defeat*
> *(How?)*
> *You can dare to win by losing all, you can face the heat*
> *Dare to beat the system, face the heat*
> *Dare to beat the system (Yeah)*

Can I beat the world's system, can I dare to win by losing all? I'm not sure I'm that committed!

Friday, February 15, 1985

Up early. Had prayer meeting until 7:30. Did homework. Went to breakfast, then English Comp at 9:50. Talked to Kendra and Christy after class. Kendra thanked me for my Valentine's card. Jeopardy with Gregg at 11:00. Lunch, then Calculus at 12:20. Got a 72 on mt test. Big trouble!

Went to the business office, then the missions office. Talked and watched TV all afternoon. Went to dinner at 5:30. Watched TV all night, along with a usual large Crusty's pizza. Tomorrow is our big date!

Saturday, February 16, 1985

Got up at 11:00. Met Todd and the rest of the missions team for lunch at 11:45. We went to the mall to buy our team outfits. Pretty cool. Got home at 5:00 (one hour later than expected). I called Kendra to ask for an extra 15 minutes—only to find out her car wasn't available! Why can't I get a car!

I sat around and moped and even cried a bit for the next hour, feeling sorry for myself. I still crumble under the heat of life. No Italian Inn for us! I still met Kendra at 6:45 and went to the Homecoming basketball game. It was fun, and we had a nice talk. Back to the dorm at 10:00, even more depressed for what could have been. Talked to Todd about it and watched TV. Kendra seems destined to be just a really good friend. I have no blessings from the LORD when it comes to girls. I am emotionally broken!

Sunday, February 17, 1985

Went to Higher Dimensions at 9:30 with Kerry and Todd. Thankfully! Great sermon. Ate lunch together. Still pretty down. Talked to Kerry about it. Still down.

Went to missions team practice at 2:00. Had a prayer time until 3:30. That helped. I repented of my selfishness and ungratefulness and felt comforted by the LORD again. We practiced until 5:00. Went to dinner with teammates Aaron, Miles, and Keith. Back to the room at 5:30. Studied, relaxed, and watched TV. Went to bed with my mind and heart back on track. I just need to keep Kendra as a good friend! Nothing wrong with that, right?

Monday, February 18, 1985

Went to Humanities at 8:50, then sent a letter to Mom. Went to breakfast, then called Dad. Jeopardy with Gregg at 11:00. We are pretty even with wins and losses. Lunch, then Calculus at 12:20. Talked to Cheryl for a bit. Back to the room, then HPE at 2:15 for an exam. Played basketball with Gregg the roommate. Greeted Kendra. Ran a mile with Tammy.

Dinner at 5:00. Went to the LRC with Kerry and Todd at 5:30. Back to the dorm for studying and TV. Called Kendra at 10:30 for a very brief talk. Went to bed at 1:00. Still hurting a bit. Two big prayer requests for February:

1. Kendra and girls in general
2. College major and future occupation

Tuesday, February 19, 1985

Went to NT Survey at 8:50, then breakfast. Chapel at 10:45. Actually pretty boring, which is not usual. Had Calculus class at 12:20, then lunch. Went to the bookstore and bought a birthday card for Kendra's mom. Just trying to be a good friend! Went to Humanities at 2:20. Studied and relaxed.

Walked to Media Writing at 5:00. Went to dinner. Left with Kerry at 7:00 and picked up my birth certificate. Pretty necessary for international travel! Studied the rest of the night. Wrote letters to Laura, Lynda, and Julie back home. Went to bed, pleading for strength from the Lord.

Wednesday, February 20, 1985

Went to NT Discussion at 8:50, then English Comp at 9:50. Talked to Kendra! She's still great, even if as just a friend! Trying to play it cool. Went to the P.O. then back to the dorm. Wish I could get more mail from my friends. Jeopardy with Gregg at 11:00. Went to lunch and then Calculus at 12:20.

In the afternoon, called Mom and checked on her. At 2:15, went to the LRC with Todd. Got only an 88 on my NT test. We watched two hours of missions tapes as part of our Summer Missions training. Went to dinner. Talked to Tina.

At 9:00, went to a missions team practice. Found out we may have a change of plans? What is that all about? We prayed together about it. Back to the dorm in the rain at 11:45. Bed. Lord, save our missions team!

Thursday, February 21, 1985

Off to NT Discussion at 8:50, then to breakfast. Talked to Tammy; came back to my room at 10:15. Left at 11:00 with Shelly, Wendy, Aaron, and Todd (half of our missions team) and went to get our passports. Due to an error, I couldn't get mine. That's not good. Went to Burger King, sat around and talked.

Back to the dorm, talked to Mom and Tina. Went to Media Writing at 5:00 and took a test. Had dinner with Cindy and had a great time. Called Mike for Cindy, which was awkward. She likes this guy, and I'm the middle man. I continue to help people with relationships without a real relationship. Went back to the dorm for study and TV watching with Walter. Went to devos at 10:45 with Kerry. It was really good. We had a great talk.

Friday, February 22, 1985

Went to breakfast at Saga, then English Comp at 9:50. Talked to Kendra and said goodbye (she's leaving for the weekend— some family thing). Jeopardy with Gregg at 11:00. Lunch and Calculus at 12:20. Relaxed all afternoon and watched TV. Talked to Tina and Tammy.

Went to dinner at 5:15. Kerry, Tina, and I went to a performance of the ORU Concert Choir at 8:00. Kerry left early. Not sure what that's about. Back to the room at 9:45. Watched "Children of the Corn" and "Vacation" in Skip the Chaplain's room. Talk about two radically different movies! Went to bed at 2:15. I need strength!

Saturday, February 23, 1985

Another lazy Saturday morning. Went to lunch at 11:30. Back to the dorm to study all afternoon. Talked to Cheryl for a half hour. It was good to connect with her again. Went to early dinner with Todd at 4:30. Went to missions team rehearsal from 5:00-7:00. I'm getting the hang of working the sound equipment. Went over to Wendy's house (a girl on the missions team) at 7:30. Her father is an ORU professor, so she lives in Tulsa. Had a great time. Looked at pictures, played Trivial Pursuit, and then a classic game of charades. Our team won twice! Left at 1:15.

Sunday, February 24, 1985

Todd and I met the rest of the missions team at 10:15. Went to church together at Trinity Christian Fellowship. Ate lunch together as a team. We are really bonding well. Back to the dorm at 1:30. Called Bry, Peck, and Dad. Everything is good back home. I'm starting to feel better about not being home for the summer. Maybe God has a better plan for my friends!

Left at 4:00 and picked up our rented sound equipment. Prayed together as a team. We all went to Grad Housing at 5:00 to set up a Chinese New Year Party! Really getting into the context of our summer in Southeast Asia! Great time. Pam, Wendy, Shelly, and I are getting very close. I talked to Wendy about Todd (they like each other). Free relationship counseling always available! Back to the dorm at 9:00. TV and bed.

Monday, February 25, 1985

Went to Humanities at 8:50, then breakfast. Jeopardy with the roommate at 11:00. Went to lunch, then Calculus at 12:20. Teacher didn't show, so back to the dorm—fifteen minute rule. Went with Gregg to get haircuts. Afterwards, I ran two and a half miles with Todd. We talked until 5:00. Went to dinner at 5:30. Studied all evening. Hall Meeting at 11:15 to talk about our Wing Retreat plans. Bed. Didn't talk to Kendra today.

Tuesday, February 26, 1985

Went to NT Survey at 8:50, then breakfast. Chapel at 10:30. Sadly, it was uninspiring. I wish for more meat of God's Word! Walked back to the dorms with Kendra. She's great as usual. Went to Calculus at 12:20, then a late lunch. Humanities at 2:20. Media Writing at 5:00. Went to dinner at 6:00, followed by studying Humanities for three hours. Relaxed and signed guys up for our Wing Retreat. What a hassle! I'm ready to retire as social director. Bed at 12:15, feeling sick.

Wednesday, February 27, 1985

Got up at 8:00. Went to NT Discussion at 8:50, then English Comp at 9:50. Greeted Kendra, but that was it. Met Tina at 10:45 and got food for the Wing Retreat. Ate lunch at 11:00. Played a half a game of Jeopardy with Gregg. Decided to sleep and skipped Calculus, since I felt so puny. Studied for Humanities all afternoon.

Took the Humanities exam at 4:15. Pretty hard. My brain felt fuzzy. Went to dinner afterwards. Finally got my corrected birth certificate and a great letter from Rachel (from back home). Promptly wrote her a return letter. Got in bed at 6:00 (sick) and watched TV. Stayed up much too late, unable to get comfortable.

Thursday, February 28, 1985

Went to NT Survey at 8:50, then breakfast. Jeopardy at 11:00. Studied. Lunch at 12:15, and then the library with Kerry ay 12:45. I still don't study well in quiet places. At 1:30, went to the

Financial Aid office, then ran around and got my college major officially changed to Telecommunications! Finally feel settled and hopeful for a career in journalism.

Went to Media Writing at 5:00, then dinner. Back to the dorm at 6:45. We had Open House from 8:00-10:00. Tina, Alyson, and some other sisters came by. Wendy from the missions team stayed the whole time and talked. Did homework until midnight. Still sick and tired. And, giving up on Kendra, as another month of school ends.

March, 1985

Friday, March 1, 1985

Went to a late breakfast with Kendra and Chrissy, sitting at their wing table. Great time. Went to English Comp at 9:50 with Kendra. Talked afterwards. Jeopardy at 11:00 with the roommate. Lunch, then Calculus at 12:20. Back to the dorm after dropping a note off at Kendra's box. Relaxed all afternoon.

Met with Kerry, Tina, Tammy, and the Retreat man at 4:00 for some planning time. Went bowling at 4:30 with Tina, Tammy, and Skip the Chaplain. Bowled badly, but it was fun. Went to dinner. Called Mom. Got in bed at 7:00, still suffering from this cold or flu or whatever it is. Our retreat starts tomorrow!

Saturday, March 2, 1985

Got up at 8:30. Packed for the Wing Retreat and got all the guys ready. Left at 10:15 with Kerry, Todd, and Tina. We picked up the food and packed the cars. The whole group (27 of us) left at 11:15. I rode with Tammy.

Got to "Shepherd's Fold Ranch" at 12:15. Awesome place. Had lunch, went paddleboarding, then horseback riding. Played basketball and relaxed. Had our first speaking time with Mr. Sowell at 5:15. He's really good! Ate dinner. Had our second and third sessions afterwards. Campfire at 10:00—great conversations.

Lessons learned today from these three talks:

   - All my dating relationships should be committed be God (they are all His anyway).

   - We need to take advice from parents and close friends.

   - Never, never, never talk against men of God.

   - Pray for my future spouse's well being.

Sunday, March 3, 1985

Had breakfast with the group at 9:45, followed by a worship service at 10:30. Ended with a time of encouraging the person next to us. Mine was Tina. She and I had a nice time of sharing. Packed up and left. Rode back to campus with Tammy. Got back at 12:45.

During the afternoon, called Peck, Bry, Mom, and Dad. All is well. Studied. Went for an early dinner. Talked to Wendy. Back to the dorm and studied some more. Watched TV and went to bed at 12:15. Ready for a brand new week with a more godly attitude!

Monday, March 4, 1985

Walked to breakfast, then Humanities at 8:50. Jeopardy with Gregg at 11:00. Lunch and then Calculus at 12:20. Picked out a thank you card for Mr. Sowell. He was truly inspiring. Went to HPE at 2:20. Ran two miles. Getting in shape for that next test.

Went to dinner. Back to the dorm at 4:00. Talked to Walter and watched TV. Went to a missions team meeting along with two other Philippines summer missions teams. It was very interesting. Learned a lot about the Philippines (one of our stops). Back to the room at 10:30. Had a Wing Meeting in the Fishbowl at 11:00. It was very good.

Tuesday, March 5, 1985

Awoke and went to NT Survey at 8:50, followed by breakfast. Chapel at 10:45. Pretty good and convicting Went to Calculus at 12:20. Talked with Cheryl. Lunch, then Humanities at 2:20. Got a 94 on my test! Studied and relaxed afterwards.

Went to Media Writing at 5:00, followed by dinner. Back to the dorm at 7:00. Studied, watched TV. Tried to go to bed early (12:15 am), but stayed up hoping Kendra would call. She didn't.

Wednesday, March 6, 1985

Went to NT Discussion at 8:50, followed by English Comp. at 9:50 (Kendra was a no-show). Played Jeopardy with Gregg at 11:00. I am getting good. Went to lunch, followed by Calculus at 12:20. Went to the LRC afterwards and studied. Went back to my room—feeling VERY sick. Can anyone say, relapse! Why do I get sick so often? Maybe my faith isn't strong enough (or my immune system).

Went dinner, then back to my room for more studying. Kendra called—but only talked for five minutes. Went to missions team practice at 9:00. Left early at 10:30, SO SICK. Got in bed, watched TV, and ate pizza (good old comfort food)! Went to bed asking the Lord for an answer about Kendra. Whatever it is, God is good!

Thursday, March 7, 1985

Got up and forced myself to go to NT Survey at 8:50, followed by breakfast. Chapel at 10:45. Pretty decent. Went to lunch at noon, then back to the room. Studied. Spent most of the afternoon in thought and prayer. I need to spend more time in prayer—not necessarily in thought.

Went to Media Writing at 5:00. Ate dinner at 6:00 with Todd, Aaron, and Michael (the guys on our missions team). Went to a meeting about Easter Seminar with Kerry at 8:00. Talked to him afterwards about my problem with Kendra. He was very sympathetic, as someone who tried to pursue Kendra, and failed.

Went to Claudius Dorm at 9:30 and met the Missions Team. Had prayer meeting until 11:00. A real blessing! Then, came back to my dorm and had devo's until 11:45. It was great too! Talked to Walter until 12:30. Lord, change and cleanse me!

Friday, March 8, 1985

Met Kendra for breakfast in the cafeteria. We walked to English at 9:50. She's busy all weekend, as usual. Bummer. Back to the dorm at 10:45. Jeopardy at 11:00. Went to lunch, followed by Calculus at 12:20. At 2:00, went back to the passport office to finish my paperwork. Went back to my room and talked to Mom. Dinner at 5:00, followed by spending the entire evening in my room. Ate, talked, and worked out our school schedules (with Kerry, Skip the Chaplain, and Todd). This is what Friday night at ORU looks like for losers. Called Wendy. Went to bed at 12:45.

Saturday, March 9, 1985

Slept in until lunch to get over my spring cold. Finally feeling a bit better. Went to the LRC at Noon and studied until 2:00. Back to the dorm. Hung out with Todd and Walter, so I didn't get the work done I needed to. No big deal; I'll catch up later.

Went to dinner at 5:15. Then, went to get basketball tickets at 6:00 with Kerry and Cathy. Finally got some great seats! Went to the dorm and picked up Wendy and her friend, Tammy. Went to the finals of the conference basketball tournament. We lost to Loyola! We went to Charlie Mitchell's (voted the students' number one favorite restaurant in Tulsa) for dessert and talked until 12:30. Back to the dorm and bed. Todd is in even more trouble with Wendy! He needs my help. I need to take my own medicine and tell Kendra how I feel about her! But dare I risk a good Christian friendship?

Sunday, March 10, 1985

Went to Higher Dimensions Church at 9:30. Great worship service as usual! Went to lunch at 12:15. Back to the dorm for some studying. Called Peck and Bry and my sister Amy. Mom and Dad called me later. I always hold my breath with them, but I was able to exhale. No drama today.

Went to dinner at 5:45, followed by missions team practice from 7:00-9:00. Back to the dorm. Talked to Walter until 10:30. Todd came by and we all talked until midnight. Wendy, Shelly, and Pam are my favorite teammates so far. I finally confirmed to myself that my major will be Telecommunications, minor in writing, with future graduate work at CBN University. CBN was where many of our ORU graduates went for further education. Thank you, Lord, for giving me clear direction.

Monday, March 11, 1985

Went to Humanities at 8:50, followed by errands and Group Advisement at 10:50. Yay! Totally unnecessary, but required in order to sign up for next semester's classes. Ate lunch at 11:15, followed by Calculus at 12:20. Talked to Cheryl. HPE at 2:30. We practiced CPR, and ran two miles. Saw Kendra running with another guy. Great.

Dinner at 5:00. Back to the dorm to study and watch TV. Wing Meeting at 11:00, followed by hanging out. Bed at 12:30. Not bummed, but "thoughtfully hurt." That's a new term I'm trying out for size. I have to get stronger in the Lord.

Tuesday, March 12, 1985

Went to NT Survey at 8:50, followed by breakfast. Went to chapel at 10:45. Kendra's music group sang for us! She looked (and sounded) great. Got a stomachache just watching her.

Went to Calculus at 12:20. Talked to Cheryl. Studied until Humanities at 2:20. Studied some more. Went to Media Writing at 5:00, followed by dinner at 6:00. Studied and watched TV all night, as well as eating the required pizza. Bed at 12:30. Trying to get over Kendra!

Wednesday, March 13, 1985

Went to NT Survey at 8:50, then English Comp at 9:50. Couldn't avoid Kendra, so we talked casually for a few minutes. Jeopardy back at the room at 11:00 with Gregg. Lunch, then Calculus at 12:20. Absolutely bombed my test! I am seriously heading towards failing my first class of my college career. How did I ever think I could be a math major?

Back to the dorm to study all afternoon, with extra motivation. Went to dinner at 5:00 with Todd. Talked more with him back at the dorm while we did laundry. Talked to Joanna on the phone. She wants to see me while we are both on break in

Arizona (ugh). Have to find a way to get out of that! She's a nice girl, but not my type.

Went to missions team music practice from 9:00-11:00. Devo's at 11:30, followed by bedtime. I've got enough on my plate with Kendra. Why is Joanna pursuing me? And, bigger news: our summer missions team is still struggling to raise all our money!

Thursday, March 14, 1985

Went to NT Survey at 8:50. Saw Kendra at breakfast and showed her that I was depressed. Purposefully. Am I really that manipulative? Went back to the dorm. Kendra called to see what was wrong.

"Nothing's wrong," I said, like we were married or something.

"Oh...okay. It seemed like you were upset. Are we good?" she replied.

"Of course!" I lied.

Thankfully, my lying lips and manipulative heart got to go to a very good chapel service at 10:45, followed by lunch. Back to the dorm at 12:45. Relaxed all afternoon, doing very little, other than pouting. Went to Media Writing at 5:00. Great guest speaker! Very motivational.

Went to dinner at 6:30, followed by a trip to the mall with Tina. Had a really good time. Back to the dorm at 9:00. Helped Walter with his homework and had a good talk. Talked to Cheryl, Tina, and Cindy. Packed. Wendy called and spilled her guts about Todd. We traded our relational problems. Busy night! Finished packing, talking with Todd and Walter. Will I have closure with Kendra before Spring Break?

Scottsdale, Arizona

March 15, 1985

Friday, March 15, 1985

Woke up very nervous about Kendra. Went to breakfast at 9:00 and ate alone. When Kendra and Christy came into the cafeteria, I immediately left. Went to the library and saw Todd. Said goodbye for the break. Waited in the pit (great place to relax and act like you are studying) until class started. Went off by myself, not planning on talking with Kendra. But, she found me and asked to talk. So much for my secrecy techniques.

We took a walk for the next hour and a half through the Prayer Gardens—always the place for relationship conversations at ORU. I was honest this time. We got everything out in the open and I felt a lot better (just stupid, still). We hugged goodbye. Back to the dorm at 11:30 and said goodbye to everyone. Met Whitney and Kerry and left campus at noon. Talked privately with Kerry about Kendra, and we said our goodbyes.

Cousin Whitney and I flew to Denver, had a long layover, and flew on to Phoenix. Gram and Gramps met us at the airport. It was awesome to see them again. Went to Red Robin for dinner and got to their house at 7:30. We relaxed and talked all night. Watched "Heaven Can Wait" later that night.

Thank you, Lord, for the opportunity to talk with Kendra. I'm going to face my weaknesses in order to get stronger. I just care about her so much! But I'm happy to be here in Scottsdale for a much-needed break!

Saturday, March 16, 1985

Slept in. Whitney made me breakfast. After watching some basketball (love college basketball), I went and laid out by the pool with Whitney. Back inside at 1:00. Relaxed all afternoon. Aunt Char and Uncle John came over for dinner at the house. Had a great time. They left at 7:30. Whitney and I spent the evening talking and watching TV. Gram and Gramps came home at 9:30 with cousin Earl. I haven't seen him since he was an annoying toddler. This should be interesting. We watched "The In-Laws" at 10:00. Bed.

Sunday, March 17, 1985

Got up early. Read the newspaper. Left for church at 7:30 with Gramps, Gram, and Whitney. Good service at Valley Cathedral. Came home at 9:30 to pick up cousin Earl. He wasn't much for church, sadly. Went to a coffee shop for brunch. Ate like an absolute pig. Earl, Whitney and I went to the grocery store afterwards. We lounged out by the pool and swam. Called Dad, Peck, and Bry. Relaxed all afternoon. Joanna (ugh) called and we talked for too long.

Whitney and I left at 4:15 and went to get dinner and rent movies. Came home, ate and watched "Sixteen Candles," followed by "Diner," and then "Deathtrap." Gram and Gramps left in the middle of "Diner," upset at us for choosing it. Forgot about the bad parts. Not cool for my grandparents thinking I'm some kind of pagan. Bummed me out the rest of the night. Went to bed at midnight. Lord, give me strength!

Monday, March 18, 1985

Got up and ran two miles with Whitney. Came home and ate breakfast. Called Joanna, then Kerry. Kerry skipped out on me today, which kind of made me mad. Went outside and laid out at 11:30. Joanna and her cousin Debbie came over at 1:00. We all laid out and talked until 3:45. It was actually a nice time. I talked a lot, which is what I do when I'm nervous.

Went to dinner with Gram, Gramps, Whitney, Aunt Char, and Uncle John at 5:00. Spent the evening watching TV. Called Kerry. Went to bed at 12:30. Really trying to face my weaknesses and fears!

Tuesday, March 19, 1985

Got up and had breakfast by myself. Cloudy day, so Whitney and I decided to go shopping at noon. I bought a camera and some film for myself. Back home at 2:00. Went back out with Whitney and Earl to Los Arcos Mall at 3:30. Got a pair of shoes and two shirts. Pretty successful shopping day for me.

Picked up a pizza at 6:00. Then went on to the Fashion Mall. Just browsed. Came home at 8:30. Cousin Wes (Whitney's brother and my favorite cousin) called at 9:00 and we had a good talk. We both wished he could have made the trip to Scottsdale to hang out. Watched TV by myself. Kerry called later. Finally went to bed at 11:30, after compiling my TOP TEN list of coolest girls at school (this is the current order of cool-ness):

1. Kendra
2. Wendy
3. Tina
4. Cheryl
5. Cindy
6. Pam
7. Tammy
8. Alyson
9. Kim
10. Shelly

Plus, Top Five at home and abroad, just for fun.

1. Lynda

2. Rachel

3. Laura

4. Sandra

5. Leanne

How many of them have me on their Top Ten list?

Wednesday March 20, 1985

Got up and ran two miles by myself. Great time to think and pray during the cooler part of the day. Came home. Gram's former pastor's wife came over (haven't seen her for years). Had a nice visit. Ate breakfast. Left at 10:00 and picked up Kerry. Brought him to my grandparent's home and we hit the pool, laid out, and played putt-putt golf on the astroturf. Ate lunch. Laid out some more. Left at 2:45 and went to a Christian bookstore. I bought three books and a magazine. Home at 4:15. We left again with Gram and Whitney. Dropped Kerry off at his mom's house.

We met Gramps and Earl at Picadilly for dinner at 5:30. Earl, Whitney, and I went shopping afterwards. I bought a tie for school—always a necessity. We left Thomas Mall at 7:15 and went to the movies. Saw "A Sure Thing." It was really good. Came home at 10:00. Watched TV and went to bed. I miss everyone at school!

Thursday, March 21, 1985

Got up early and continued my discipline of running two miles. ORU has made me into someone who tolerates physical exercise. Yay, me! Returned home, relaxed, and watched TV. Still would rather watch TV than exercise. Had McDonald's for breakfast. Nothing better than two Egg McMuffins. Studied until 11:00. Laid out at the pool. Burnt to a crisp. My fair skin is no match for the Arizona sun. Left at 2:30 with Whitney and Gram and went to Fiesta Mall. Bought a card and teddy bear for Kendra. It's her birthday today! Met Gramps, Earl, Aunt Char and Uncle John at Italian Grotto for dinner. Had great linguine and clam sauce. Home at 7:15. Watched TV and relaxed. Went to bed early.

Friday, March 22, 1985

Got up and ran two miles with Whitney. Home and breakfast. Went to the pool at 10:00. Laid out until noon and swam. Relaxed inside in the air conditioning. Went and filled up Gram's car with gas. Called Mom. Left at 4:45 for dinner (the whole gang) at CoCo's. My favorite Scottsdale restaurant since I was a kid!

Said my goodbyes to Aunt Char and Uncle John. They are really my favorite aunt and uncle. Back home at 6:00. Relaxed the rest of the evening. Packed clothes and wrapped Kendra's present. Sadly, Whitney and I have been at odds today for some reason. Maybe I get on her nerves. Can't wait to get back to school! Lord, make me ready to face Kendra. I want to write so badly (actually be a real writer)!

Tulsa, Oklahoma

March 23, 1985

Saturday, March 23, 1985

Got up at 5:40 am! Left at 7:00 with Gramps, Earl, and Whitney for the airport. Our plane took off at 8:00. I got to talk about Jesus to the guy sitting next to me! It was so cool. Changed planes in Denver. Felt nauseated. Too much turbulence for my touchy stomach. Got into Tulsa at 1:00. Mark picked us up and we got hamburgers at Wendy's.

Back to my dorm at 2:15. Unpacked. Talked with Walter, Dave, Darrel, and Skip the Chaplain. Got my mail from the post office. Went to a late dinner at 7:15 with Skip the Chaplain and Darrel at Monopolies. Came home at 9:00 and crashed hard.

Glad to be back home!

Sunday, March 24, 1985

Relaxed and watched TV almost all day. No church for me. Called Mom, Dad, Peck, and Bry at commercial breaks. Waited excitedly for everyone to get back to school. Wrote Kendra a birthday card. Kerry returned at 3:30. Talked and hung out.

Went to dinner at 5:30 with Walter and his friend Kim at Hamburger Haven. Came home at 7:00 after a fun conversation. Gregg the roommate returned at 8:30. He agreed to deliver my birthday present to Kendra. Everyone else returned to the brother wing. Visited. Bed.

What will happen to our missions team?

Monday, March 25, 1985

Got up and went to Humanities at 8:50. Studied. Back to the grind of Jeopardy with Gregg at 11:00. Went to lunch and then Calculus at 12:20. Got a 67 on my Calculus test! Ugh. Back to the dorm at 1:15. Went to HPE at 2:30. Got tested on CPR. Passed. But would I be courageous enough to help someone?

Dinner at 5:00. Back to the dorm at 5:30. Talked with Todd. Shocker of the night: He has to leave the missions team due to lack of money-raising! He's the one that brought me in! And he's our main male vocalist! So bummed (for both of us). Did homework the rest of the evening. Watched the Academy Awards, which is always my favorite awards show. Hung around with the guys and talked. Called and talked to Wendy for a half hour and Kendra for a couple of minutes. Pizza at midnight. Save our missions team, Lord!

Tuesday, March 26, 1985

Went to New Testament Survey at 8:50. Saw Cindy for the first time since break. Went to breakfast and visited with Tina. Went to a great chapel service at 10:45. Talked to Wendy on the way back. Went to Calculus at 12:20, followed by lunch. Back to the dorm. Called Mom. Went to Humanities at 2:20. Did homework and watched TV. Went to Media Writing at 5:00. Dinner, then back to the dorm. Bad headache all evening. Tried to study, but couldn't focus. Give me strength, Lord. Kerry will probably start dating Kendra again! Why am I surprised? He's so much cooler than me!

Wednesday, March 27, 1985

Got up and went NT Survey at 8:50, followed by English Comp at 9:50. No Kendra. Played Jeopardy at 11:00. Lunch, then Calculus at 12:20. Took another exam. I need at least something in the 80s! Back to my room at 1:15. Called Wendy and talked. Studied with Kerry until 4:00. Talked to Walter and Todd. Went to hair check at 5:00, then to dinner.

Back to the room at 5:45. Went to NT Review at 6:30. I boldly confronted Kerry about secretly seeing Kendra without talking to me first. At least I respected him enough to ask him before! But, I have no choice but to sacrifice her for my friendship with Kerry. At least that's what I'm telling myself tonight. Went to Timko Barton Hall at 8:45 for our missions team practice from

9:00-11:00. Back to the room and studied until midnight. Talked to Walter until 12:30. Bed.

Thursday, March 28, 1985

Got up and went to NT Survey at 8:50. Saw Kendra. Went to breakfast, then straight to the Missions office. So far, I have raised $460.00. Not too shabby. Chapel at 10:45. Another really good one. Lunch with Todd afterwards. I still feel so bad for him. His dream of a summer was crushed. Back to the room and called Mom. Studied. Went to the NT exam at 4:30.

Dinner at 5:30. Back to the dorm. Kendra called (for Kerry) and we talked for a minute. Guess she figured he's always in my room (which he is). Wendy and I met at 9:00 and we talked until 9:30. Met the rest of the missions team for practice (except Keith and Pam). Great time of sharing and praying. Back to the dorm at 11:30. Talked to Kerry, Walter, and Todd. Kendra: Why not be a friend now?

Friday, March 29, 1985

Went to breakfast at 9:15. Kendra ate with me, and we actually had a light and fun conversation. Maybe we can be friends. We walked to English Comp at 9:50. Parted after class. Jeopardy with Gregg at 11:00. Went to Calculus at 12:20. Sent Pam her birthday card. Lunch with Todd and Aaron. Met Kerry at the library at 2:15. Researched for our respective papers together. Back to the dorm and had a nice talk with Walter. Dinner at 5:15.

Relaxed and watched TV all evening. Played Risk at 11:00 and ate pizza with Scott, Todd, Skip the Chaplain, and Walter. Bed at 1:30.

Saturday, March 30, 1985

Got ready for my three-mile run this morning! Every student was required to do this run (with a decent time) to pass the PE requirement. So, I followed the large crowd to Mabee Center and ran. Did pretty good for me—about 25 minutes. Talked to a lot of people. I actually had fun! Watched the 10K run (saw Kendra, who loves to run). Lunch at noon. Dropped off a friendly note to Kendra.

Back to the room and studied until 2:30. Watched the NCAA basketball semi-finals. Called Gram. Talked to Tina. Went to dinner at 5:00. Watched more basketball. At 7:00, went to the "Souls-a-Fire" concert with Tina, Todd, and Mitch. It was awesome. Lasted until midnight! Walter is in the group, and he is fantastic. Back to the room and bed. Kerry went out with Kendra tonight. Here we go again!

Sunday, March 31, 1985

Got up and studied all morning instead of going to church. They are getting lazy at checking the floors, so I took advantage. Not a good habit, Kwas! Went to lunch at 11:30. Came home and called Mom and Dad. Also called Bry. Went to missions team practice at 2:00 (which is just like church for me). Great time. But sadly, Todd officially announced that he was dropping out of the team. We all cried together.

The whole team went to dinner at Taco Bueno at 5:00. Back to the dorm at 6:00. Watched TV and relaxed all evening. Talked to Gregg, Walter, and Todd until midnight—talked about Kendra and Kerry mostly, of course. Went to bed at 12:30. Will Kerry and Kendra be real friends of mine in my future? Wendy, Shelly, and Pam are great. Lord, I need to know what to do!

April, 1985

Monday, April 1, 1985

Went to Humanities at 8:50, then to the LRC to study afterwards. Jeopardy with the roommate at 11:00. Lunch at 11:30. Got my fall semester's schedule. It's all messed up! What's going on here? Went to Calculus at 12:20. Back to my room at 1:15. Practiced CPR with Gregg. Went to HPE at 2:30.

Dinner at 4:45. Back to the dorm at 5:20. Studied until 9:00. Watched TV. Got a very encouraging card from Shelly (on my summer missions team). She's an awesome girl. Talked to Wendy for a while (my other favorite on our team). She is worried that our missions team may fall apart. Had Wing Meeting at 11:00. Called Shelly at midnight and thanked her for the card. Bed.

Tuesday, April 2, 1985

Went to NT Survey at 8:50. Skipped breakfast (too much to do), returned to the dorm, did homework, and prayed. Jeopardy with Gregg at 11:00. Went to Calculus at 12:20. Finally got my passport, plus $100 in support from Gram! Talked to Kerry, but not about our relationship—he thinks I'm mad at him. Went to Humanities at 2:20. Came back to my room and relaxed.

Went to Media Writing at 5:00. Professor didn't show. Came back and talked with Todd and Walter. Started studying at 7:30. Wendy called later. Studied more. Ate pizza (after midnight). Bed at 1:15. Lord, help me keep up my studies! Are Christian friends really friends forever (like Michael W. Smith claims)?

> *And friends are friends forever*
> *If the Lord's the Lord of them*
> *And a friend will not say never*
> *'Cause the welcome will not end*
> *Though it's hard to let you go*
> *In the Father's hands we know*
> *That a lifetime's not too long*
> *To live as friends*

Wednesday, April 3, 1985

Got up early and studied until 8:30. Went to NT Survey at 8:50. Got a 91 on my test. That helps my chances for an improved GPA! Went to English Comp at 9:50. Was absolutely rude and ignored Kendra. I just can't hide my feelings. Jeopardy at 11:00. Went to lunch at 11:30. Went to Calculus at 12:20. Talked to Cheryl a little bit. Back to the room at 1:15. Studied with Kerry and Todd.

Went to a Humanities test at 3:45, then to dinner at 4:45. Returned at 5:15. Talked with Kerry until 7:00. Great talk. It really cleared the air. We are still going to be friends, but with "lower" expectations. Yes, the lower expectations are on my part. I continue to want too much from other people. Later on, talked to Tina about it. Went to the Depot at 7:00. Talked to Wendy until 8:45. Missions team practice from 9:00 until 11:30. It was great Back to the dorm. Talked to Todd until 1:30. What a day of talking! Maybe I should write a book on communication.

Thursday, April 4, 1985

Went to NT Survey at 8:50, then to breakfast. Kendra asked to have breakfast with me. We walked to chapel together early so we could talk. Nothing was really accomplished, but she is still awesome. Lunch at 1:00 with Gregg, Todd, and Wendy. Met Kerry at the LRC afterwards and got my fall class schedule fixed. Thank you, Lord. Back to the room to write a paper.

Went to Media Writing at 5:00. Dinner at 6:15. Back to the room at 7:00. Talked to Dad. He has raised $860 for me—from all his business connections! So thankful for the support of my parents. Missions team practice at 9:30. The group is very upset, since our travel plans are up in the air. Talked and prayed, submitting ourselves to the Lord's will. Ran back to the dorm in the rain at 11:30. Need to invest in an umbrella. Wrote a letter to Kendra. Bed at 1:15.

Friday, April 5, 1985

Woke up early and finished my letter to Kendra. Went to breakfast with Kerry at 9:15. Went to the Mabee Center and signed in at 10:00. It was time for "ORU Seminar Days" with visiting

Seminar Students. Went back to Security and stood with four other guys, carrying people's luggage to various dorms all day. Saw a lot of my friends in their dorms. Signed out at 8:00. A good day's work to make some very necessary moolah. Back to the dorm. Talked to Aaron. Kendra called, but I was too tired to talk. Fell asleep at 11:00. Seminar guests showed up on our floor at midnight. Went back to sleep, exhausted.

Saturday, April 6, 1985

Got up at 7:30, very tired. Went to Timko Barton at 8:30 for a missions team meeting (everyone was there, except Wendy). We talked about our plans for the summer until 9:30. Everything is still in a stater of flux. Back to the dorm. Talked to Walter. Started writing my paper at 10:30. Stopped for lunch at noon. Talked with some of our seminar guests. Some pretty interesting people.

Went to dinner at 5:00. Back to the dorm. Talked to Walter. We decided to be roommates next year! I have gotten closer with Gregg, but he's not sure he is even coming back next year. Watched TV and talked until 9:00. Wrote another paper from 9:00 until 11:30. Stopped to call Wendy—she has pneumonia! Went to bed at midnight. Kerry's out with Kendra again tonight! If I really trusted the Lord (like I say I do), I should be happy for them, right?

Sunday, April 7, 1985

Got up at 4:30! Yes, that's right, 4:30 am. Duty calls. Off to the Mabee Center at 5:30. Worked the luggage drop off at Towers and then took the shuttle out to the airport. Seminar Days are over! Finished up work at 11:15. Lunch at noon.

Back to my room and laid down for a while. Went to missions team practice at 3:00. Prayed until 4:30. Shoved down some dinner, changed, and met the team again at 5:15 (sadly, Wendy is still sick). Went to Will Rogers Methodist Church. Our sound system broke partway through (not my fault), but the performance still went well. Back to the dorm at 10:00. Relaxed. Pizza at midnight. Called Mom and Dad. They are coming on Friday for a visit (since I'm not coming home this summer). Lord, help our team!

Monday, April 8, 1985

Went to Humanities at 8:50, then to the bookstore. Bought Reena a card (she is supporting my missions trip. So awesome). Jeopardy at 11:00, followed by lunch and then Calculus. Afterwards, went to the LRC to study. Went to HPE at 2:20. Afterwards, did homework and talked to Aaron and Wendy. She's finally feeling a bit better.

Went to dinner at 4:45. Back to the dorm at 5:30, crashed until 6:30. Studied all night and watched TV. Had a wing meeting at 11:00. Homework and pizza until 1:00. Called Dad and Wendy. Went to bed at 1:30. Now, I'm sick. I'm tired of being sick so much. Why am I so physically weak? And, worse than that, our missions team may actually have to disband! Stinks! And, worse than that,

Kendra hasn't said a word to me since Friday. Okay, that may not be the worst. But sad.

Tuesday, April 9, 1985

Went to NT Survey at 8:50, then breakfast. Went to the business office and paid next year's room deposit. Chapel at 11:00. It was okay. Calculus at 12:20. Then, reserved my room on 7th Ed again for next year (with Walter). Back to the room. Talked with Kerry. Humanities at 2:20. Got a very sorry 86 on my exam. Back to the room to sleep (plunging deeper into my sickness).

Media Writing at 5:00. Went to dinner at 6:00. Back to the room for TV watching and relaxation. Keith called to tell me that Aaron and Mike dropped off the missions team! I actually cried. Talked to Wendy about it. The rest of the team had an emergency meeting at 9:00, but I was too sick to go. I studied and sulked the rest of the night. Just so sad. Lord, why did you call me to this missions team in the first place, if it is all going to fall apart?

Wednesday, April 10, 1985

Went to NT Survey at 8:50, followed by English Comp at 9:50. Kendra was a no-show. Jeopardy with Gregg at 11:00, followed by lunch. Went to Calculus and took an exam at 12:20. Back to the dorm. Called Mom. Went with Gregg to get haircuts and bought a gift for Walter (a thank-you for being my next roommate). Back to the dorm at 3:00, watched TV and talked.

Talked to Aaron and Wendy about the missions team. It seems to be the only thing on my mind right now.

Went to dinner at 5:00. At 9:30, went to a meeting with our missions team leader (Greg), plus Pam, Wendy, and Shelly. The five of us are the only team members left. We talked until 11:30. We may be going to England now (instead of Southeast Asia)! It actually looks pretty promising. More to come. Talked to Dad about it. Ate pizza. Went to bed at 1:30.

Thursday, April 11, 1985

Went to NT Survey at 8:50, then breakfast. Off to chapel at 11:00. Good one. Went to lunch at noon. Studied all afternoon. Talked to Wendy. We both feel very hopeful. Went to Media Writing at 5:00. God a 98 on my paper! At least one class is going my way. Is that confirmation that I should be a Journalism Major?

Went to dinner at 6:00 and talked with Reena. She is such a supportive friend. My first real friend from India! Back to the dorm at 6:30. Relaxed and watched TV all evening. Very tired and kind of down. I think it's the sickness more than anything. Bed at 12:30. Mom and Dad are almost here! Kendra is still invading my thoughts.

England: Here I come?

Friday, April 12, 1985

Went to an early breakfast. Ate with Kendra and Chrissy. We had a good talk. Talked with Kendra more on our way to class. Back to the dorm at 10:15. Jeopardy at 11:00. Went to lunch. Met with Wendy and Shelly. Pam decided to join the Philippines team! Happy for her, but sad for us.

Went to Calculus at 12:20. Got an 80 on my test—a bit better. Back to the dorm at 1:15. My parents met me in the Fishbowl. They met Todd and William. Then, I went with them to get their car fixed, which gave us time alone to talk. They dropped me off at 3:00. I met Shelly and Wendy at 3:20. We met the rest of the England Summer Missions Team. They seem really cool!

Afterwards, met Kendra at 5:30. My parents picked us up and we went to dinner at the Italian Inn. I chose this restaurant since it was where I wanted to take Kendra on our first real date. It was sort of like a double date, even though she is dating Kerry. Have to say that Kendra was very cool—funny and sweet to my parents. We dropped her off and drove back to their hotel. We relaxed and visited. They took me back to my dorm at 9:00. Todd, Walter, and Kerry came to the room and we talked and laughed until 11:15. Kerry played it cool about Kendra.

Bottom line: I am still in love with Kendra. This is not good.

Saturday, April 13, 1985

Left with Mom and Dad at 10:45 to go to brunch at Denny's. Went to the mall and shopped for some things for my trip. It was fun, but I was tired. We got back to the hotel at 3:00. They let me use their car, so I dropped them off and picked up Todd. We went to Western Sizzlin' at 3:30 for Walter's surprise party, hosted by his friend, Kim. In a shocking turn of events, Dad called in the middle of the party to let me know that my little brother Josh fell out of a tree at home and broke his arm! So, they had to leave at 4:00 to return home. I was absolutely crushed. I was enjoying their attention. But, on a positive note, Walter was surprised!

Then, Kerry came up to me and said, "You need to back off, man. You know I like Kendra. You can't keep moving in on her like this."

"We are just friends, Kerry," I claimed. "No need to get so upset." "If you really are my friend, you would back off!"

Wow. Could this day get any worse? I went back to my room at 6:00 and packed some stuff. I still had my parents' hotel for another night. Kerry graciously drove me and Todd back to the hotel. We watched TV and talked. Walter came over at 7:00. Gregg stopped by at 9:30. Wendy called, and then also came by at 11:00. We all watched movies and talked. I talked to her privately about Kendra. She was very kind and understanding. She left at 1:00 am.

Gregg, Todd, and Walter all stayed over. We talked about our lives, and growing up, until pizza time at 2:00. So tired!

I have FINALLY decided to cut off Kendra FOR GOOD! No talking, ever. Time for a break. This weird "love triangle" has to stop—for the best of everyone. But I'm still in love with her. Updated girl list:

1. Wendy
2. Tina
3. Shelly
4. Pam

Sunday, April 14, 1985

Got up at 10:30. Packed up my stuff and got back to the dorm at 11:30. Called my parents. Thankfully, everything is fine with my brother. Tried to call Kendra so I could tell her my decision, but no answer. Talked to Wendy. Called Bry back home and had a good talk.

At 2:45, met Wendy, Shelly, and Mike at the EMR dorm. We went to Greg, our new mission team leader's house. Mike and I grilled. We met the rest of the original England Team we are merging with. Had a great time of sharing. Back to the dorm at 7:00. Relaxed, and talked to Todd and Walter. I still feel sad that Todd can't go with us. Wrote Kendra a final letter to cut it all off. Went to bed at 12:30.

Lord, heal my heart. Can't wait to go to England!

Monday, April 15, 1985

Woke up early. Dropped off my letter at Kendra's dorm. Came back to the dorm and studied. Jeopardy at 11:00, followed by lunch at 11:30. Skipped Calculus to rest and study. Went to HPE at 2:30. Went to the synthesis study meeting at 3:45 until 5:15. Todd and I went to the wing picnic afterwards. Back to the dorm for more studying. Kendra and Cheryl both called, but Gregg said I wasn't home (when I actually was). I just couldn't handle it today. Watched TV and talked to the guys the rest of the night.

Tuesday, April 16, 1985

Went to NT Survey at 8:50, followed by breakfast. Went to chapel with Walter at 10:45. Went to Calculus class at 12:20, followed by studying, then Humanities at 2:20. Cashed a check and bought some birthday cards. Back to the dorm at 3:15. Called Cousin Whitney and talked for a while.

Went to Media Writing at 5:00, followed by dinner. Spent most of the evening writing a paper. Called Peck. Saw Pam at dinner, as well as Wendy. Really miss Pam no longer being on the missions team. Ate pizza at 12:30 and went to bed. Kerry and I are still avoiding each other. Lord, give me strength to see Kendra tomorrow.

Wednesday, April 17, 1985

Went to NT survey at 8:50, followed by English Comp at 9:50. Kendra was in class, but we never looked at each other! Are we back in high school or what? Played Jeopardy at 11:00, followed by lunch. Went to Calculus at 12:20. Back to the room to read all afternoon. Talked with Walter and Todd. Went to dinner. Saw Alyson. Got an apology letter from Kerry, which was encouraging.

Back to the dorm at 5:30. Finally spent time talking to and praying with Kerry. We will be friends again, but not ever close friends. Haven't we already done this? What does that mean? Couldn't study after that, so just watched TV. Had a good conversation with Shelly. She gets me. Unfortunately, couldn't catch up with Wendy today—it's her birthday. Lord, heal my heart like you healed my brother's broken arm!

Thursday, April 18, 1985

Went to NT Survey at 8:50. Saw Kendra, but we didn't talk. Went to breakfast, then chapel at 10:45. Sadly, it was uninspiring. Lunch afterwards, then back to the dorm for homework. Finally talked to Wendy and wished her a proper happy birthday.

Went to Media Writing at 5:00 and gave my speech. Went to dinner and talked to Aaron for a while. Wasted my evening mostly with TV. It's what I do when I'm depressed. Talked to Wendy again. She and Shelly met me in the Fishbowl at 9:00 and we talked for a while. Ate pizza at 12:30. Need just a little more strength!

Friday, April 19, 1985

Went to a late breakfast and skipped English Comp. Just couldn't do it this morning. Picked up a card for Wendy at the bookstore. Went to Calculus at 12:20. Met Wendy for lunch. Back to the dorm. Went to the business office with Gregg the roommate. I went on from there to a missions team meeting at 3:30. Great time!

Had dinner at 6:15 with Susanne and Greg from the team. Great conversation. Saw Kendra, but ignored her. It's been exactly one week since our last talk. So much has changed since that double date with mom and dad! Back to the dorm at 7:15. Talked with Walter and Todd all evening, watching TV in between. Talked to Wendy a couple of times too. Most of my talk with Todd was about relationships. What else? Bed at 12:45, worried about Kerry and Kendra. But thankful for my renewed missions team!

Saturday, April 20, 1985

Got up at 9:30. Susanne called at 10:30. We met at 11:00, prayed, and worked on the prayer letter for the missions team. She's sort of the co-leader of the team, and really awesome. Went to lunch and back to the dorm. Started writing yet another paper. Took a break to call Wendy.

Left campus at 5:30 to go out with Wendy and Shelly. We boycotted the ORU Spring Banquet and had a great time by ourselves. We went to Flakey Jakes for dinner. Then, walked around the mall until 9:00. Went to see "The Breakfast Club" at 9:30. What a great movie! It really hit home. Went to Peppers and talked about it afterwards. Back to the dorm at 1:00. Talked with Todd and Walter. Thank you, Lord, for tonight! Wendy and Shelly are quickly becoming true, great friends.

Sunday, April 21, 1985

Slept through church. Am I becoming a heathen? Hid out in the dorm, then went to lunch at 11:30, pretending I had been to church. Back to my room to work on my paper all afternoon. Called Dad and Wendy. Went to dinner at 5:00. Back to more work on my paper. Bry called and we talked for awhile.

At 9:45, Kendra called and we met at 10:00. We walked all around campus until 11:00. We decided to try to save the friendship. She still really cares about me, but just as a friend. We prayed together. Back to the dorm, and a conversation with my go-to "counselors," Walter and Todd. Finished my paper at 12:30. Went to bed wondering how I can stay friends with Kendra. I just can't be friends with Kerry! Is that right, Lord?

Monday, April 22, 1985

Went to Humanities at 8:50, followed by breakfast. Still recovering emotionally from yesterday's confrontation with

Kendra. Back to my room and fell asleep. Greg the missions team leader called to let me know I was running sound tonight. Went to our team prayer meeting at 10:45. Only Susanne, Robin, and Liz showed up. We had a great time of prayer—then we sang and even danced before the Lord! Went to the bookstore at noon, followed by a boring Calculus class at 12:20. Went back to the dorm, relaxed and watched TV. Talked to Shelly and Mike.

At 4:45, got a call from Greg that I had to meet him at 5:00 to run sound for the music team. Threw my good clothes on and met him at the entrance at the LRC. We wandered the catacombs, finally found the elevator and went to the 6th floor—to a beautiful banquet room. Greg left me all the sound equipment and told me to set up. I was frantic. This equipment was totally new to me. Some random guys helped me out. Finally sat down to eat with the team. Found out that Amy left the team now! We are a team of eight. But, it was a great steak dinner and conversation.

Had to run like a mad man back to Towers at 7:30 with Greg to get my stereo. I was so sweaty—then had to run sound for the next two hours. The performance went pretty well—Liz was the best. She's a senior who has recorded her own album. At 9:30, Mike and I walked Wendy, Shelly, and Robin back to their dorm. Came back to my dorm to tell the guys all about my wild night. Hall meeting at 11:00. Talked more, then bed. Kendra and I will regain our friendship, right Lord?

Tuesday, April 23, 1985

Went to NT Survey at 8:50, followed by breakfast. Avoided Kerry and Kendra. Got a funny letter from Cousin Wes. Went to chapel at 10:30. Talked with Wendy. Went to Calculus at 12:20, followed by lunch. Ate with Wendy. Got my paycheck and passed my monthly hair check. Went to Humanities at 2:20, then back to the room to relax. Went to Media Writing at 5:00. Got an A for the semester! That feels good.

Dinner at 6:15, then back to the room. Studied for another dreaded Calculus exam. Talked to Shelly. Walter's friend, Debbie, called and we talked for two hours! Good, but very long. Why do people naturally think I'm their counselor? Bed at 1:00. Need divine help on this Calculus exam to pass the class!

Wednesday, April 24, 1985

Went to NT Survey at 8:50, followed by English Comp at 9:50. Kendra sat next to me, and we had a very nice (friendly) time. Jeopardy with the roommate at 11:00. Went to lunch, then studied for Calculus. Took my exam at 12:20. Went to the Missions office afterwards. Back to the dorm. Wrote letters to Wes and Amy. Mailed letters and went back to the missions office. Talked to Greg about the sound system. We need something better! Back to the dorm. Called Mom. Dinner at 5:00. Afterwards, talked with Todd and Walter. Played two games of Risk with Gregg and Todd. Watched TV and ate pizza at midnight. Bed. Freshman year is quickly winding down.

Thursday, April 25, 1985

Went to NT Survey at 8:50. Last one! Went to breakfast afterwards. Chapel at 10:30, then lunch. Back to the room for TV watching and relaxation. Went to Media Writing at 5:00 (sadly, last one). Can't wait to take more communication classes.

Went to dinner at 6:00. At 6:30, went to the mall with Gregg the roommate. We saw "Police Academy 2." Very stupid movie. Back to the dorm at 9:30. Wendy called at 11:00. She asked to meet and talk about something very serious. We walked and talked until midnight about her weight problems. She wants me to help keep her accountable. I'm not sure if this is a privilege or a potential problem. Saw Kerry and Kendra in each other's arms (yuck) in the Prayer Gardens. Bed at 1:15 am.

Friday, April 26, 1985

Went to breakfast, then English Comp at 9:50. Saw Kendra, but we didn't talk. Jeopardy at 11:00. Went to lunch, then Calculus at 12:20. Go a 77 on my exam (ick). I will need a miracle on the final to pass this class. Returned to the dorm, mad at that class and myself. Left at 2:00 to run errands with Walter. Went to missions team meeting at 3:30. Very good. It got my mind off Calculus.

Back to the dorm at 5:30. Went with Gregg to Burger King at 7:00. Brought it back to the dorm. Ate and watched TV with Walter. Talked to Cindy for the first time in a while. Great talk. I miss her and Tina. Fell asleep at 11:00. Woke up at 1:00 and talked to Wendy until 1:45. We argued about girls, of all things. Does she like me? She can make me so mad at times!

Saturday, April 27, 1985

Got up late. Went to the mall with Walter at 11:00, for some shopping and lunch. Back to the room at 2:00. Relaxed and talked to Todd. Wendy and I walked three miles together at 4:00, to keep her disciplined in her weight loss. Dinner together in the cafeteria at 5:00.

Played Risk with Walter, Todd, and Mike from 6:30 until 9:30. Long game! Played Trivial Pursuit afterwards, until midnight. Wendy and I met and talked, ate pizza. Not exactly the most nutritious idea (for her). Bed at 1:30. Kerry still thinks I'm mad at him. Wendy is hard to have as a friend, but also probably good for me. She certainly speaks her mind!

Sunday, April 28, 1985

Got up at 10:30. At this point in the semester, church feels optional to me, which isn't good. Went to lunch at 11:30 with Gregg the roommate. Back to the dorm. Called Dad, Bry, Peck, and Grandma. Everyone's doing well. Started packing up my dorm all afternoon. Talked with Wendy and Shelly.

Went to dinner at 5:30 with Todd and Walter. Back to the dorm. Went through all my clothes with Gregg, Todd, and Tompa. We traded some, giving what we didn't need anymore to Goodwill.

I got a nice pair of pants from Tompa. Watched TV and relaxed the rest of the night. Debbie (Walter's friend) called at 10:30 for more counseling. I met Wendy at 11:00 and we walked for 45 minutes. Saw Susanne. Stayed up late, talking to Walter. Only three days left of exams! I miss Kendra.

Monday, April 29, 1985

Went to our missions team meeting at 10:50. We all talked until noon. Got a card from Mom and Dad. Back to the dorm. Talked with Wendy and Shelly. Tried to study all afternoon with Todd and Gregg, but we got way too distracted.

Left at 4:30 for my first final of the semester: Humanities. Then, went to dinner. Had a lazy evening, watching TV. Talked to Wendy for an hour. Talked to Cousin Whitney too. Bed. Four final exams left! Wendy still makes me really good and angry. But, she tells me that our fighting clears the air and makes us better friends. We'll see.

Tuesday, April 30, 1985

Got up late. Played Jeopardy at 11:00. Went to lunch, then studied all afternoon. Dinner at 4:45. Took my second final: Media Writing, at 7:00. It wasn't hard. Back to the dorm at 7:30 and studied some more. Talked to Wendy and Shelly. Argued theology with Todd and Walter, but it was productive. Ate late night burgers and went to bed at 1:30. Feeling weird on this last day of the month.

May, 1985

~

Wednesday, May 1, 1985

Took my English Comp Final at 8:00. Saw Kendra. Back to the room at 10:00. Studied. Played a last Jeopardy with Gregg the roommate at 11:00. End of an era. Went to lunch with Wendy. Back to the room for more studying. Took my Calculus final at 1:00. Hopefully, I did enough to get a C in the class—or maybe a low B.

More studying. At 4:30, took my final final—NT Survey! Saw Kendra again. Went to dinner at 5:30. Back to the room—was totally bored all night. Hard to come down from studying and taking finals. Said my final goodbyes to Skip the Chaplain and Walter. Watched TV and ate pizza. Watched Gregg pack, then went to bed at 1:30. Everyone's leaving! I want to say goodbye to Kendra!

Thursday, May 2, 1985

Didn't wake up until 10:00. I needed the sleep. Said final goodbye to Gregg and we hugged. He's definitely not coming back to ORU next year. This place was not a good fit for him. Played Jeopardy with Tompa, then we went to lunch. Came back to the dorm and bummed around all afternoon. Packed some. Talked a bit to Todd and William.

Went to dinner at 4:45. Back to the dorm. Called Wendy. Met her at 6:20 and went to our last official missions team meeting. We all got our plane tickets! Back to the dorm at 7:30. Watched TV and talked to the few guys who were left here in Tulsa. Wendy picked me up at 9:40. We went to Riverside Park and walked our three miles. Got into a long conversation about my past—especially my girl experiences (or lack of). It ended pretty well. Back to the dorm at 11:00. Talked to Todd. Pizza at midnight. Bed. Want to see Kendra one more time!

Friday, May 3, 1985

Got up at 7:00. Went to the bookstore with Todd and Kerry to sell our books. Got some money for my summer expenses. Back to the dorm. Said goodbye to Tammie, then Bill. Packed until 11:00, then played Jeopardy with Todd. Went to lunch. Packed all afternoon. Brought boxes down to storage at 4:15.

Ate dinner at Saga at 5:00. Gregg and Walter both called— they got back home safely, to Colorado and New York respectively. Called Dad. Wendy called and we went out at 8:00. Ran errands, and then watched the movie, "Gotcha." Went to Mazzio's afterwards for pizza and more talking. Back to my dorm at 1:00 am. Talked to Todd and said goodbye to Steve. Went to bed at 2:15. Worn out emotionally. Saw Kerry and Kendra together again today. Wendy is just seriously weird in some ways!

Saturday, May 4, 1985

Got up at 10:30. Had lunch at 11:30 with Robin. Saw Daphne and Reena. Back to the dorm and relaxed. Helped my next door wingmate, Art, move out at 3:00. Watched the Kentucky Derby. It always reminds me of my grandfather and our shared love for racing thoroughbreds. He had a horse at the Derby a few years ago! Talked to Todd.

Wendy picked me up at 5:15 and we went over to her house. Had a great dinner with her parents. Great conversation. Enjoy her professor dad a lot. We left at 8:00 and went to the mall. Went to the movies and saw "Stick." It was really good. Burt Reynolds is one of my favorite actors. Met Wendy's brother there. Came back to the dorm at midnight. Bed. Last night on the ORU campus for my freshman year!

Sunday, May 5, 1985

Graduation Day 1985! Got up at 9:00. Decided not to go to the Baccalaureate ceremony. Packed my bags and watched TV. Called Bry and Peck. Talked to Wendy. Met Tina at 1:45 and we went to graduation together, since we had brothers and sisters graduating. First time to go to such a long graduation ceremony! At the end, said my goodbyes to Tina, Cindy, and Todd. Finished packing.

Chuck the RA officially checked me out at 7:00. I'll miss him—he was a great RA. Went to the Fishbowl with Tompa, and we said our goodbyes. Met up with Cousin Whitney and Mark, and my Uncle Bill, Aunt Jane, and Cousin Sarah. Had a lot of fun with them. Went back to Whitney and Mark's apartment. Sat around and talked. Everyone left. Called Wendy at 11:00. Went to bed at 11:15. Will stay with Whitney and Mark for two weeks, until my missions trip begin. Why couldn't I see Kendra to say goodbye to her? Your will be done, LORD.

Monday, May 6, 1985

Got up at 10:00 with a terrible, pounding headache. Must be a post-graduation hangover (no, I didn't have any alcohol). Had breakfast with Whitney. Watched TV all day long. Mark came home at 6:30 and we had dinner. A bunch of Mark's friends and I played softball, which was good exercise. Wendy called. TV the rest of the night. Bed.

Tuesday, May 7, 1985

Got up late again. Read my Bible and prayed for a while. Ate breakfast. Watched TV all day long with Whitney. Called Mom and Dad. Mark came home and we had dinner. Mark and Whitney left, so enjoyed the quiet by reading and writing letters. Jeff (my former PE professor) came over and we talked. Bed. Mark and Whitney are so great to let me stay here.

I want to start writing things that are substantive soon!

Wednesday, May 8, 1985

Got up at 10:00. Took a long walk to the Family Practice Center and Sipe's for Whitney, then to the post office. Saw Kendra's car in the parking lot and ran into Kerry on the way. How weird! Back to Mark and Whitney's apartment at 12:15. Watched TV and relaxed all day. Wrote letters to Randy, Julie, and Marcie from back home. Mark came home and we had dinner at 6:30. Watched more TV. Wendy called at 10:30 and we took a walk until 11:30. It was fun. We caught up on our week. Came back to the apartment and talked until midnight. Bed. Whitney found out she is pregnant!

I finally feel relaxed.

Thursday, May 9, 1985

Up at 9:00. Left at 10:15 with Wendy to run errands. Went to the mall and used Mom's Sears' credit card. Bought most of the rest of my stuff for the trip (thanks Mom!). Wendy and I got into our biggest fight of all time. Very hurtful. I actually didn't talk much, since she is way more verbal than me. She dropped me off at 2:30. Mom called and we had a good talk about how to handle Wendy. Relaxed the rest of the day. Wendy called and we went to the bank. We both tried to put it behind us. Home for dinner. Watched TV. Bed at 12:15. Wendy is very hard to like. I miss my mother.

Friday, May 10, 1985

Ate breakfast. Wendy picked me up again (it stinks not having a car at college) and we went back to the bank (closed yesterday) to get our traveler's checks. Back to the apartment at 9:30. Did laundry until noon. Lunch. Whitney left at 12:30 and I relaxed by myself all day. Kind of nice. Mark and Whitney went out on a dinner date, and I ate dinner alone. Also kind of nice. More TV. Wendy and Shelly came over at 9:15 and stayed until 10:00. Bed at 11:30. Wendy is so, so on my nerves. I think I am way too mature for a real girl-guy relationship!

Saturday, May 11, 1985

Had the apartment to myself again. Relaxed and cleaned for Whitney. Watched the White Sox game. Wendy called. She came over at 4:30, but left shortly after. We are just not getting along. I called Shelly and vented a bit. Listened to music, read, and wrote a little. Wendy came back over at 6:00 and we went to Sears to shop some more. Rented a VCR and 3 movies. Back to the apartment to watch "An Officer and a Gentleman." We ordered pizza and Shelly came over at 8:45. Next up, we watched "Against All Odds." Wendy left at 11:00. Shelly stayed and finished the movie—until midnight. Bed at 12:30. I can't believe I am going to London!

Sunday, May 12, 1985

Ate breakfast and read. Watched sports. Called Mom and Dad. Watched "An American Werewolf in London" after lunch. Perfect preparation for my summer trip, right? Called Bry and

Peck. Worked out. Still alone, I ate dinner and watched TV. Then Wendy came over at 9:00 and we finished watching "First Blood." At 10:00, we finished "Against All Odds." She left at 11:00 and I stayed up for a while. Good day. But I miss Kendra.

Monday, May 13, 1985

Got up at 8:30. Did my laundry and ate breakfast. Began packing. Left at 11:30 with Wendy. We ran errands and returned the videos. Returned, had lunch, and packed some more. Watched TV and fell asleep. Finished cleaning the apartment and packing. Watched TV all evening. Called Mom and Dad at 11:00 and said goodbye. Kind of sad. Wrote a card to Kendra. Bed at midnight, feeling weird. Am I ready for this trip?

Tuesday, May 14, 1985

Ate breakfast, cleaned up and took out the garbage. Mailed my card to Kendra. Relaxed and waited for Wendy and Shelly to pick me up. They were late—I hate being late. For me, being ten minutes early anywhere is being on time. We rushed back to her house, got Wendy's mom, and sped to the airport.

Checked baggage (big hassle since all our luggage was overweight). We ran to our plane and made it in our seats with three minutes to spare! Short flight to Dallas. We ate there and went to a coffee shop. Waited for our plane to depart at 5:20. Met Steve and Jackie from the Nigeria Summer Missions Team! Then, we met Susanne at our next gate. Boarded and flew all night. Had dinner. Watched the movie "2010." Had a pretty good time. Not much sleep. Landed at 8:30 am, London time.

London, England

May 15, 1985

Wednesday, May 15, 1985

We arrived in London at 8:30 am (London time). Six hour time change; nine hour flight. Went through passport check at Gatwick Airport, met Liz, and went through customs. Met Greg and Robin (Robin and Liz lost their luggage). Greg, Susanne, and I took a lot of the luggage to the St. Jude's vicarage (pastor's house) and unloaded. A big hassle. We met the vicar's wife, then went to a bank to cash our checks. London is so cool! Took the Tube (subway) to Victoria Station and then the train back to Gatwick at 12:15. Met the rest of the team there. We all gathered the rest of our luggage.

Took the train back to Victoria Station and then the Tube to the vicarage. Had lunch there at 1:30, and met a bunch of people. Food was weird, and not in an interesting way (like cold quiche). Looked around Earl's Court for a bit. Then, we packed our overnight bags, got into a van, and David the Vicar drove us to a home 45 minutes outside of London. We arrived at Highmoor Hall in Nettlebed at 4:45. It was built in the 1600s! The place was awesome—like a mansion! We will be staying here for three days. It's old, cold, and roomy! We walked through it and took pictures. I spent a little time with Liz.

The whole team met up at 6:30 and talked. Everyone was a bit punchy, operating with no sleep. Ate dinner together at 7:00. Our last meal for the next two and a half days! We are all required to fast to get our hearts and minds ready. It was an awesome meal, like a restaurant. Talked some more. Went to bed at about 9:15. Exhausted.

Thursday, May 16, 1985

Took a shower in a huge, cold bathroom. It had a couch in there! Had our first team meeting at 9:00. Greg spoke and we had praise and worship. At 11:00, we all went our separate ways for time alone. I sat in a dark room with old furniture, read my Bible and prayed for an hour. Then I took an hour-long walk.

The team met together again at 2:00. Greg preached, we prayed and sang. The verse given to me to study was **1 Corinthians 13:8**.

Love never fails. But where there are prophecies, they will cease; where there are tongues, they will be stilled; where there is knowledge, it will pass away.

Very timely for me. Went off alone again. Afterwards, talked with Shelly for an hour, then hung out with Mike and Robin. We all reconvened at 8:00 for sharing and singing. Prayed for a long time for London. It was really good. Greg, Mike and I washed our drinking glasses at 10:30 (we are the only three guys on the team). Went to bed at 11:00. Tired, but, satisfied.

Friday, May 17, 1985

Met as a team at 10:00. Greg preached, we sang together. Prayed in the Holy Spirit for one whole hour! I have never done that before. God has revealed a lot to me over the last month. We spent time alone. I laid in my bed and read until 4:00. Found out that four of the team broke the fast. Only Greg, Liz, Susanne and I remained. Wimps.

We had another team meeting at 4:00. Another hour of praying in tongues. Broke up at 6:00. I stayed and talked with Liz, Mike, and Robin—about food mostly! Maybe fasting doesn't do what it's supposed to do. Talked with Wendy and Susanne for a bit. Met again at 8:00 for our final meeting. All praise and worship until 9:00. Greg, Susanne and I stayed and had a great talk until 10:30. Stayed up long into the morning talking to Mike and Greg, sharing our stories. Food tomorrow!

Saturday, May 18, 1985

Had breakfast! Felt like a new man! Susanne, Robin and I sat in the sun and talked until 11:30. Then, Robin and I talked and sat on the swing. Had an awesome lunch at 12:30. Didn't know food could taste so good. Cleaned up the dishes. Liz and I had tea and had an awesome talk outside. At 2:00, Robin, Mike, Susanne, Liz, and I took a long walk into the town of Nettlebed. Found a drugstore and bought pop and candy bars. Cheap. Walked back to Highmoor Hall and got back at 4:30. Relaxed. Packed up.

David the Vicar, his wife Francis, and Angela their daughter came at 5:00 to pick us up. We drove back to Earl's Court and the vicarage at St. Jude's Anglican Church. We were given a tour of an old medieval looking church. Had an awesome dinner at 7:30 with the family. Afterwards, tea and talking.

At 9:45, Greg and Susanne made the decision to split the team up for our lodging. Wendy and Susanne would stay with girls from Youth With a Mission (YWAM). Robin, Shelly, and Liz would remain at the vicarage. Mike, Greg, and I moved into a flat above the vicarage. Greg has his own room; Mike and I stay together on our own twin mattresses on the floor. Liking Mike more and more. We met Mark, Steve, and John who rent rooms in the same flat. We all talked together for a long time, ironed our clothes and packed. Settled on to my mattress at 1:00 am.

Help Lord! I need you now more than ever, and so does everyone else.

I don't know what I'm doing here.

Suzanne, Wendy, and Shelly were crying about the split.

Greg, our team leader, doesn't know what we are actually going to do here either.

But, Lord, you will come through. I know it. I know it. I know it.

Sunday, May 19, 1985

Got up at 9:00, flustered. Greg, Mike, and I left at 9:30 and walked to the bus stop. We took a double-decker bus to pick up Wendy and Susanne at their flat. I guess Greg felt sorry for them. Came back to the church and met up with the rest of the group. Church service went from 11:00 to 12:15. Typical Episcopalian service. Huge church with maybe 60 in attendance. Had coffee and talked afterwards. Met a lot of neat people. Went back to the vicarage for lunch at 1:30. Had a nice lasagna. Had a good team meeting until 3:15. Greg was more positive and things are looking up.

We all changed and left at 3:45. We took a tour all around Earl's Court (on foot). We looked in some stores, saw some good Italian restaurants, and even went through Kensington Gardens. Just made it back for the evening worship service at 6:00. It was led by a YWAM team and was more charismatic and fun, but some very poor Bible teaching. Afterwards, we had coffee and biscuits (cookies) and chatted. Went back to the vicarage at 8:15 and had dinner. Good bread and cheese. Talked and relaxed. Wendy and Susanne went back to their place. The rest of us took a walk back up to Earl's Court Road. We went to a Wendy's (yes, the American restaurant!) and had milkshakes. On the way back, Liz and I shared a lot. She is becoming a very good friend. Back to the flat and bed by Midnight. Feeling better, but still weird. Guess it's culture shock.

Monday, May 20, 1985

Got up at 7:15. Took a bath (no showers here!). Had a bowl of Muesli for breakfast. Went to the church at 9:00 and all of us met in the vicar's office. We sang and prayed with David the Vicar, Francis, and some others. We finally talked about what we would be doing this summer. For a planner like me, that was a relief. At 11:00, just the missions team met and talked. Left at 11:30, and got some stamps and envelopes. We all walked to the YWAM "Kitchen" for lunch (roast beef sandwiches). Afterwards, took the Tube to Victoria Station. Grabbed a tour bus at 2:30 and toured all of London. Awesome sights! Came back at 4:15.

Later, we took the Tube to Leicester Square and then walked around Piccadilly Circus. At 5:00, we ate dinner at the Three Lanterns. Had some awesome spaghetti. At 6:00, we split up. Liz, Greg, and Susanne went back to the vicarage. Robin, Shelly, Wendy, Mike and I took a walk. We went to see "American Dreamer" at 6:15. Great movie. Afterwards, looked around some more, ate some ice cream. Grabbed the Tube at 9:15, and actually found our way back to Earl's Court at 9:45. We went to the vicarage and visited with the girls until 10:00. Then, Mike and I went upstairs to our flat and sat around writing letters. We took our letters to the post box later that night. Bed at midnight.

Tuesday, May 21, 1985

Breakfast. Met at 9:00 for prayer. Afterwards, the whole group met with two YWAMers for prayer and preaching. I was angry the whole time for some reason. Boy, I can get in a mood. Afterwards, we walked to The Kitchen for lunch. Still mad. Went to Sainsbury's grocery store and shopped (bought some good snacks). Back to the flat. Wrote a letter to Bry. Five of us proceeded to deep clean the whole flat. It was very hard work! But it needed it.

Went back to The Kitchen at 6:00 for dinner. The choice for dinner was chicken or lamb. I was determined to choose lamb as much as I could! Love lamb! Back at the flat, Mike and I hung out with Angela, the Vicar's daughter. We showered her with American boy attention. We made her laugh a lot. Later, Shelly, Wendy, Mike and I walked into town and bought postcards. Back to the flat at 9:30. Had an awesome talk with Greg and Mike. Not mad anymore. I really think it's spiritual warfare. You can feel the spiritual darkness here! Had some quiet time by myself until midnight. Prayed with Mike. Bed at 1:00.

Wendy really got on my nerves today. What else is new?

Liz is still cool. Greg is cool.

Mike and I are a lot alike when it comes to girls. We are getting close.

Lord, help me! You want me to change so much.

Can I handle this spiritual darkness?

Wednesday, May 22, 1985

Morning quiet time, and breakfast. Had prayer meeting at 9:00 with the team. Awesome time. Went to The Kitchen at noon for lunch. Mike and I walked back to the flat and had good quiet times again. Then, we went to the YWAM Coffee Bar at 1:30. We worked there until 5:00. This was to be the main work for the team—relational counseling/evangelism of people from the streets of Earl's Court. It was a wildly draining experience! First, I met Zac, a 26-year old ex-junkie who is now an on-fire Christian. We prayed together and talked a lot. I even helped him bandage up a man's gross bloody wrist! Later, I met Dennis and had a deep discussion with him. He asked hard questions for which I didn't have answers. But it turned out to be a good debate on religion.

Went back to the upstairs flat at 5:15 and wrote a letter to Peck. Went to dinner at The Kitchen at 6:00. Walked back with Liz and had a good talk. Went to the vicarage and sat around and talked. Went back to the Coffee Bar at 7:30 and worked there until 10:30 with Susanne, Shelly, and Liz—plus Ron and Angel from YWAM. I brought my Christian music cassettes with me and had a much better time. Talked with Richard and Derek, two guys around my age. Richard was a lot of fun to talk to. Cleaned up at 10:30—I washed the toilets. Met Mike and came back to our flat. Talked and prayed. Bed at midnight.

Lord, you are more precious than silver!

Thursday, May 23, 1985

Got up at 7:30. Met at 9:00 for Team Meeting. Donuts! They always makes me feel better. Went to The Kitchen at noon for lunch (usual soup and bread). Back to the flat at 1:00 with Mike and Liz. Talked. At 1:30, went to the Coffee Bar with Robin. I worked until 4:00. Had another interesting talk with Dennis, then later with Richard. Back to the flat at 4:00. Had a planning meeting with Wendy, Shelly, and Greg until 5:30. We talked about how to minister to a house group of mental patients.

Went to dinner at The Kitchen at 6:00. Lamb again! Back to the flat with Liz at about 7:00. Left at 7:30 with Greg, Wendy, and Shelly and walked to our House Group. Started at 8:00. It was absolutely wild! Sue and Ruth (from YWAM) led it. Sam, the REAL crazy guy from the Coffee Bar was there. Some of the others were pretty nice and docile, but all mentally disturbed in some way. For some reason, I liked being in the midst of insanity and confusion.

We walked home at 10:15. On the way, Greg and I stopped to help Billy home, the resident alcoholic. He staggered along with us, and relieved himself on a car or two. It was pretty hilarious, but sad. We came back to the vicarage and sat around. At 11:00, everyone got together for a party for Greg's birthday! We ate cake and talked for a while. Said our goodnights and up to our flat. Bed by midnight.

Friday, May 24, 1985

Up at 7:30. Prayer meeting with church staff at 9:00, then team meeting at 9:30. Talked, and prayed in the Spirit (tongues) for an hour. Finished at 11:30 and walked to The Kitchen for lunch. Walked back with Mike and went straight to the Coffee Bar to open up. Wendy came in for a bit and visited. Had another long, intellectual talk with Dennis. I think I'm getting to him (hopefully the Spirit is). Talked to Richard too. Left at 4:00 with Ron from YWAM. He took me to get my hair cut. Very short. And, first time from a barber with only a straight razor! I checked my neck on the way out.

We went straight from there to The Kitchen for dinner at 6:00. Left at 6:45 with Wendy and walked to my flat. Actually had a really good talk about ourselves and our relationship. I shared my top ten list of problems with her. We then opened up the Coffee Bar at 7:30. The whole team worked, except Robin. Greg, Mike, Ron, and I played the worst game of Monopoly ever. They all ganged up to destroy me—I actually got my feelings hurt. It was cutthroat, for no reason. I quit the game at 10:00. I have always been a sore loser. Then, Liz brough this homeless woman to me and she talked to me for about a half an hour about all her problems. Very sad life. We hustled her out at 10:50. Then, still hurt, I came back to the flat at 11:00. Went to bed hurt and tired.

Saturday, May 25, 1985

Slept in until 10:00 (PTL). Cooked a great breakfast of bacon and eggs with Mike and Greg. Left at noon with Mike. We took the Tube to Leicester Square and started walking south (I think). Took lots of pictures of famous sites: Trafalgar Square, Parliament, etc. Then we took a wrong turn and got lost. Walked a long time—way too many miles. Mike was complaining the whole time like a baby. I finally figured out how to get us back to Victoria Station. Then, we took the Tube from there to Oxford Circus in the West End. We walked around and shopped until 3:00. Saw a lot of punk rock style people. Mike got his hair cut while I waited. Hopped the Tube back to Earl's Court. Made it to our flat at 4:30 and had a well-deserved rest.

Later, went down to the vicarage and talked to all the girls for a while, including Angela, the vicar's daughter. Changed into dress clothes. Left at 5:30 with the whole team and walked to Jake's restaurant, but it was closed! We walked around until we found the Chelsea Pasta Bar. It was so good—seafood fettucine! Walked back at 7:30 and changed clothes.

We opened the Coffee Bar at 8:00. I played Uno with a couple of homeless guys for a while and then talked to Richard and some Scottish guy. He was rough. Somehow, we all hurt Richard's feelings and he got mad at us. This was a discouraging setback in our relationship. But, we found out that Charlie became a Christian today! Left at 10:45. Said goodnight to the girls. Hung out with the guys. Mike and I prayed until midnight. Went to bed pretty discouraged for some reason. Maybe I'm just overtired.

Sunday, May 26, 1985

Got up at 7:30 to see Mike off. He was going to the church early to give his testimony. Mike sees himself as a future evangelist. I went back to bed. Got up at 9:00 and had breakfast. Went to church at 11:00. Heard a really good sermon on forgiveness by a visiting pastor.

"Jesus said that if you don't forgive others, He won't forgive you. Do you get how serious that is?" he said.

I shook my head. I had never thought about that in depth before.

"Think about someone you have not forgiven. Forgive him or her right now!"

Many people came to mind. Kerry. Kendra. My dad. My sister. Boy, I have work to do.

Went to the vicarage afterwards. Had a great turkey dinner with the whole gang. Washed dishes afterwards with Mike and Angela until 3:00. Went upstairs to my flat and wrote letters to Todd and Tina, postcards to Gregg, Alyson, and Daphne.

The rest of the team came up to the flat at 5:00. We had a very long meeting. Everyone aired their feelings, like it was a group therapy session. It felt like some kind of revolt was coming against Greg, our leader! NOBODY is happy; everyone is discouraged with the present conditions and the lack of a plan. Guess we weren't really listening to the morning sermon. We all went to evening worship in pretty bad shape. We took communion, and the service was dry and boring.

Afterwards, we had coffee. I talked to Ron for a while, then Angela for a long time (she was fun). Left there and had a bite of dinner at the vicarage. At 9:00, Mike, Liz, Robin, Angela, and I walked to Pizza Hut and had TERRIBLE pizza. The British just can't do pizza I guess. It was gross, but we had fun. We talked a lot about dating. Back to the vicarage at 10:15. Played Uno with Shelly, then sat around and talked until midnight. Up to the flat. Mike and I talked about our situation and prayed together.

The devil is really attacking us! Lord, help!

Our unity is broken.

I really can't stand Wendy. Lots to forgive.

Liz is still cool.

Monday, May 27, 1985

Got up at 10:00. Took a walk with Mike at 11:15. I think it is always cloudy in London! Met the whole team at the vicarage at Noon. Today was our day off! We took the Tube to Wimbledon. Arrived at 1:15 at the house of some people Greg knew. We had lunch and sat around and talked. We took a walk and got to see Wimbledon Tennis Center—even Centre Court! It was so cool. They were great to us.

Left at 5:00 and took the Tube to Leicester Square, where we split up. Mike, Wendy, and Robin went to see West Side Story.

The rest of us five stayed together. We walked around for a long time, but couldn't find a suitable movie. So, we ate dinner at Wendy's and sat around until 7:30. We even bought a hamburger for a homeless guy! At 7:30, the three remaining girls went back to their flat. Greg and I stayed out on our own. We finally found a movie. Stood in line for an hour—a 9:00 showing of "The Killing Fields." It was awesome, but very depressing. We caught the Tube home and arrived back at the flat at 11:45. Talked and had prayer time. Bed at 12:30.

Virtually ignored Wendy today.

Had a great talk with Greg. He is trusting me more and more.

He thinks Wendy, Susanne, and Mike are immature. I agree.

I don't know what to do about Mike. He's driving me crazy.

Lord, bring unity, maturity, and vision!

Tuesday, May 28, 1985

Got up at 8:00. Bath and breakfast. Had prayer time with the church staff at 9:30. It was kind of funny. Had our team meeting at 11:00. Greg preached a really good sermon that everyone needed to hear. I just hope they listened! We had lunch at noon at The Kitchen. David the Vicar and Angela joined us. Liz and I talked. Came back with Mike. We opened up the Coffee Bar at 1:30. I ran to Sainsbury's for milk. Mike, Shelly and I talked with Graham and Richard for a while, then Dennis. I think I'm getting somewhere with Dennis. We worked hard and closed up at 5:00.

Back to the vicarage. Mike and I helped YWAM set up the barbecue and tables in the gardens. At 6:00, the whole YWAM team and our team (and Angela) had a cookout. It was fun. Mike and I took a lot of pictures. Talked to Ron and had fun with him. At 7:30, everyone started to leave. We cleaned up until 8:00. Then Mike and I hung around the vicarage with Angela, since we had the evening off. We talked and laughed. At 8:45, Mike and I left for the movies. We saw "Beverly Hills Cop" at 9:15. Ron met us there. It was hilarious. Got out at 11:00 and walked back to the flat. Mike and I talked to Mark for a while. Had some cereal and prayed. Bed.

Wendy and I are cordial, nothing else.

Still praying for unity!

I miss home. I need mail!

Wednesday, May 29, 1985

Got up at 8:00. Bath and breakfast. Met with the group and the church staff at 9:00 for prayer. Had our team meeting at 9:45. Did a lot of praying and talking. Liz gave me a letter from my mom! So thankful to hear from her. Meeting ended at 11:15. Greg and I walked up to Earl's Court Road and bought three bouquets of flowers for the girls who cooked for us every day at The Kitchen. Went straight there, gave them the flowers and had lunch.

At 12:30, Greg and I left for more shopping. We shopped at Harrod's (huge, famous, expensive store), then some other shops. Bought mugs and flowers for all the girls on the team. Back to the flat at 2:45. Then, we went to the Coffee Bar at 3:00. I ran to the store and bought poster board. Cut and glued some gift boxes out of it (Mike helped). When Robin came to work, I snuck the gift boxes into the flat. Then, I went to work cutting and arranging flowers and writing cards (Greg made up all the DEEP poetry and I just copied it in the cards).

At 6:00, we met the girls and gave them the gifts. They were thrilled—and all hugged us. We all walked to The Kitchen together and had dinner. Greg and Mike got into a minor fight. Came back to the flat at 7:00 and cleaned up. Went back to the Coffee Bar at 7:30 and worked for a while. Then went to Peter's (an old man) flat, picked up some old clothes, and went back. Left the Coffee Bar at 9:45. Picked up Robin and walked to The Kitchen. We waited for Shelly, then walked home together. Bed.

Wendy and I are just being polite at this point.

Thursday, May 30, 1985
Had an early meeting at 7:30 with the guys of the flat in the vicarage. At 8:00, we moved into the church and had our team meeting (without Wendy and Susanne). Mike bought us donuts, and we had a good prayer meeting, ending at 10:00. I went back to the flat and wrote postcards to Randy, Cindy, Joanna, and Lynda. Sent them.

Walked to The Kitchen at noon for lunch. It was the worst soup ever. Just hot, colored water. Walked back with Wendy and

Shelly, but didn't say much. Got changed, then rode the Tube with Wendy and Shelly. I got off by myself at Knightsbridge and shopped—mostly at Harrod's. Way too expensive for me, so I didn't buy anything. Got a headache and stomachache, so I walked home. Went straight to bed at 3:00 and slept until 5:00.

Walked to The Kitchen with Mike for dinner. Walked back with Liz at 7:00. Had a meeting with Greg, Wendy, and Shelly. Then, at 8:00, had our small group time. Greg preached and Wendy led worship. She did her usual yelling at us, and just being overbearing. Left at 10:15 and walked home. Wendy and I got into a fight and we didn't talk after that. Back to my flat. Mike was sleeping. Greg, Mark (our flatmate) and I woke him up by telling him he forgot to pick up Robin (joke)! After he settled down, Mike and I sat up and talked—mostly about Wendy. He gave me some good insights. Asleep by midnight.

Wendy and I have to have a real heart-to-heart talk soon.
I need some spiritual and emotional energy!

Friday, May 31, 1985
Met with the church staff at 9:00 for prayer. Had a team meeting at 9:30. Hard for me to sing praises to the Lord this morning. Afterwards, Mike and I went back to the flat and talked. Planned out the day and started cleaning up. At 12:30, Mike and I walked to Sainsbury's to buy groceries. Back to the flat and started prepping. Greg bought a grill and Mike ran more errands. I bought

the dessert—strawberry torte! I put on an apron and started cooking: steaks, green beans, potatoes, salad, soup—and sparkling grape juice. The three of us dressed in our Sunday best and surprised the girls.

The girls came over to our flat at 5:15 (we were barely ready). I never worked so hard in my life. Mike and Greg served the girls each course, while I kept plating the food. Maybe I have a future in the restaurant business. They were clearly overwhelmed! The girls also bought us mugs, candy, and flowers. We joined them for the main course and dessert.

At 7:00, Mike, Wendy, Shelly, Susanne, Greg, and I took the Tube to Victoria Station. We walked from there to the Westminster Theater and saw "Man of Two Worlds"—a one-man drama, all about the Apostle Paul. It was very good. Left at 9:45 and took the Tube home. We cleaned up dishes and sat around and talked. After the girls left, the guys talked until midnight. Bed.

Wendy and I are civil again.

The girls loved our meal! It was fun.

June, 1985

Saturday, June 1, 1985

Left the flat at 9:00 with Greg, Mike, and Robin. We grabbed some breakfast, then caught the Tube. Took it out to Brent Cross and then caught a bus to Brent Cross Shopping Mall. Biggest mall I have ever seen. We split up—I went by myself. Spent all my money! Bought a shirt, sweater, jacket, jeans, and three books. Met the others at noon.

Mike and Robin took off by themselves. Greg and I had lunch then took the Tube home. Back at the vicarage, I showed my purchases to the girls, and we talked for a while. Ron (from YWAM) came over at about 2:00. Ron, Liz, and I took a long walk to Hammond Park. We sunned ourselves and took pictures of each other. Fun. Back to the flat at 4:15. Relaxed, and played Uno with Robin and Shelly.

At 5:00, Greg and I left for the movies. We saw "Witness." Awesome movie. Back at 7:15. Had dinner at the vicarage. Went to my flat alone and talked to Mark. Cleaned up and watched a bit of TV. British TV is fun. At 9:15, Greg returned, and we talked with John (another cool guy) until 10:00. I ironed clothes, read some, and went to bed.

Love Liz and Ron.

Lord, what are we doing here? What is our purpose?

Sunday, June 2, 1985

Got up at 9:00. Bath and breakfast. Went to church with the whole team. It was boring as usual. Had parish lunch afterwards in the church gardens. The food was bad, but the conversations were great. At 2:00, went to my room by myself. Wrote a letter to Mom. Read some. At 3:30, we had a team meeting. We talked about our future plans, then spent some time praying. Each one of us got prayed over by the rest of the team, which was much needed.

At 6:00, we went to evening worship. The girls from our team led worship, which was awesome. The Lord really ministered to my soul. Wendy even gave an awesome testimony. A visiting ORU humanities study group came and attended the service with us! Afterwards, we had coffee and then dinner at the vicarage. Some of the humanities team joined us and we visited. It was fun.

Everyone left at 9:00 except Liz and me, and David and Francis (vicar and wife). Liz and I made tea and the four of us watched TV and talked. Very cool. Felt like a double date. David and Francis left at 10:00. Liz and I stayed up talking by ourselves until 11:00. Said goodnight and came up to my flat. Bed.

Day off tomorrow!

Liz is still cool.

Monday, June 3, 1985

Met Liz, Mike, Robin, and Susanne at 10:00. We decided to split up. Liz and I went together. We took the Tube to Bleeker Street and exchanged money. Then, we went to the planetarium and saw a laser show (sort of boring). Then, we went to Madame Tussaud's Wax Museum. Very famous, from what I understand. It was awesome! We took pictures with all sorts of famous celebrities! My favorite was with Ronald Reagan. Left there at 12:30 and walked through Regent's Park. We got to the London Zoo at 1:00. Lunch, then looked at animals, including some exotic ones I had never seen! At 3:30, we caught a boat ride down the canal to Camden Town. It was a boring town, so we caught the Tube and came home, very tired!

I talked with Greg and helped him with our side-trip travel plans. We may end up going to Italy! At 6:00, Liz, Greg, and I took the Tube to Leicester Square. We had a great dinner at The Pasta Bar. Walked around and met up with Robin and Mike. The five of us went for coffee and dessert. At 8:30, Greg, Liz and I went to the movies to see "The Mean Season." It was good. It ended at 10:45 and we took the Tube home. Said goodnight to Liz. Greg and I stayed up and had a good talk. Bed.

Need to start conserving my money!

Liz acts like she likes me, but I don't know. She could just see us as good friends.

Mike and Robin do everything together. Are they an item?

Greg is the coolest leader of all time.

Tuesday, June 4, 1985

Got up at 8:00. Bath and breakfast. Met with church staff at 9:00. Had our team meeting from 10:00 until noon. We talked about our potential travel plans to France, Switzerland, and Italy. Greg delivered a great sermon about dedicating ourselves to God—very convicting! Went to lunch afterwards. I was unusually quiet. I left lunch abruptly, for some alone time. Later, Liz asked what was wrong with me. At 1:30, went to the Coffee Bar. Prayed and opened at 2:00. Derek, Richard, and I played two games of Monopoly until 5:00. Talked with Greg and Mike.

Went to dinner at The Kitchen at 6:00. Liz thought I was mad at her, but I reassured her that I wasn't. I really was more afraid of giving my heart away too soon (again). I was quiet again at dinner. Walked home with the group, and I had another personal quiet time for a while again. At 8:00, an Australian girl named Kim came over to visit John (flatmate). He wasn't home, so Mike and I talked to her until 9:30. It was fun. What an accent! I left at 9:45 and picked up Shelly from The Kitchen at 10:00. We had a good talk about me and Wendy. Talked to Robin and Angela when they returned our laundry. Talked to Mike. Bed at 11:30.

Lord, help me to have more quiet time with you! I love you so much!

I need to talk to Wendy

I need a strong friend again.

Jesus, just love me tonight. I am so unworthy sometimes!

Wednesday, June 5, 1985

Got up at 7:45. Quiet time. Met with church staff at 9:00. Met with our team at 10:00. Did a lot of business assignments: I'm in charge of sound for the concert, as well as the singles' group on Saturday. We prayed for a while. At noon, I skipped lunch and went back to the flat with Liz. We each had a bowl of cereal and talked about things. It was good. She left, and I had another quiet time and then I talked to Mike and Robin. At 1:30, went to the Coffee Bar to open at 2:00. Spent most of the day playing chess with Derek, followed by Monopoly with him and Mike.

Left the Coffee Bar at 5:00 and went to the vicarage. Grabbed Wendy and brought her back to the flat. I talked to her about "us" and apologized. We are friends again! Went to dinner at 6:00. It was very good. Left there with Robin and talked about Mike for a while. Learned some things about the two of them. Back to the vicarage and visited with the girls.

Went back to the Coffee Bar with Wendy, Shelly, and Susanne at 8:00. All the YWAM people left to do street witnessing, leaving the four of us in charge. It was a real hassle. I talked with

Richard for a long time and had some other really strange conversations. Got Liz to sign a cassette tape of hers for Richard. Back to my room at 10:30. Talked to Mike. Bed.

Will be co-teaching the Singles' group with Liz on Saturday! Mike and I had a great talk about relationships!

Thursday, June 6, 1985

Met for prayer at 7:30. Greg and I walked into town and bought donuts for everyone. Ate at 9:00 at the Coffee Bar with the whole team. Sang and prayed until 10:30. Back to my flat to read and relax. Liz came up and bugged me (in a good way). Went to The Kitchen at noon for lunch. Back to the flat to relax again. Went to the Coffee Bar at 1:30 and opened up at 2:00. Liz came in and we talked about the concert. I was tired and upset for some reason, so I upset her too. She left. I spent time with Derek and Richard. Talked a bit to Dennis too. Closed up at 4:00. Back to the flat. Hung out with Greg and Susanne as they made travel plans. Liz came up and gave me chocolate chip cookies to cheer me up. Nice.

Went to dinner at 6:00. Returned with Liz and Wendy. Read some by myself until 8:30. All the girls came over and Shelly baked apple pies. Wow, she can cook! Robin and I talked by ourselves for a long time. At 11:00, Shelly and I had a good talk. The girls left at midnight. Mike and I stayed up and talked a bit. Bed.

What I do about Liz? I don't want to start liking her. She's a senior!

Sometimes, I just feel useless.

Friday, June 7, 1985

Got up at 8:00. Bath and breakfast. Met with church staff at 9:00. At 9:30, our team met to go over more travel plans. Sang and prayed. It was good. At 11:00, Liz and I went to Kentucky Fried Chicken and brought chicken nuggets back to my room. We sat around and ate, discussing our "friendship theologies." Since we were all alone, it turned out to be a great time of sharing our hearts and minds.

"I don't let many people into my life. I guess I have very high standards of friendship," Liz shared. "I get that. I hope you will learn to trust me," I replied. "I can see that happening. I would love to become close friends." "I'm cool with that." (Yes, that's exactly what I said.)

At 1:30, we talked to the others. I met with Robin about sound. At 2:15, I went to the Coffee Bar. Spent time mostly with Derek, then played Monopoly with him and Mike again.

At 4:00, went upstairs to the flat and had dinner. Shelly and Wendy made good soup, sandwiches, and apple pie! Sat around and had a good conversation. Liz gave me one of her flowers we got for the girls. Nice gesture. The girls got sort of crazy afterwards (must have been the pie). Later, all of us (except Robin) walked to the YWCA. We held a prayer meeting from 8:00-10:00 for the Earl's Court area. Liz led worship. Greg, Liz, Shelly and I walked home at 10:00 in the rain. We stopped for a coke at McDonald's. Back at the flat. Bed at 11:30.

Liz and I will make a great team, as well as friends.

Robin and I get along well, like brother and sister.

Only Susanne left to get to know better.

Lord, take care of Liz and let me help her in any way possible.

Saturday, June 8, 1985

The whole team met at 9:30 at the church with Frances. We cleaned the upper balconies of the church (gross) and mopped and dusted. Had fun, even though it was hard work. We finished at 12:15. I washed up and changed. Liz and I took off and walked up to High Street Kensington to look at books in a Christian bookshop. Looked at other shops and returned to the vicarage at 1:30. Had lunch together on our own. Then, the two of us shut ourselves up in the living room to plan the singles meeting. Read through "The Friendship Factor" by Alan Loy McGinnis together. Fascinating book. Talked until 5:15! Good time of preparation.

Dinner at 6:30, prepared by Angela. I took a few minutes alone to get ready for our small group meeting. Most of us gathered at 7:30, but we waited until 8:00 (fourteen in all). Liz and I taught together until 9:00. We made a good team. We had some refreshments, then led a discussion until 10:15. Some people stuck around later than that. Finally, everyone drifted home by 11:45. Great day!

Liz can teach! So can I.

What about a major in sociology, Lord?   Just a thought.
Suddenly, I am unsure about my Telecommunication major.
Liz and I are getting closer.

Sunday, June 9, 1985

Sunday! Got up at 10:00, well-rested. Church at 11:00.
Good worship service. Talked afterwards, and then lunch at 1:45 at
the vicarage. Awesome meal. Up to the flat at 2:15 for some rest.
At 3:00, Mike and I walked to St. Stephen's Hospital (and got lost
again). Visited Zac for a while, who is recovering from surgery.
Back home at 4:30. Greg drafted me to write for the church
newsletter. I whipped it out in about an hour. Fun to use my writing
gifts.

Went to evening worship at 6:00. Very good service! Liz led
praise and worship, Greg preached, and we had communion in a big
circle where we served one other. At the end of the service, everyone
stayed for coffee and conversation. Angela, the vicar's daughter,
received the baptism of the Spirit at the end of the service! Mike
prayed with her, she cried, and we were all so happy.

At 8:15, we came back to the vicarage and ate dinner (Shelly,
Wendy, Mike and me). We talked a lot. I started feeling bad—some
old regrets popping in my head. Mike and I took some dinner up to
Greg and Robin who were working with John (an English lawyer
who has started hanging around with us) on my article for the
church newsletter! John was tearing it to shreds, so I left angry.

Just wandered around awhile, deeply hurt. I'm a good writer, right Lord?

At 9:30, the missions team met to talk about our trip again. We have cut it down to Germany, Italy, and Switzerland—which is fine by me. I still felt weird. At 10:30, I tried to call Mom and Dad, but no one answered. Back to my room. Visited with Mike and Robin. I sulked. Liz came in and sang some songs which made me very reflective. Liz cried, and Greg came in and laid hands on her. She feels totally burned out. Everyone left at 11:45 except me and Mike. Greg wants to talk to us about who knows what. I'm heading for a breakdown myself!

Monday, June 10, 1985

Got up at 10:30. Everyone had left for some sightseeing on our day off, so I gradually got up and bathed. At breakfast and left at 11:30. Said hello to Angela in the vicarage and walked up the street to WH Smith. I bought Liz a card and came back to my room at 12:25. Wrote the card and brought it to her room to put it on her bed. Talked with Mark and Steve, our flatmates. Went to my room and relaxed and thought. Read some. At 4:30, went to the vicarage and talked to Wendy, Shelly, and Liz. I sat around, sort of depressed—came back to my room at 5:00. I talked to Greg. Then, Wendy and I talked. I told her what was wrong. She told me that she had feelings for me! I admitted some for her too. Really weird!

Liz and I left at 6:15. We took the Tube to Leicester Square (my new favorite place). Found Garner's Steakhouse and ate dinner. It was awesome and the conversation was great. Expensive too. Lingered until 8:30. Then, we went to the movies at 8:45: "American Dreamer" (what, again?). It was great again, and Liz liked it a lot. Took the Tube home and said goodnight at 11:00. Back to the flat. Talked to Greg. Bed.

Am I falling for Liz?

What about Wendy?

I am feeling somewhat secure again (said the insecure guy).

Tuesday, June 11, 1985

Got up at 8:00. Bath and breakfast. Went to church staff meeting at 9:00. Got mail from Peck and Joanna! Met as a team at 10:00. Prayed, then talked a lot of business. Went to lunch at The Kitchen at noon. Not good. Walked home with Greg. Talked to Wendy. Waited for Robin.

At 1:15, Robin, Greg, and I left with Liz's broken electric piano in tow. We took the Tube to Bond Street—walked all over until we finally found the repair shop. Found out it couldn't be fixed. That made me so mad! We took the piano home. Robin and I took off together. We went to Euston Station by Tube and had a good talk. We found a sound system store. Got a good price to rent a piano. Back at 4:15. We called some other stores, but decided to stick with the one we found.

Went upstairs with Mike at 5:30. I preached my sermon to him and we discussed it until 7:00. He gave me some good critiques. I don't think I'm a preacher! Then, we went downstairs and had dinner in the vicarage, combining all the house groups (80 or so people). Richard and Derek came. Met in the church for praise and worship. I sat with Liz. A pastor named Sandy preached and it was good. The Spirit moved. We prayed for Derek about his smoking addiction. Everyone was ministering to someone. I left with Wendy and went back to the Vicarage. We talked until 10:30. She went to bed. Liz and John the Lawyer came in. We sat around and talked and had tea. Went to my flat at 11:15 and talked to Greg until Mike came in.

Do I really know the real Liz? Greg opened my eyes a bit about her

What about Wendy?

Wednesday, June 12, 1985

Got up at 8:00. Bath and breakfast. Church staff meeting at 9:00. Met with the team at 9:30. Very good meeting! We talked business, then prayed. Prayed one-on-one as well. I had Greg. I ignored Liz, on purpose. So much for being a friend. Back to my room at 11:30, to read letters from Dad, Mom, and Rachel—pictures too! Went to lunch at The Kitchen at noon. Back to the flat. Talked with Robin for a bit. Had her make phone calls for me. At 2:00, we walked to the printing shop to get our flyers done. Then, we went to work at the Coffee Bar. Played Uno with Derek and Mike. Wrote a letter to Rachel. The whole place had a big discussion, led by Sue. I think Dennis is getting closer to accepting Christ!

Closed up at 5:00 and went to the flat. Unbeknownst to me, sparks were flying as seven of the team members met. Mike walked out, then Wendy. Everyone is hating on Liz for some reason! I talked with Greg and Mike. Went to dinner at 6:00.

I talked to Liz and told her nothing was wrong with me (a lie). I ignored her at dinner. Walked back with Wendy. I spent the evening alone, reading, praying, and thinking. Drove myself a little crazy thinking about all the drama. At 9:15, I opened up to Greg about Liz. At 11:00, Robin, Mike and I walked Susanne and Wendy to the bus stop. Came back—Greg was having a long talk with Liz. Tough to be team leader. Asleep by midnight.

What is up with Liz? The rest of the girls do not like her. I guess I get it. It's time for our relationship to change. Thank you, Lord, for my family.

Thursday, June 13, 1985

Got up at 9:30. Robin came at 10:30 to cook Mike and me breakfast, At 11:00, Liz and Shelly came upstairs. We took the Tube to St. Paul's. We found the Christian bookstore and I bought a Steve Taylor cassette: "Meltdown." His music is so cool. Didn't talk to Liz the whole time we were hanging out. Left the girls and spent the afternoon in the flat. Had lunch at 2:00 with Robin, Mike, and

Greg. They left. Angela and her friend visited with me for a while. Relaxed, but found myself going crazy again.

At 5:00, Greg and Mike came back. Went to dinner at 6:00 at Wendy's with the whole group (plus Richard and Derek). Talked to Susanne mostly. Walked home with Liz at 6:30. Didn't say much, but promised to talk with her later. Spent an hour by myself in Greg's room, praying, reading, and crying. Good. At 7:30, Greg, Wendy, Shelly, and I went to our crazy, mental patient house group. Wendy did a good job teaching. Back to the flat at 9:30.

The whole team met at 10:00. We decided to cancel our side trip to Germany, Switzerland, and Italy! Sad! It hurt, but not too bad. Afterwards, Liz and I talked until midnight. It was awesome—straightened out a lot of things. Always so good to clear the air.Opened my eyes about Greg, though! He's the real problem. Back to my room. Talked to Mike and Greg. Bed.

Have to deal with Greg now. Lord, I need your help!

Wendy is jealous! Need to work with her.

Liz is back to being an awesome friend!

Friday, June 14, 1985

Met for prayer with the staff at 9:00. Had our team meeting at 9:45—John the Lawyer joined us for some reason. Greg taught and we had more prayer. I received a phone call during the meeting from the Bank of Montreal saying I had $300 there. Wow! When I returned, John the Lawyer blew us away by giving us a word from the Lord:

"Get moving!"

What does that mean? More would have been helpful. I left the prayer time a little early to help Francis bring groceries home from Sainsbury's. Met the others for lunch at the Kitchen. At 12:30, Robin and I took the Tube to Bank Street. Found the Bank of Montreal and got $300 in English pounds! Went back to the flat by Tube. Had a great conversation with Robin. At 2:30, went to work at the Coffee Bar. Talked with Derek and Richard. Wrote a letter to the family. Talked to Dennis and got totally frustrated with him. Left at 5:00 for some relaxation time in my room.

Went to dinner at 6:00 at the Kitchen. The lamb was so good, yet again. Left afterwards with Liz. Walked and talked. We met the whole team at 7:30. Had a great group talk about our feelings (good therapy, I think). Went to the Coffee Bar at 8:15. Talked to Derek and Wendy the whole time. At 9:00, Liz and I met up in my room. Talked until 11:30 about our meeting tomorrow. We are really one-minded in our ideas about relationships! She's so cool. Talked with Greg later. Waited for Mike to get home from talking to Robin. Bed.

What's going to happen with Robin and Mike?

I'm learning a lot from Liz.

Wendy and Liz talked about me. Wendy told her that "I'm a romantic." Is that a good or bad thing?

Why am I a teacher? I'm an introvert!

I need to be nicer to Greg. He is our leader.

Saturday, June 15, 1985

Got up at 9:00. Bath and breakfast. Met with our team (and John the Lawyer—I guess he is a permanent part of the team now) at 10:00. He ran through upcoming events with us, including our places in Steve Ryder's Crusade. I left at 11:30 and went to the vicarage. Talked to Robin a while about her relationship with Mike. At 12:30, we had lunch. It's Robin's birthday today! Shelly cooked, and it was awesome. John the Lawyer attended as well, of course. At 2:15, I went to my room to relax. Fell asleep until 4:00. Woke up and continued planning my talk entitled: "Moving into Marriage". Ironic, right? Liz came up at 4:30 and we planned and made posters.

At 6:00, Liz left and I went to dinner at the vicarage with the others. Shelly cooked again and it was awesome again. Talked to Wendy for a while. Came back to my room to pray and read. At 7:00, Liz and some others came up to the flat. At 7:30, everyone else came too—15 in all (Richard, Derek—and, yes, John the Lawyer as well). It was a good time of teaching and discussion. Afterwards, I talked to Shelly, then John for a bit. I'm beginning to like him a little more. Then Liz, Robin and I left and walked to McDonald's for a Coke. It was fun. Back to my room at 11:00 and talked to Greg and Mike. Bed by midnight.

What major should I pursue, Lord? I thought this was settled.

Wendy? Liz? Just friends.

I've finally decided: I'm glad I have never kissed a girl. I will not kiss until I can commit to one woman!

I've learned so much from Liz.

Oh, to be 21. (Just kidding)

Lord, I'm finally learning. Help it to sink in!

Sunday, June 16, 1985

Got up at 9:30. Went to church at 11:00. Wendy sang and Liz spoke. It was good. If I believed in women preachers, she would be a good one. At 12:30, we all went to the vicarage. Sat with Liz on the couch and talked. Had a great lunch at 2:00 with the vicar's family. At 2:45, Greg, Wendy, Robin, Mike and I took the Tube to Hammersmith. Met David the Vicar, Angela, Shelly and Liz there at 3:15. Found Covenant Community Church and worshiped there from 3:30 until 5:30. I talked with Wendy. Liz is still hurting because of Greg. I rode home with David and some others.

Went straight to the 6:00 worship service at St. Paul's. It was led by YWAM, and was very good. Liz sat next to me and was clearly in emotional pain. During the prayer time, she went to the front and was prayed for. At 8:00, Liz and I walked back to the vicarage. We had a light dinner with the whole family. At 8:30, the mission team met in our room. Liz blew up at Greg, and most of the team joined in—this time, all against Greg! What's going on here? We talked to Greg about miscommunication, pressure, and shortage of time. We settled down, and got the "tough week" schedule presented to us. Wrapped up at 9:45. Liz and Greg went off to talk. Mike and I talked, and he prayed for me. He left, and Greg came to our room to talk to me. (He and Liz reconciled.)

"Don't read me, bro, don't try to read me. I know you think you are God's gift to counseling, but don't read me!" Greg fumed.

"Okay..." I said. "Didn't realize I was doing that."

"Just talk to me. You want to know something, just ask."

"Got it."

I also got a letter from Wendy telling me how much she cares for me. The hits just keep on coming. Bed by midnight.

Greg really annoys me. He really got to me tonight.

I need peace. Too much pressure!

One week of a beard. It has to go.

I hurt for Liz.

Monday, June 17, 1985

Got up at 8:45. Bath and light breakfast. At 9:45, most of the team left. I stayed back with Liz. At 10:15, the DREADED John the Lawyer came to the flat. He took Liz and me to Leicester Square via the Tube. We walked to the National Art Gallery in Trafalgar Square. I have to admit, it was fun to see so much incredible art. At 1:00, we left and went to Pizza Hut for lunch. My bad mood hit me, and I became distant—suddenly feeling like the third wheel. Not fun. After lunch, we walked all the way to Westminster Abbey. From there, we took the Tube to Kew Gardens and stayed there the rest of the afternoon. At 4:30, John the Lawyer left us. Liz and I took the Tube back to the flat. Arrived mentally exhausted.

Found out the team was NOT going to the Full Gospel Business Men's Fellowship International dinner. So, I planned to catch a movie with Wendy and Shelly—I needed to talk with them anyway. But, no! Greg ORDERS me to tag along with him and Liz to the FGBMFI dinner instead. Why me? I swore (in my mind only), and quickly changed clothes. We arrived at the Café Royal at 6:30 and mingled. Had a pretty good dinner. Rodney and his wife sat with us, as well as the dreaded John the Lawyer. Praise and worship was pretty good, testimonies were good, and the speaker was awesome. But...I was still not in the mood. Even some healings occurred, and they didn't affect me. We left at 11:00 and rode the Tube back to our flat. Liz told me that the dreaded John the Lawyer was angry that I came along. So was I! I went to my room. Heard that Mike had a great day at Windsor Castle. More anger. No more talking for me. Bedtime.

God, why am I here?

I am useless. In Liz's life especially.

I can't stand Greg. This was just some sort of manipulative revenge.

But of course, life goes on, and tomorrow I will put on my mask and serve again!

To top it all off, I'm getting a cold! Typical...

Tuesday, June 18, 1985

Got up at 8:00. Staff meeting at 9:00. Afterwards, I helped David and Robert move stuff all over the church. Still angry and depressed. At 11:00, we met as a team in our flat. Just business. Afterwards, Mike made us some scrambled eggs and we ate. I sat around and pouted for a while. I found David the Vicar to get an insurance letter written. Met Wendy. She is still angry too. And, for some reason, she still likes me. After talking a bit with Robin, I left at 2:00 with Greg (yuck). We went to the bank, then took the Tube to Easton. Found the audio store and paid the bill for the good sound system. Still angry. Back to the flat at 4:00. Woke Susanne up by accident.

After a quick nap, I left with the whole team (except Liz) for dinner at Pizza Hut. Good food; bad mood. Back to the flat at 6:15 and got dressed. Talked to Greg and told him I was worn out (since I've had no real time off). He really didn't care. Told me to toughen up. At 6:45, left with Greg, Mike, Susanne, John and Karen in John's car. Went to the Steve Ryder Revival that started at 7:30. Horrible praise time, but a great sermon. I started to fall asleep, though. Over at 10:30 and back to the flat. Bed.

Lord, heal my cold.

What about Liz, John, Greg, and Wendy? Life itself?

Wednesday, June 19, 1985

Woke up with my bad cold at 8:00. Ran to the drugstore and dropped off my film. Had a staff meeting at 9:00 followed by a team meeting at 9:45. Greg gave a good sermon (mostly aimed at me, I thought). We prayed in the Spirit until 11:30. Then, all of us (except Wendy and Shelly) went to brunch at Benny's. I had a great big English breakfast. Everyone left separately. Liz and I left at 1:00. We talked as we walked to the bank and the drug store. Back to the flat. Went to work at the Coffee Bar at 2:00. Discovered that I didn't have to work (or Mike either), so we went back to our room. Nice communication. Read and tried to sleep. Susanne and Greg were in the flat making noise, then Robin came up and bothered me.

At 5:15, Robin, Mike, Wendy and I left and ate dinner at Wendy's (the restaurant). Wendy and I took the Tube to Piccadilly Circus. Walked around and talked for a long time. She told me she still had feelings for me. I STILL just don't know. A pigeon pooped on me, totally embarrassing me. There is nothing going right for me. We saw the movie, "Starman." It was good. Left at 10:00 and took the Tube home. Said goodnight. She got mad at me for not walking her to the bus. I was tired (and talking to Derek!). Then, the craziness continued. Went up to my room. The dreaded John the Lawyer arrived HOPPING MAD. Greg tried to talk him down. Mike and I joined in prayer for that conversation! Afterwards, Greg talked to me a little about it. Still don't understand what the big idea is. I just think he is arrogant and controlling. But maybe I am too. Bed at 11:30.

What more can go wrong?

Rebuild my life, LORD!

Thursday, June 20, 1985

Got up at 8:15 (missed the 7:30 meeting because of my cold). Had our team meeting (minus Wendy and Susanne) at 9:45. We talked, then prayed. At 10:30, we walked through the church, praying over each pew. They prayed for me and Shelly too. At 10:30, I went back to my room. Ran into town to buy Kleenex and pick up my photos. Not bad. Returned and hung out with Mike and Greg. At 11:00, we met the girls. Walked to Spats for lunch. My mind was stuck on Liz. Walked back to my room, prayed for a while, then went to work at the Coffee Bar. Talked with Dennis. Later, helped Greg unload the sound equipment and set it up in the church.

At 5:00, Mike, Greg, and I cleaned up and got dressed. At 6:00, we went to the church and met all the other ministry workers. Prayed together and got briefed. I was assigned to be an usher. Of course. At 7:30, the Steve Ryder Crusade resumed. Good praise, good sermon, good crowd. Steve (a former bank robber) was slaying people in the Spirit left and right. One of the ushers next to me just fell out and was unconscious for fifteen minutes. At 10:15, it was over. Mike, Greg and I went back to our room and changed clothes, then went back to the church to break down the whole sound system. Afterwards, most of the team (plus John the Lawyer) went to Wendy's. We ate and talked. Back to our room and was asleep by 1:00.

Wendy didn't talk to me at all today.

Lord, heal my cold!

John the Lawyer is settling down. I'm trying to like him.

Friday, June 21, 1985

Slept in until 10:15. Team meeting in our flat at 11:00. Talked and planned until 12:15. Went to Garfunkel's for lunch. It was good. Talked with Liz and walked back with her. I later walked alone to the drug store. Saw Shelly there. Then, went to WH Smith and bought some cards. Back to my room at 2:30. Relaxed and jammed to some music. At 4:30, I went downstairs and our sound equipment was finally delivered. I helped the guy set it up until 5:30. Talked to Robin for a while.

Back to the flat. Helped Mike cook dinner. At 6:45, went back to the church to finish setting up the sound equipment. At 7:20, went to the Coffee Bar and had dinner. Good time, even with John the Lawyer there. At 7:45, we started practice, which took a long time. The girls practiced worship songs, then Wendy sang her set (she was frustrated). The team did the "hands" skit, which I like. Then, Shelly sang a few awesome songs, followed by Liz. The entire time, John the Lawyer was talking to a demon-possessed woman in the back of the church. He and the vicar cast the demons out! Wild! Liz and I prayed for them while it was happening, together in our pew. She was really great tonight.

At 11:30, Liz, Greg and I finally left. She went to her room, and we went to our flat. Greg, Mike, John and I sat around and talked. Went to bed. Pretended to sleep. Listened to Greg and Mike talk poorly about the team, especially about me! That's it. Lost all respect for Greg. Haven't respected Mike for a while anyway. Fell asleep angry.

Concert tomorrow!

Are we going to Paris on Monday?

Saturday, June 22, 1985

Got up at 9:45. Bath and breakfast. Talked to Greg and Mike. Found out that Greg has called off the Paris trip! I was so mad. Lost even the last bit of respect for him as a leader. Stalked out after breakfast. At noon, went to the church. There were too many people there, so I just started walking. It started to rain (of course), so I ducked into the Forum Hotel. Sat in the lobby until 1:30, writing cards to all five girls. It was fun, and it released my anger. Returned to the church at 1:45. Spent the rest of the afternoon there, preparing for the concert and praying. Richard and Derek hung out too. Shelly practiced for a bit, then Liz, then Wendy last. I talked to each one of them about Greg—and Robin too. None are all too happy with him either. Robin brought me some food at 4:00.

At 5:30, I went back to my room, changed clothes, and rushed back to the church. Prepared more and prayed more. The whole team showed up at 6:45 and prayed. At 7:30, our biggest concert so far began. But only about fifty people showed up (so disappointing). I went a bit crazy coordinating the whole thing. The girls were awesome and the skit went well. Even John the Lawyer did okay with his message. Shelly's rendition of "Stubborn Love" by Kathy Troccoli is better than the original!

Ended very well at 10:15. I broke everything down with Greg, Derek, and John. Mike prayed with Richard. Back to the flat. I said goodnight to all the girls and gave them their cards (not to be opened, of course). Liz went out with Greg and John the Lawyer (yuck). She'll have to get her card later. Bed.

I think I did pretty well with the sound coordination.

I don't like Greg. Nope, nope, nope.

Liz and John the Lawyer clearly like each other

Sunday, June 23, 1985

Got up at 10:00. Went to church at 11:00. Good worship service. All the girls thanked me for their cards. Went to the vicarage at noon. Sat around and talked until 1:30—mostly with Liz. At 1:30, we had a great lunch made by Shelly. She's just the best cook! Liz left at the end of it with John the Lawyer (I am so jealous). Supposedly, she went to his house for the day. I went to my flat and read and visited a Scottish girl named Angela and her son Jonathan. It was fun. Wendy hung out too.

At 6:00, we went to evening worship. Sat next to Wendy. At 8:00, we went back to the vicarage for a late dinner. Long lost Greg showed up (the girls were acting weird). I sat on the couch with Liz, had tea, and talked. I got a little upset when she told me she couldn't go to the movies tomorrow—she committed to go out with

John the Lawyer instead. I left her and visited with the rest of the girls. Went to my room later and wrote a letter to Liz. Bed by 10:15.

Going to Wimbledon instead tomorrow!

Wendy is cool, I guess

I'm fighting an impossible fight for Liz—against a British lawyer and evangelist!

Greg has really detached himself from the group. Guess I can't blame him.

Monday, June 24, 1985

Got up at 6:00 am! Wendy, Shelly, and Robin came over at 6:30. While Mike was still in the bath, we left at 7:00. We took the Tube to Wimbledon and arrived there to queue up at 7:30. (There were already a ton of people in line). Mike found a way to beat us there and got in front of the line. Queue order dictates what main match you get to watch! The three girls and I waited in the queue until 11:00. We finally got in and bought tickets for Court One (Mike got a ticket to Centre Court, of course). We were sort of mad, especially after waiting in the rain for most of three hours! We had lunch together, then Wendy and I took off together and walked around. Met the others at Court 13 at 12:15 to watch a match. It got postponed because of the rain, so we left. Wendy and I drank a glass of brandy and then all of us had a glass of sherry. It felt pretty naughty.

At 2:00, our Court One matches were supposed to start, so we took our seats. It rained all day! We waited and waited and waited. Shelly and I went and bought some souvenirs. Got strawberries and cream with Robin, like good American tourists. While Mike, Shelly, and I were waiting, a reporter from USA TODAY interviewed us (and got our names too). The rain finally let up and we saw Ivan Lendl beat Mel Purcell of the USA (it was close). We did pop over to Centre Court for a moment so I could at least see my tennis idol, John McEnroe, play a little bit.

We left at 9:00, cold and hungry—but happy. Got off the totally crowded Tube at 9:45 and split up. Shelly and I went to Wendy's for dinner—ate fast and came back to our flat exhausted. Talked a while. Bed at 11:30.

Great, great day! Tennis dream come true.

I'm sure Liz and John the Lawyer had a great day too.

Tuesday, June 25, 1985

Got up at 8:00. Rushed to prayer meeting at 9:15. At 9:45, Liz, Shelly, Robin, Mike, and I waited for the other three, talking and praying (mostly about Greg). I ran out and got a USA TODAY, but our story wasn't in there. At 11:00, the rest of the group showed up and we had a short meeting. The team split up again—Greg and I went back to the flat and he CONFRONTED ME AGAIN! I stated what was wrong and we decided that our problem was simply a mutual personality conflict. We prayed together. I guess that cleared the air. I'm trying to respect my leader, Lord! I got two letters in the mail—from Randy and Peck. They were a breath of fresh air. At noon, I walked to the film place and copy shop with

Susanne. We talked and returned for lunch with the others at our flat at 1:00.

At 1:30, we went to work at the Coffee Bar and opened it up at 2:00. Richard came in and announced he didn't believe in God! What? I talked to Derek about it for a while. Three other younger kids hung out with us: Gary, John Ross, and Emily. They were wild, but I engaged them by drawing and talking. At 5:00 we closed up shop and I talked to the girls for a while. Then at 6:00, helped Liz cook spaghetti. She did a great job and we all ate together. Liz and I got changed and we left at 8:00 together. We took the Tube to Leicester Square (where else) and went to see "The Breakfast Club." Great movie. Afterwards, we went to Pizza Hut and had dessert and coffee. Had a good talk—found out a lot more about her background. We came back at 11:50 (missed curfew). Bedtime.

Lord, help me with Liz.

Make Richard come to his senses!

Give me strength this week

I can work with Greg, right?

I miss my high school friends!

Wednesday, June 26, 1985

Got up late at 8:30. Had prayer meeting at 9:00. At 9:30, we met as a team. Talked about our trip to Scotland, prayed, and worshiped. Greg talked about us "seeking the Kingdom of God first." It was a very good meeting. Got a letter from Mom. At 11:15, Robin and I went to Sainsbury's and brought lunch and dinner groceries. We came back and I made a fruit salad with Angela. Wendy and Robin made scrambled eggs. At 1:30, Mike, Greg, Shelly, Wendy and I went to the Coffee Bar to work. We prayed, cleaned up, and opened at 2:00. Richard was in much better spirits. Derek and I played chess and talked. I avoided Dennis. Wendy and I chatted too.

At 4:30, Wendy and I left to make dinner. Robin and I couldn't light the grill, so we pan fried bratwurst (she's a good Wisconsin girl). It turned out really well. We sat around and ate in the vicarage. Liz wasn't there. At 6:00, Mike and I had the night off, so we went to our room and talked. I wrote letters to Mom and Peck—and read some. Prayed too. Very relaxing evening. Talked with Robin at 10:30. Found out that Liz was with John the Lawyer from 4:00-8:00. Now, they are talking to Greg in the other room. Wonder what that's about. So mad. Bed at 11:30.

I commit Liz to you again, Lord

"Be anxious for nothing"

Smiles and joy tomorrow—only from you!

I need sleep. I love spending time with you, Lord!

Thursday, June 27, 1985

Prayer meeting at 7:30 in the vicarage (only Liz of the girls showed up). At 8:00, Liz, Greg, Mike and I walked up to the Appleyard Café for breakfast. It was very expensive with not much food. Came back to my room and rested for a bit. At 10:00, Greg, Mike and I went and bought flowers for Susanne and Wendy, then rode the bus to their flat to pick them up. We just missed them! Frustrating. Took the bus back to the church and ran into Wendy at a hair salon. Gave her the flowers. Walked home. Greeted everyone. Then went to buy some camera film at Sainsburys. Back to my room for some relaxation. At 12:15, went to pick up Wendy, but she had already left. Frustrated again! Came back to the vicarage.

Later on, the entire team, plus Angela the vicar's daughter, walked to Kensington Gardens with some Kentucky Fried Chicken for lunch. Not enough food again! The girls and guys picnicked separately. What, are we in elementary school? At 1:30, I walked back with Mike. I had the afternoon off, so I really mellowed out. Read for a while, prayed, and just sort of spaced out. Some wild feelings in my heart. Mike came back to our room at 5:00 and we talked.

At 6:00, we went downstairs and talked to the girls, then ate dinner that Francis made (very good, and plenty this time) at 6:30. I talked to Richard afterwards. At 7:15, Greg, Wendy, Shelly, and I discussed our house group, then went over to Ruth's house at 8:00. It was weird as usual (even more so). These really are mental patients in need of Jesus! I got mad at Wendy during the meeting, so we talked afterwards. All okay again. Up to my room at 10:15. Read and wrote and went to bed at 11:30.

Ignored Liz all day for no reason.

I want to go home. Maybe. I don't know.

What do I do about Liz, Lord?

Friday, June 28, 1985

Got up at 8:00, in surprisingly good spirits. Team meeting at the vicarage at 9:00. Didn't talk to Liz. Mike and I left at 9:45 and walked to the Olympia Hotel (a very yucky place) to pick up Zac. We took the Tube Fulham Breadway, followed by the bus to St. Stephen's Hospital. Got there at 11:00 and waited in the ER until noon for Zac to get his stitches out. Rode the bus back and stopped for coffee; then took the Tube and dropped Zac off. He's going to be okay. We walked home, exhausted. Got back to the vicarage at 1:00. Wendy made us lunch. Prayed together afterwards and opened up the Coffee Bar. Mike, Susanne, and I ran it today. I talked with Richard, and finally beat Derek in chess. Talked to Lorraine for a while too. Closed up at 5:00 and went to my room. Wrote a letter to Randy and relaxed.

At 6:00, I went downstairs. Saw Liz leave with John the Lawyer and found out that she really likes him and is going after him! A crushing blow to my heart. Yes, I'm dramatic. Ate dinner with the other four girls, Angela, and Frances. At 7:00, Robin and I took a walk, sat in the Gloucester Hotel and talked about Liz and John the Lawyer. Came back to the flat and sat around and talked to the others. At 9:15, Mike and I took a walk and talked. Robin came to my room and took my note and a candy bar to Liz. Packed up some of my clothes. Bed.

Okay, Lord, I'm hurt, mad, feel used, sad, rejected, and feel real SMALL and FRIENDLESS. But...I'm used to it.

Saturday, June 29, 1985

Got up at 8:30. Bath and breakfast. At 9:30, Mike and I went downstairs and had rolls with Shelly. I got a pretty good letter from Liz. Waited for the others. At 10:15, Greg, Wendy, Susanne, and Robin finally came to the flat with the van. We sat around until noon waiting for Greg to make final plans. Liz came back, after spending the morning with you-know-who. We all finally left at noon. Drove to Oxford. Stopped for sandwiches in the van. Liz talked to me for a bit. She gave me the heart-breaking news that John the Lawyer was her dream man in all respects—and he was coming home with her to Florida in August!

We arrived in Oxford at 2:00. We all split up. Mike, Wendy, Shelly, and I went off together (now known as "the rebels"). We walked all around Oxford. Saw the various colleges and churches. I bought a mug, postcards, and two sweatshirts. It was a lot of fun. At 6:00, we all met back at the van. Drove back to the flat. Shelly, Liz and I relaxed on the couch. The five of us then took the Tube back to Piccadilly Circus. Walked around and found a little Italian restaurant for dinner. It was pretty bad. Left there at 9:00, walked around for a while and took the Tube home. Got home at 10:00. Packed some more and cleaned up the room.

Scotland tomorrow!

Liz and I are now friends again, for good.

Funny, weird, funny.

Tomorrow is a new day!

Scotland

June 30, 1985

Sunday, June 30, 1985

Got up at 6:30. Bath and light breakfast. Dressed and finished packing. At 8:00, Mike and I helped Greg pack up the van. Found out the girls had been up since 4:00 thinking we were leaving at 5:00. Typical miscommunication by Greg. They were mad as hornets! Had more breakfast and hung around until 9:45 when we finally left. Got on the road. I sat in the back with Wendy and Robin. Had fun. Had lunch in the van. Made a few pit stops. I made Wendy mad at me, she made me mad, and we stopped talking—again. Talked to Liz for a while to stay away from Wendy.

At 5:00, we finally made it to our Bed and Breakfast at Windemere. It's a great little town in the Lakes District. We dropped our luggage and drove into town. We split up at 5:30—Liz and I went together this time. We walked into town and had dinner together at an English pub: roast beef and Yorkshire pudding. Had an incredibly awesome talk—aired out absolutely everything. Walked around afterwards and I bought a roadmap. Met everyone at the van and went back to the hotel at 8:00. Mike and I watched TV in our room and talked. Said goodnight to the girls. Robin came and talked to us for a while. Greg and Liz were talking in the hall. Early bedtime for me!

Liz and I are all straight now as friends.

Robin is fun.

Wendy is a big problem. I want our friendship, but I don't know how to handle it!

This town is so cozy.

July, 1985

Monday, July 1, 1985

Got up at 7:00 after a great night's sleep! Bath. At 8:15, Greg, Mike, and Susanne and I went to breakfast. Awesome English breakfast. The others joined us later. We packed the van, then had devotions together. We were still a bit uptight as a team. At 10:15, we got on the road again. I sat next to Liz in the back. Greg drove like a raging maniac! The entire time, he was going 85 mph around sharp turns. Only angels saved us from certain death. We all were getting motion sickness. Thankfully, we stopped at the Beatrix Potter home (famous author of the Peter Rabbit books) and looked around. It was fun. We stopped a few times for potty breaks, but only stopped for lunch at 4:00! We ate at a small hotel.

Stuck around the hotel until 5:30, then back on the road. More wild driving! Jesus, take the wheel! I tried to make the best of it with the others. At 8:00, we made it to Fort William and the Moorings Hotel. The three rebel girls (Shelly, Wendy, and Robin) were so ticked at Greg. We got our rooms. Mike and I bunked together. At 8:45, Wendy, Shelly, and I decided to eat because we were starving. We ate at the hotel restaurant. The girls vented all their anger to me (about Greg). Afterwards, we went to their room to talk some more. After a bit, Wendy kicked Shelly out and we had our BIG talk (finally). It was good, and we cleared up a lot. Our friendship is still worth it! Headed back to my room. Mike and I talked and had some coffee. Bed.

Lord, help Greg's driving and our attitude!

Wendy is my friend. Liz is still cool.

Tuesday, July 2, 1985

Up at 7:30. Finally got a shower! Went to breakfast with Mike at 8:30. Met the rest of the team. Big English breakfast. Afterwards, we had nothing to do, so the five rebels hung out (Wendy, Shelly, Robin, Mike, and me). We walked outside, then ended up in our room. At 12:45, the entire team got in the van and rode into town. We had a terrible lunch—Greg made a bad choice. We shopped a bit. At 2:30, Greg dropped us off at Fort William. We split up—Wendy, Shelly and I went together. More shopping in some fun Scottish shops. I bought a double sheepskin rug that was so beautiful!

At 5:00, we ate dinner at a little café that was pretty good. We hung around in town and talked until Greg picked us up at 7:15. Wendy kissed me a few times, on the lips, which was pretty weird. When we got back, the three of us talked in the girls' room. We drank two bottles of wine that we bought in town. Big mistake. Wendy got sort of buzzed—and I didn't feel so hot either. Mike and Robin popped in at 8:30, so I left with Mike and went back to our room. At 9:30, I went to the TV living room with Robin, Wendy, and Shelly. Wendy laid on my lap while we watched TV. Then, to my shock, we started making out (must have been the alcohol). Shelly and Robin left—understandably. I was so nervous—it was too much. We went back to my room to find Mike, Shelly, and Robin talking. It was very embarrassing. The girls left, and Mike and I talked. Went to bed, freaking out.

Lord, what do I do now?

I did not want that to happen! No! No! No!

Wednesday, July 3, 1985

Got up at 7:30. Showered. Packed while Mike got ready. Still freaked out. Went to breakfast at 8:30, joining the others. Mike and I left and finished packing. Helped the rest of the girls pack their stuff in the van. Got on the road at 10:30. Sat next to Wendy in the back seat. It was very awkward, and still too physical. We stopped for lunch at 1:00. I bought some posters of Scotland. Later, we stopped at the castle at Loch Ness and took pictures. Tried to spot Nessie, to no avail. At about 4:00, we stopped at the North Sea. It was fabulous. We walked around on the beach and collected shells and rocks.

We left there, and Greg sped on (as usual) to Peterhead, Scotland. We were all getting sick—Shelly almost threw up. We arrived at Maggie and Derek's home at 5:30. We relaxed and watched some Wimbledon. My favorite player, John McEnroe, got beat! We ate fish and chips for dinner. At 6:30, Derek came home and we visited. They have two kids. Sat around, watching more TV.

Later, Wendy and I went to the living room and talked. It was very good—we are still just pursuing a friendship, but occasional kissing is okay (according to her). We prayed together about it. At 9:30, the girls went to another house to spend the night. Mike, Greg and I jumped in the sauna for a while. Bed.

Wendy and I are cool, for now.

Greg is still a loser, but I've forgiven him.

Wish we could have spotted the Loch Ness monster!

Thursday, July 4, 1985

Got up at 10:30! Stayed in bed listening to Mike and Greg talk until 11:15 (mostly incoherent babble). Took a bath. At 12:15, we had a great big breakfast, made by Maggie. The rest of the afternoon was free time. Watched Wimbledon for a while. The three rebel girls had a long talk with Greg, venting their anger towards him. I ended up watching Liz and Susanne ride horses while playing with some dogs. At 3:00, I played with the two daughters of our hosts, Bonnie and Melissa. At 4:00, Greg talked with me. He vented his anger LOUDLY at me for telling the girls "things" about him. I didn't say much. I had no defense. The peace of God was in me, I think.

At 5:15, we ate a good dinner as a team. Afterwards, we met as a team. Greg preached and we prayed together. At 6:45, Derek came home and we all left in the van at 7:15. Arrived at the New Hope Bible School for a meeting that began at 7:30. I stayed in the sound booth as the other seven were on stage. The music and worship was awesome. Lots of dancing. Greg preached. It was so refreshing and alive. The service ended at 9:45 and we socialized until 10:15. Derek drove us back to his house. Sat around and snacked for a while. We sang patriotic songs for a bit, since it was the Fourth of July! Mike, Susanne, Liz, and I sat up and talked, gave back rubs to each other, and watched TV. Bed.

Greg, I will love you, but I don't like you.

Liz is cool.

Mike? I don't know.

Shelly sang awesome tonight!

Friday, July 5, 1985

Got up at 10:00. Bath. Watched BBC News for a bit. At 11:30, we had a big English breakfast together (the five of us who are staying here). Greg picked up the three other girls. Wendy and I sat around and watched more TV. At 1:15, Greg, Susanne, Wendy, Shelly, Robin, and I went to the Wool Mill. I didn't buy anything this time. Robin left the group to meet up with Mike and Liz. I was mad. No loyalty! The rest of us drove back to the house. Sort of a boring afternoon—watched Wimbledon and some other shows. The rest of them returned—I snubbed Robin for snubbing me (very mature of me, of course).

At 4:30, changed into my dress clothes. We ate dinner as a team with Derek and Maggie. At 6:30, had a team meeting and prayed. At 7:30, we made it to Fellowship Church. Wendy sang, Liz led worship, and Greg preached again. It went well. Afterwards, a man played the bagpipes for us. Over and over again. So cool. We all returned to the house at 10:00.

Wendy and I went off to pray. It was a good time of prayer, but then we made out at the end of it! That shouldn't have happened! Afterwards, Robin came in and we talked. I was still shaking—couldn't explain it. Robin and I talked out our differences, and committed to remain as friends. After that, I spent some time alone with Liz. It was the best time. It helped show me what to do with Wendy. The hard part is putting it into effect. It's nice to have Liz as a good friend and sounding board. Back to my room and bed at 12:30.

I don't like how Mike and Greg team up against me.

I have to control the physical part of my relationship with Wendy, even though I don't want to. I have to.

I have to put all of my friendship sermons into practice.

I'm glad Robin is okay.

I have to do something nice for Shelly, since she is so cool.

You don't have to touch to show you care!

Saturday, July 6, 1985

Got up at 7:30 to bath. Had a light breakfast. Left with Susanne and Greg at 8:00. Went to pick up the three rebel girls. We all then drove to Aberdeen. Cool city. Split up. I went with Wendy and Shelly. I bought a scarf and blanket for myself, and a sweater for my sister, Amy. It was rainy, but still fun. Met back at the van at 11:45. We drove back to Peterhead, getting lost on the way. Didn't get back until 1:45! I told jokes and was the life of the party van—acting so strange for me. Got back and snacked for a bit, then watched Wimbledon all afternoon. I fell asleep for a bit.

At 4:30, I get dressed, feeling sort of left out of the group. Had dinner with the whole team and family—fish and chips, of course. Watched some TV. At 6:30, we met as a team, prayed and talked (felt on the outside even more). Left for Zion Tabernacle, and got there right before the worship service started. I ran sound in the booth—Greg didn't even introduce me! Wendy led praise and worship. Liz prayed for people. Mike preached for the first time and did a very good job (people raved). I felt more left out. We all left at 9:15 and went to some old fisherman's house for some fellowship and dinner. A lady played the accordion, and a woman named Freda gave her testimony. They were sweet. We left at 11:00. Wendy was bummed because I didn't talk to her. Bed at 12:15.

I feel left out of this whole Scotland trip.

Haven't told Wendy to stop kissing me, but I have to.

I need a vacation—big ministry at home is coming. I feel it.

I need to stop feeling sorry for myself!

Sunday, July 7, 1985

Got up at 8:15. Bath. Breakfast at 9:00 with Maggie and five of the team. Still feeling mellow and depressed. Went to the living room alone afterwards. Liz came in at 9:30 and we talked about my problems (mostly). At 10:00, the five of us staying together met and prayed. We left at 10:30 (Derek driving the van) and met the three rebel girls at church. The service began at 11:00.

It was good—I actually got to sit with the team. Greg preached a fiery sermon and we sang A LOT. We sang one refrain of a song twenty times, while everyone danced. The people are great at Zion Tabernacle. Got out at 1:15. Back to the house for a late lunch with the family and Freda at 2:15. Still not talking to Wendy. Watched Wimbledon afterwards for a while, then took a walk with Susanne until 4:00. We walked down to the beach of the North Sea. Came back and watched the Wimbledon Finals. A seventeen-year-old named Boris Becker won the men's final! Didn't see that coming.

The team met at 5:00 and we talked and prayed together. Left at 5:45 for church. When we got there, Wendy corralled me, and we talked everything out. No more kissing (sad, but cool). The service started at 6:00 and went until 9:00! It was the best. Each one of us was on the stage, and gave our personal testimony. I started because they wanted to hear from me first—they called me Al Capone (being from Chicago). It was fun. A lot of singing again. Later, I ran the sound system so Liz and Shelly could sing. We danced a lot too. Left at 9:15, sadly. Derek drove and we picked up fish and chips. Went to the house and ate. The three rebels left for their house. We watched TV. Mike and I cleaned out the van and then packed. Bed at midnight.

Wendy and I are cool. No more kissing!

Back to London tomorrow!

London, England

July 8, 1985

Monday, July 8, 1985

Got up at the obscene hour of 4:45 am. Dressed fast, packed the van, and left to pick up the three rebels. Got on the road at 6:00. Tired! Rode in the back next to Wendy and Liz. Stopped for a yucky breakfast at 8:15. Slept a few times. Arrived in Edinburgh at 11:30 and stayed until 1:15. Hung out with Wendy and Shelly. Looked at the castle (didn't get to tour it, sadly). Shopped at various wool mills. Bought a few souvenirs. Got lost a few times. Back on the road. Slept some more.

Had a very late dinner at 8:00, right before getting on the M1 for London. Had some good talks all along the way. Arrived in London at 11:30, at Wendy and Shelly's flat. Got back to the vicarage and unpacked our stuff. I did not receive any mail all week I was gone! So frustrating. I vacuumed out the van and went to my room. Talked to John and Mike for a bit. Sleep by 1:30.

Back to work tomorrow!

So tired!

Wendy is just plain weird.

Liz is just fine.

London! (I like Scotland better)

Tuesday, July 9, 1985

Got up at 8:00. Bath and breakfast. Went to prayer and staff meeting at 9:00. Mike and I went upstairs and relaxed at 10:00. Left at 11:45 and brought my film to the chemist. Walked on to The Kitchen for lunch. It was good to be back, even if the soup was just hot water. Back to my room and relaxed. Wendy came up and we talked for a while. Went to work at the Coffee Bar at 1:30. Sang and prayed, then opened up at 2:00. I spent a lot of time talking to Wendy and Shelly, then Derek. We played chess. Closed up at 5:00.

Back to the flat. Helped Shelly bake a strawberry shortcake. Talked. Went to dinner at The Kitchen at 6:00 (all except Liz—she went out with John the Lawyer. He picked her up in a tux. Classy?). Afterwards, walked back with Shelly and Mike. Talked in our flat for a while. Then, Shelly and I finished the strawberry shortcake (I whipped the cream by hand). At 8:00, everyone but Liz came up and ate the dessert together.

Afterwards, Wendy and I took a long walk around Earl's Court and talked some more stuff out. Came back to the vicarage and continued talking until 9:30. She and Susanne left, so I stayed and talked with Shelly until 11:00. Great talk. I really learned a lot about her AND how to talk to Wendy. Went to my room. Wrote a cute note with Scripture to John the Lawyer and Liz and posted it on the vicarage door. If you can't beat them, join them. Off to bed.

Wendy really knows how to anger me!

I hope we can straighten all this stuff out once and for all.

Six more days, then home!

Wednesday, July 10, 1985

Got up at 8:00. Bath and breakfast. Prayer meeting at 9:00. Liz got my note and loved it! Had our team meeting afterwards and it went very well. We made plans for our last week on the field together. Helped Wendy move in to our flat at 10:45. This could be a problem. Went to lunch at The Kitchen at noon. Very good. Came back to the flat and did some laundry. Wendy and I went and exchanged some money. At 1:30, went to the Coffee Bar. Prayed and opened up at 2:00. I played Monopoly with Mike and Derek, then chess. Ron came back for the first time in forever! I was so happy to see him. We talked. Wendy and I finished our laundry. At 5:00, Liz and I talked to Ron about the Lord.

At 6:00, went to dinner at The Kitchen. Walked back to the Coffee Bar and re-opened at 8:00. Ron returned, and we listened to teaching tapes and talked the whole evening. Found out why he left and how he was doing. Talked to Wendy later about a tough conversation with Lea.

At 10:30, came back to the flat. Robin and Shelly bought Chicken McNuggets and we five rebels (plus Susanne) enjoyed them. Wendy and I hung out in her room. Liz was out with John the Lawyer again. Shelly and I had a nice talk too.

"You know, every time we hang out, Wendy gets jealous," Shelly said shaking her head.

"I get that. But why? She knows we are just friends!" I proclaimed.

"It's just insecurity. But she is my best friend, so I have to be considerate."

"I understand," I said. But I really didn't.

Went back to Wendy's room. She was crying, so I consoled her. Had a great talk about Biblical friendship. I was so happy. Said goodnight at 12:15. Sleep by 1:30 after more prayer.

Shelly is an awesome friend to both Wendy and me.

I'm so glad Ron is back!

Thursday, July 11, 1985

Got up at 7:00. Bath. Prayer meeting at 7:30 with the whole team. Mike prophesied over David the Vicar! God has big plans for him in the future. Had breakfast in the vicarage, then upstairs for our team meeting. It was great. I was prayed over for a long time, along with Shelly and Liz. My "word from the Lord" was about waiting for God's plan and using His strength. I needed to hear that. We finished at 11:00.

I went and got my photos of Scotland. Came back and talked to Wendy in our kitchen until 1:30. It was so very good. Went to the Coffee Bar and prayed. Opened up at 2:00. Shelly and I talked until 3:30. It was awesome. Wendy came, and the three of us talked. We talked about a healthy diet (I gave my "milk sermon," the one about how humans can't really digest cow's milk, so it causes all sorts of problems. At least that's what I learned doing a research paper in high school!) I left at 3:45 with Greg and Mike, helping move a desk for a lady. Came back and talked to Ron for a while. Brought him back to the flat, and we hung out with Wendy and Shelly for a while.

Walked to dinner at The Kitchen at 6:00. Great lamb! Mike and I had a weird fight over dinner because of a picture of Wendy and him. He took it from me and ripped it up, as well as the negative. I was so mad that I walked out. Went to my room angry, so I started to listen to some music. Wendy came up and consoled me. We went to our house group at 8:00. Wendy taught the group. Shelly and I just talked to each other. We all took pictures of each other.

Came back to the flat at 10:30 and talked more to Wendy. She left when Mike showed up at 11:00. We had a knock-down, drag out fight about the whole picture thing. He even PUNCHED ME A FEW TIMES. I finally got to the root of his anger problem, and we sort of made up. Bed at 12:30.

Mike, I really hope you grow up soon.

Shelly, you are the neatest

Wendy, you are getting cooler

No Liz interaction today.

Robin, your immaturity costs (Susanne too).

Greg, whatever.

Got a letter from Kendra today! It was cool, but just pretty factual and sterile. I still liked it.

Friday, July 12, 1985

Got up at 8:00. Bath. Staff prayer meeting at 9:00. Afterwards, we met in our room and discussed business until 10:15. Wendy and I talked until 11:00, then I wrote a letter to Kendra. At noon, we all went to Thelma's for lunch. It was great! I opened a bottle of champagne (spilled some) and had two glasses myself. Very fun celebration! Sat next to Liz. Left there at 1:30 and mailed letters at the post office. Went to the Coffee Bar at 2:00 to work, even though I was very tired (can't hold my liquor). Counseled a few people and took pictures. Closed up at 5:00.

Left at 5:15 with Wendy and Shelly. Took the Tube to Leicester Square and walked around. Had dinner at Burger King. Went to the movies at 6:50. Saw "Runaway"—very good. Wendy was mad the whole time. Again. Left at 8:30 and walked around some more. I bought maps, cards, and a mug. Wendy and Shelly stopped talking to each other. Shelly ran off and Wendy and I came back to the flat together at 9:30. We talked until 12:30! It was good.

She is so jealous of Shelly, but knows it's stupid. She is trying to live in Biblical friendship. Afterwards, I talked to Mike, trying to live our Biblical friendship myself. Bed at 1:15.

Shelly is still cool.

Wendy: I pray for you and care for you.

Rough! Boy, am I emotionally tired!

Saturday, July 13, 1985

Got up at 9:45. Bath. Mike and I had eggs for breakfast and then relaxed. I left at 11:30 with Shelly and Susanne. We walked up to High Street Kensington and shopped. I bought trinkets for the family, Bry, and Peck. I also bought a very cool Swatch Watch for myself! They are the latest "thing." Back to the flat at 2:45, very tired. I talked to Shelly about Wendy while we ate lunch. Back to my room at 4:00 while Wendy and Shelly talked out their problems. Mike came in and we talked.

At 5:00, Mike and I walked up to the video store on South Kensington. We rented two movies and returned. Got some dishes for the party with Greg and Mike. Sat around talking to Wendy until 6:30. At 7:00, all of us met (except Greg and Mike who were late). Robin and I went on ahead to Jakes to reserve a table. The others arrived, and we had a great team meal together. I saw Liz for the first time in a while. Finished at 9:30. All of us (except Greg and Liz) walked to Ron's flat (Greg came later, as well as Liz and John the Lawyer). We watched two movies together. First, "Nighthawks" until midnight. Then, Greg, Mike, and Robin left. Next movie:

"Table For Five" until nearly 2:00 am. Two great movies and a lot of fun. I walked Susanne, Shelly, and Wendy home. Bedtime.

Two days left!

Sad, but happy!

I miss Liz.

Sunday, July 14, 1985

Got up at 9:00. Bath and breakfast. Went to church with the team at 10:00. Wendy gave a good testimony and David the Vicar preached a very good sermon. I talked to some visiting Americans afterwards! John the Lawyer and Liz were together. At 11:00, we had Parish lunch in the garden. I talked to a lot of different congregants and took some pictures. Ron and I had a great visit. At 3:00, Wendy and I came back to the flat. She cut my hair. Afterwards, I went to her room and we read *The Friendship Factor* together. We talked about it until 5:45. Such a good book. Some of my favorite bits:

> *"The best friendships do not require that anyone keep the upper hand."*

> *"Conversation with your longtime friends will indeed get sparse if you restrict yourselves to facts, as that couple evidently did. But when you and your mate get together in the evening and you talk about your feelings, there will always be plenty to discuss, for every one of us has a hundred different emotions during the day. The world of our feelings is a*

multifaceted, rapidly changing world, and to meet with a friend to talk about these things—that is intimacy."

Went back to church at 6:00. It was a packed house! The girls sang and Greg preached. We had communion as well as a healing service. A lot of people were prayed over. John the Lawyer was there again. The service ended at 8:00. Talked to Ron for a while, then left with Wendy and Shelly.

At 8:45, the whole team walked over to Graham's flat for our last party together! Richard, John, Derek, and some others were there too. We had some cheap wine and Richard cooked some great spaghetti! It was a lot of fun. Left at 10:15 and walked home with Wendy and Shelly. Read some more of *The Friendship Factor* with Wendy until midnight. It was fun, and we had good conversation about it. Talked to Mike for a while and went to bed by 1:00.

Miss Liz (soon to be Mrs. Liz).

Shelly and Wendy—I will miss you both!

The Friendship Factor!

Monday, July 15, 1985

Got up at 8:15. Bath. Woke up Wendy. Went to our last staff prayer meeting at 9:00. Very sad, but very good. Afterwards, Wendy, Shelly, and I went to Sainsbury's and bought some food gifts. Back to the flat. At 11:30. Susanne, Wendy, Shelly, and I went to McDonald's for lunch. I bought McNuggets for me and Shelly, and we all talked. Then, we went to WH Smith's and shopped. Back to the flat. Wendy helped me pack for the next few hours and we had a lot of fun. I watched Wendy pack for a while, then went into the other room and wrote some cards. Ron came over for a bit. Wendy and I read more of *The Friendship Factor* together until 4:30. Then, she finished cutting my hair. Sat around and talked for the next few hours with various members of the team.

At 7:15, Wendy and I ran up to the store and bought ice for the party. Came back and had a pizza party! It was good fun and great food. Strawberries and cream for dessert, just like good Londoners! Afterwards, the eight of us sat around in our room and gave our reflections. Each one of us shared our summer with the others. Susanne cried a lot about regrets, and the rest of the girls cried too. All of them told me how much they appreciated me, which felt so good. We ended at 11:00. Some of us continued to sit around, writing in each other's journals.   The party broke up around 1:00 am. Wendy and I hugged for a good ten minutes, saying our goodbyes to each other. It was sad. Back to my bed. Wrote a card to Liz. Sleep.

Last night in London!

Reflections...

Feeling so sad, but happy!

Will miss everyone!

Here is what some of the team wrote in my journal:

John Darling,

First of all, thanks so much for being such a true and faithful friend. I have learned so much from you this summer and I have been truly blessed by our friendship. You are the closest guy friend I have ever had. You are the only guy that I have ever opened up to this level. I let you see my vulnerable side, such as seeing me at my worst (when I get up in the morning, when I wear my glasses, wet hair, no make-up, etc.). It sounds like dumb things, but I've always been afraid to let guys see that side of me because of what they'd say. I never thought a guy would care about me enough that things like that wouldn't matter. But you have proved that I was so wrong. You have always been so encouraging and complimentary, never caring what I looked like or how I dressed. You have also seen the best and the worst of me as certain members of the team seem to have brought out the feistiness in me like never before in my life! Yet you remained my friend and love me for who I am! Thanks so much for always being there and being so positive. Thanks for helping me to learn to love myself. Through you the Lord has shown me that, when I get ready for marriage, a guy CAN be my best friend before being my boyfriend, husband, etc. Thanks again for being such a terrific friend. I love you!

Love, Shelly

John,

    A true friend…this summer we've laughed and cried together. You've shown me aspects of friendship that I've never understood before. The Friendship Factor <u>does work</u>, as long as the foundation is Jesus Christ! Thank you for helping me make it work this summer.

Love in Christ,
Robin

P.S. I will include a special chapter about you in my book: "The Acquaintance Factor".

P.S.S. I'm thinking about writing a second book: "How to lose friends and make enemies". Would you collaborate with me? Can we talk about it later? I can fit you in tomorrow around noon!!

Later Gator,
Robinsky

Dearest Jonathon,

    Remember the cup? Memories. John, what can I say? <u>You are special</u>. Kid, we've been through SO much. You and I have truly had to work at our friendship, but it is worth it. I'm glad now that we didn't decide to "chuck" our friendship when the going got rough. Believe me, I really wanted to that night at the Lakes! I'm glad you encouraged me not to. Thank you for teaching me the Friendship Factor and showing me that it really works. I've really enjoyed reading The Friendship Factor with you. I think it brought us closer. John, you're so cute and special to me. Sometimes I just look at you and say to myself, "Boy, he's handsome. Babe, you're really growing on me." But, I am learning to "check" each feeling that comes up about you. It's so tempting to let my mind run, but I won't. With God's help, I won't! I want to do God's will so badly. I know God has us *in the palm of His hands. He loves us so much and wants the best for us. John, I look forward to seeing where our friendship takes us, but I also know that either way, we'll still have our friendship. Remember: "Friends for Life!" You are so dang special to me, you dumb-dumb!! Wow, you've grown this summer by leaps and bounds! You're becoming such a leader. I'm so proud of you, kid! Oh—I appreciate your compliments so much—a lot more than you'll ever know. John, I love your holey beard and your zits and I also love your skinny body!*

P.S. You were so cute singing in tongues in Nettlebed!

Love in Christ, Wendy

Dear John,

I love to start letters like that! Well, it's been quite a summer, huh? I have learned a lot this summer. Thanks for being patient with me. I'll never forget you, the "professional" navigator/map reader, holding your peace when I advised the wrong turn after Aberdeen.

I also appreciate the way you refused to add to the confusion in our meeting that began to turn to SNAFU. You have "wisdom beyond your years"—I had to add that after tonight's comments. My mind is drifting off to sleep, and you're wanting to go to bed, so I better close…

Love you! Susanne.

My dear John,

Not my dearest John, but what can I say? Would you like to have one of the most successful lawyers in England on your case? Quite a little pun there.

This summer has been too fun to fit on one little page like this. Remember Rebecca Ryan? I thought I was her for a while—it must have been from drinking out of unrinsed coffee cups. No! Don't think about that! Arghh!!!

Your little notes were some of the most special times of encouragement that I ever received. You always had the right thing to say during times when I needed to hear it. Certainly, I am convinced of all the guys on the team, you have the best understanding of what it is to treat a girl like a brother in Christ. I hope Kew Gardens won't make you doubt my ability to be your sister.

As a sound man, spiritually speaking (musically is taken for granted), I like the way you think! Keep on eating the Word. The more you sell out for Jesus the more He can entrust you with deeper revelations of Himself!

May your whiskers ever multiply, and may you NEVER be walking under a tree when a pigeon—well you know what I mean. Praise God for friends. I love you and I'll be looking for you at "THE WEDDING" (how about a music video and dancing and stuff).

Liz

Crete, Illinois (Home)

July 16, 1985

Tuesday, July 16, 1985

Got up at 7:00. Bath. Finished all my packing and cleaned up my room. Packed all the team luggage into David's car (Richard and Derek came by to help). Said goodbye to the Vicar and his family, and our flat (so sad). Shelly, Robin, Derek, and I left and took the Tube to Victoria Station. John the Lawyer and Liz met us there. John the Lawyer announced their engagement! Wow. What a summer romance. We waited and met Mike who had most of our luggage. I checked in. Everyone else came—they were running late. We all caught the 10:00 train and arrived at Gatwick at 10:30. Sat next to Liz and John the Lawyer. Got off the train on a dead run. Left my luggage in the train, praying that it would follow me somehow. Waved goodbye to all and kissed Wendy goodbye. Just made my plane (what, again?) and got to sit next to Liz.

The plane took off at 11:30. It was a long, long flight! Liz talked mostly about John the Lawyer and I talked about Wendy (she thought we were going steady!). Slept a lot, even through the movie.

Upon arrival at Atlanta at 3:00, it was hailing—so we were diverted to Memphis. Sat for an hour, then flew back to Atlanta. So long! Got in at 8:00 (5 hours late, and 1:00 am London time). Got off and got our luggage. All of it arrived, praise God! The Lord provided smoothness the rest of the way through customs. Said a sad goodbye to Liz and ran to my gate. The plane was delayed. We finally got off the ground at 9:15 (8:15 Chicago time). I'm missing everyone, especially my friend Wendy!

Got in at 9:45. Mom and Dad picked me up. Luggage came and we drove home. Talked a lot. Home at 11:15. The boys and Amy were still up, and Julie, Bry, and Peck were there! I talked to them for a while, then Bry and Peck left with their gifts. Stayed up talking to Julie and Amy (gave a good testimony, I hope) until 1:00. Relaxed on the couch until 2:00 am. Then bed.

Culture shock setting in already

I miss my London family. Even with all the drama.

Wednesday, July 17, 1985

Got up at 10:00. Julie stayed over with Amy, so I talked to her for a bit. Gave Josh and Matt their gifts. Relaxed all morning. Mom made us a late breakfast. Afterwards, I started washing my clothes. Lunch at 1:30. Amy came home at 2:15. We played teaching cassettes and had a good talk about friendships until 4:15. Talked to Mom and her friend Pat afterwards. Peck called. Talked with Amy some more.

Dinner at 5:30. Cleaned the kitchen and talked to Mom for a while about Dad. They are still struggling. I'm back to reality again. Peck came over at 7:00. We talked all evening, with a few interruptions (like walking the dog). He told me all his summer stories, and I talked mostly about friendships and girls. It was fun. He left at 11:00. I wrote Wendy and watched TV. Prayed and read. Bed at 1:00.

Thursday, July 18, 1985

Had a morning prayer time and studied until 9:00. Went downstairs and relaxed, watched TV, and had breakfast. Mailed my letter to Wendy. Talked to Mom. Had lunch at 12:30. Played with the dog and the brothers. Gramps came over at 1:30. We hung out and talked and watched the Cubs game (I cheered for the other team in my heart). He left at 3:30. Mom and I watched Jeopardy. Went upstairs and read. Dad came home and we had a family dinner at 5:30. Relaxed. Peck called. Watched TV with Mom and Dad until 8:30. Amy came home. Talked to her and watched TV until 10:30. Listened to a teaching tape and fell asleep at 11:30, very tired.

Reality is hitting me.

Bry still hasn't spoken with me!

Friday, July 19, 1985

Got up at 7:00. Listened to a tape on Christian sex, then read and prayed. Showered and dressed. Had breakfast. Bummed around all morning, watching TV, reading, and listening to teaching tapes. I am a sponge about relationships. At 1:45, drove (for the first time in months!) and picked up Amy from work. We went to Jewell and bought groceries, then went to the bank. Home at 3:00. Talked to her for a while, then Peck called and we talked.

Read and prayed until 5:00. Had dinner. Dad came home and we talked. Left at 6:30 and drove to Peck's house. Met Bry at 7:15 at River Oaks. We saw "Back to the Future." It was a cool Spielberg flick. Went back to Peck's house afterwards. Talked to Leanne and Sandy for a while. Then watched TV and played Trivial Pursuit the rest of the night. I got home at 1:00. Bed at 2:00.

Worried about Bry. My friends haven't grown at all since Christmas.

I miss everyone on the team. I don't like it here so much.

Saturday, July 20, 1985

Got up at 9:30. Read the newspaper and ate breakfast. At 10:30, went outside and helped Dad clear the land. Jonalee and Beth stopped by and we talked a bit (they are still typical high schoolers!). Came inside and talked to Dad. Watch TV and had lunch. At 12:30, Walter (my future roommate) called. We had a great talk. He's really grown spiritually! Watched sports the rest of the afternoon. Peck called and we talked.

At 6:15, rode to town with Amy and rented a few movies. Home at 7:15. Ate pizza and watched "Police Squad!" with Mom and Dad. Funny! Dad left at 8:45 when it was over. At 9:00, Bry and Peck came over. We watched "Dreamscape" and played with my dog Mugsy until 11:00. They left at 11:45. I went to my room, wrote, and went to bed.

Church tomorrow! Will I see my "favorite" girl, Marcy?

I'm beginning to handle this stuff better, I think.

I miss ORU, Walter, Wendy, and the team!

Sunday, July 21, 1985

Got up at 8:15. Shower. Breakfast. Read the paper. Left at 9:45 for church with Dad, Amy, and Matt. The service was pretty typical. Talked to Marcy for a minute and greeted our pastor. Stopped for groceries on the way home. Had lunch. Relaxed and wrote a letter to Shelly. At 3:30, I called Wendy and had a nice talk. She is not fitting in so well also, and is missing me! Peck called and we talked. Then called Robin, which was also fun. Froze bags of green beans with the family afterwards. Had dinner. Watched TV until 8:00. Then Bry and Peck came over. Watched "Flamingo Kid" and then returned the movies. Peck left at 11:00. Had a good talk with Bry about priorities. Preached a good "sermon" to him and told him my "kissing" story. He left at 12:15. Bed at 12:45.

Bry needs the Holy Spirit.

I miss Wendy

Will I talk to Marcy any more? I hope not. I have to leave high school behind.

Monday, July 22, 1985

Got up at 6:00. Did a Bible Study with Dad until 6:30. Fed, walked, and bathed Mugsy. Relaxed and watched TV until 9:00, then had breakfast. Spent the rest of the day alone. Amy's friend called and we talked. Sent letters to Shelly and Liz. Read the Bible. Slept a little and had lunch. Peck called.

At 5:30, everyone came home. Got ready to go out. Amy and I left at 6:45. Went to the movies at 7:25 and saw "Prizzi's Honor." It was pretty good. Went to Taco Bell afterwards. Came home at 10:30. Talked to Mom and Dad for a while. Walked the dog. Watched David Letterman and went to bed at 12:30.

Tired of being at home!

Lord: help, help!

Tuesday, July 23, 1985

Got up at 9:30. Read the paper, ate breakfast and watched TV. Mom came home at 11:15. We left with the boys at 11:45 and went to Burger King, then Southlake Mall. I got jeans, shorts, a shirt, a photo album, and a wallet. Picked up my photos. Came home and relaxed. Peck called and we talked. The whole high school gang is still gossiping about me. And, it still hurts. Why? No trust. Got ready to go out, then Robin called. Made plans for Saturday and she also invited me to Milwaukee! Cool! Can I leave now? Ate a quick dinner, talked to Mom and Dad and went to Peck's house at 6:00. Talked and watched TV. Bry came over at 8:00. Played Trivial Pursuit and Scrabble and watched the White Sox win. It was fun, but sort of meaningless. Came home at midnight very tired. Went to bed.

Tired of this place and these high school people.

Lord, help me work on your strength

I want to see Robin, then Wendy,

Money is TOO tight. Need to find a job at school (yuck).

Wednesday, July 24, 1985

Had Bible study with Dad until 6:30. Fed and walked the dog, read the paper, and relaxed. Went back to my room and finished cutting magazines for Wendy's letter and mailed it at 10:00. Had breakfast and showered. Watched TV until lunch. Bummed around the rest of the day: sleeping, reading, doing some work. Got a great letter from Wendy! Talked to Amy for a while. Peck called. Had dinner at 5:30. Peck came over. Watched the White Sox game with Dad and played cards. Peck left at 10:15. Watched more TV. Went to bed.

Randy is at camp.

I need to get busy doing SOMETHING.

Lord, take care of money.

I want to go back to ORU. I miss Wendy!

Thursday, July 25, 1985

Got up at 8:45. Had breakfast and read the paper. Played some basketball after fixing the net. Did some work around the house. At 11:00, mowed the grass. Came in, had lunch, and watched TV. Relaxed the rest of the afternoon. Read the Bible and listened to the stereo. Watch more TV (what else to do?). Peck called a couple of times to make plans for the weekend. Had dinner at 5:45. Watched TV the rest of the night (real fun). Watched David Letterman, thinking of Wendy. Went to bed.

I want to go so badly.

This house needs settling down.

Lord, I want to make an impression here.

Mugsy bit Matt today. Bad dog!

I'm really bored as you can see by the above statement.

Friday, July 26, 1985

Got up at 9:00. Relaxed. Played some basketball. Had breakfast and played more basketball. Came in and worked out for a while. Got two more letters from Wendy! They were both awesome! Watched TV and had lunch. At 1:00, showered and got dressed. Spent a couple of hours looking through old high school stuff, re-living some memories. Played with the dog. Peck called. At 3:30, wrote a letter to Wendy and sent her some comics. At 4:30, got ready to go out. Had some dinner.

Left at 5:15 and met Bry at Peck's house. The three of us went to the White Sox game. We had great seats and we met some high school friends there. Th game stunk at first, but the Sox came back and won. 9-8! Drove back to Peck's house at midnight, then went straight home. Bed.

Wrote Wendy a pretty negative letter (about home)—I really miss her.

Saturday, July 27, 1985

Got up at 7:00. Showered and had breakfast. Left at 8:15 and picked up Peck and Bry. Drove to Six Flags Great America, arriving at 10:00. Spent the whole day there! I have always loved this place, even though I hate rollercoasters. Met Robin (yeah!). She came down from Milwaukee and brought her friend, Lynn. Went on four water rides—my favorite and a few others. Saw "The Imperials" in concert. Ate, played games and bummed around. Had pictures taken of all of us and had good talks with Robin. Said goodbye to the girls and left at 11:00 PM. Got home after dropping off the guys. Read a great letter from Shelly! Bed.

I miss Shelly and Wendy a lot.

Lord, give me strength!

Sunday, July 28, 1985

Left at 9:45 with the family and got to church. Met Gram and Gramps there. Good preaching. At 11:30, we left and wet to Tivoli for lunch. Good food, but a depressing conversation about money tightness (by my parents). Came home at 1:30. Relaxed, read the paper, and watched "Planet of the Apes" on TV—that movie always lifts my spirits.

Helped cook dinner and ate at 6:45. Called Wendy. Had a good talk; didn't want to get off the phone. Unloaded my problems on her. Went downstairs and had a decent talk with Rachel. She has really grown spiritually! Back upstairs to watch Miami Vice with Mom and Dad. It was kind of fun. Got ready for bed. Bed at 11:00.

Wendy, your voice was great to hear.

No support here. Amy is still waiting for me to crumble and revert to my old, selfish self. I won't!

I need strength for three more weeks!

Lord, why?

Monday, July 29, 1985

Got up at 6:00! Showered and had breakfast. Left at 6:45 with Dad. Went to the chiropractor, bank, and Gramp's office. Spent time writing my team letter at the office. Left at 10:00. Picked up my photos, then went to River Oaks Mall and bought a book and card for Wendy. Came home at 11:30. Relaxed. Had lunch and watched TV. At 1:00, went to my room and read and slept until 3:00. Watched more TV.

Mom left at 4:30, leaving Amy and me in charge of the boys. The four of us had dinner at 5:15 with Laura (we all actually got along). Talked to Laura for a while. Peck came over at 7:15, after I finished playing games with the boys. Peck and I played football and Yahtzee until 10:30. Amy came home with her boyfriend, Chris. I talked to her about ORU when Peck left. Mom and Dad came home at 11:30. Watched TV and went to bed.

Got a letter from Liz today! Things are going great with John the Lawyer.

Feeling okay today. Got to write some more letters.

Tuesday, July 30, 1985

Got up at 9:00. Ate breakfast and read the newspaper. Wrote a letter to Wendy (what, again?). Cleaned up my room until Noon. Watched "All My Children" (my favorite daytime soap opera from high school) and had lunch. Helped Mom clean the house. Read and slept for a while. Watched a little more TV. Peck called. Ate dinner at 5:30 as a family. Left at 6:15 and went over to Peck's house. Played Yahtzee until 7:30, then Bry came over. We went to the movies and saw "European Vacation." It was ok. Not as good as the original "Vacation." Got back to Peck's house at 10:00. Played Scrabble and snacked until 11:15. Went home. Watched David Letterman and wrote letters to Shelly and Liz. Bed.

I want to go away—far from here!

I miss everyone, especially Wendy

I miss London!

Wednesday, July 31, 1985

Left at 11:15 with Mom, Amy, and the boys. Met Grandmas Joyce and Georgia and Aunt Dorothy at Sauk Valley Restaurant for lunch. Came back home at 1:00. Peck called. Spent the next two hours showing the old ladies (I say that with all due respect and admiration) photos from my trip. It was fun. Peck came home and the Grams left. Peck and I went on the roof and cleaned out the gutters. Dangerous, but fun.

At 3:15, we left and went to Lincoln Mall and shopped. I bought some more cards for Wendy. Got home at 6:00. Ate dinner.

Watched the White Sox game. Dad, Peck, and I played Yahtzee and cards. Peck left at 10:00. Watched TV with Dad and Mom, then watched David Letterman. Bed at 12:30.

Tired. I miss Wendy! Only a few weeks left!

August. 1985

Thursday, August 1, 1985

Got up at 8:45. Wrote letters to Liz and Cindy. Ate breakfast and read the paper. Why is there never any good news? At 11:00, I started to work on my parents' 1983 tax returns. It was a real hassle. While I used to think I would study to be an accountant one day, this quickly reminded me why I changed my mind. Mom came home at 2:00 and made me lunch. Got into a little fight with her and felt bad after. It's too easy to pick a fight with mom. I should know better. Finished working on the computer. Watched TV. Had dinner at 5:30. Peck called. Watched the White Sox game the rest of the evening and other TV shows with Mom, Dad, and youngest brother Matt. The four of us also played Scrabble. Sox lost. To my room and bed.

Friday, August 2, 1985

Ate breakfast and read the paper. Showered and finally shaved my holey beard off. I felt like a brand new man! Mom and Matt left—I babysat Josh all day. Got out my coin collection. Sorted and cleaned my prized possessions. So many of them were collected by my grandfathers. Peck called. Ate lunch at 1:30. Cleaned up the house. Peck called again. Mom came home, and I left at 4:30 with the car.

Arrived at Peck's house. Played Kizmet and watched TV. Had great Aurelio's Pizza for dinner. Went outside and played basketball. Bry came at 7:00 and we continued playing. Goss and Jeff (friends from high school) came and played for a while. Made small talk. They acted so nervous around me, like I had three heads. Inside at 8:45. Bry and I played Scrabble. At 9:30, Darcy came over and Peck talked to her. Bry and I got into a HUGE debate—until Peck came in. Bry is rejecting Christianity and becoming an agnostic. Wrapped up the night by watching the White Sox and playing Trivial Pursuit. I finally won one. Home at 1:00 am. Bed.

Got two letters from Wendy (and she called, but I wasn't home) and a nice postcard from Angela (the vicar's daughter)
I'm mad at the Devil for blinding Bry's eyes. Bry is searching for knowledge through the wisdom of this world.

His college philosophy class darkened his thinking. Why can't he see?? I'm tired of my friends being in bondage!

Saturday, August 3, 1985

Slept in. Got into Mom and Dad's bed and watched TV— Mom served me breakfast in bed. So nice. Showered and read the newspaper. Wendy called at noon. It was a good talk (sort of). Got a letter from her about my schedule, and a cool one from Shelly. Watched the White Sox game with Dad. Everyone left at about 4:00. I relaxed, fed the dog, and watched TV. Peck called. Worked on my photo album. At 7:00, everyone came home. Had dinner.

Watched TV with Mom and Dad until 9:00. Peck called again. Rented a movie. Peck came over at 10:00. We decided not to watch the movie, but had a long talk about Bry instead. We are both worried about his soul. He left at 11:30 and Amy came home. Watched Saturday Night Live together. Bed.

Bry, you are cashing out our friendship

Wendy, I miss you. And Shelly too.

Sunday, August 4, 1985

Left at 9:45 with Amy and went to our church: Homewood Reformed. Pastor Charnin gave a very good message. Went to Dad's office afterwards, picked up chicken, dropped off the movie, and returned home at 12:15. Had lunch with the family. Watched the White Sox game and relaxed. Tom Seaver got his 300th win. What an amazing milestone! At 4:00, called Robin and had a very good talk. Peck called. Had dinner at 6:00. Went to Peck's house at 6:30. Played Kizmet and watched "The Blues Brothers". Bry came over at 9:00 and we played Life. How appropriate. He need's to find new life! Mike came over at 10:30 and we played again. Left at 11:30. Home at midnight. Wrote a card to Wendy. Bed.

Not much time left at home! Feel like I really wasted it.

Was kind of snubbed by Bry tonight (oh, well).

Monday, August 5, 1985

Got up at 9:00. Showered and ate breakfast. At 9:30, started working on the computer again for Dad and his tax issues. Worked fast and stopped at noon for lunch. Peck called. Worked more on taxes until 2:30. Went to Peck's house. We went to try to sell my coin collection to make some money. Failed. Went to Southlake Mall. Shopped until 7:45. Didn't buy anything (since I have no money!). Back to Peck's house. Ate dinner and played a game of Careers. Amy called me to tell me Wendy called the house. Home at 11:00. Wendy called back and we talked for a while. Bed.

Wendy just wanted to hear my voice. She was afraid I was pulling away. She felt stupid. Not quite sure what to do with that.

Tuesday, August 6, 1985

Got up at 9:00. Showered and had breakfast. Started working on the computer again at 10:00. Quit at noon and had lunch while watching "All My Children." Why am I still hooked on this stupid soap opera? Mom and the boys left. I relaxed for a while and slept. Called ORU, but they were too busy to change my schedule. Played with Mugsy. Spent the rest of the afternoon working on my photo album. Everyone came home. Josh and I fought—my little brothers love to provoke me. Bry called, which was a relief. Then, I talked to Peck.

Wolfed down some dinner. Went to Peck's house (Bry and Jeff were there). We played baseball until 8:30 (Peck and I won). Came inside and played Trivial Pursuit and talked. Bry and Jeff left at 9:30. My sister Amy came by and we traded cars. Peck and I played games again until 11:30. I drove home. Wrote a letter to Wendy and Shelly. Bed.

Lord, mend my schedule, please!

Got to get things done. Fast. The clock is ticking.

Wednesday, August 7, 1985

Got up at 9:15. Showered and ate breakfast. Read the paper. At 11:15, started calling ORU about my schedule. Anyone? No dice. Stopped trying at noon. Worked on the computer. Peck called a few times. Tried to call the school again and finally got through but they couldn't make changes for lack of course numbers. Why is class registration so hard! Called Robin (good chat), but she didn't have the course numbers. Called Wendy, but she was not home. Finished working on the computer and got a printout. Dad's 1983 taxes are done! Watched Jeopardy and talked to Peck.

Had dinner at 5:30. Went over to Peck's house at 6:30. We went to Washington Square Mall together. Walked around, then saw "Pee-Wee's Big Adventure." It was hilarious. Went back to his house and played Mille Bornes again. Left at 11:15 and came home. Wendy called, and so did Gregg (the roommate) and Randy from ORU. Gregg and I talked from midnight to 1:00 am. Bed.

I miss Gregg. What a unique roommate he was!

Lord, repair my class schedule. Help me get it over with!

MLB baseball strike is tentatively over! I've missed my White Sox!

Thursday, August 8, 1985

At 10:00, called Wendy and finally got my course numbers. Left at 10:30 with Mom and the boys, and picked up our two grandmas. Went to Chicago Ridge Mall and had lunch. Got my photos developed. Gram bought some clothes and other things for me. She is so great. Dropped the grandmas off and returned home at 3:30. Fixed my courses and called ORU. Finally got my schedule straight! So happy. Peck called. Relaxed. Had dinner at 6:00. Got into a BIG argument with Dad (so dumb again). Bry called. Peck and Bry came over at 7:00. We played "People Trivia" for a while and hung out. Boring. Bry left at 10:00, then Peck at 10:45. Amy came home at 11:15. We talked until midnight. Stayed up and watched David Letterman. Bed.

Praise the Lord for my schedule resolution!

Running out of time here!

Friday, August 9, 1985

Got up at 10:00. Had breakfast, then mowed the lawn. Came inside at 11:30 and showered. Had lunch and watched TV. Worked on my photo album until 4:00. Got letters from Shelly and Derek from London! Amy came home. Had dinner at 4:30. Chris picked up Amy and me at 5:00. Then we picked up Laura. Got to Poplar Creek at 7:00. Got great seats to see Russ Taff in concert. He was awesome! His Walls of Glass song was so convicting:

Why do you buy
What the world says
It thinks you should be?
Living your life through the pages
Of some magazine?
Why try to have it all right now?
Why leave behind what is real
For store-bought treasures?

The dream's not true
The dream won't last
You're just building your life
On illusion
Those things will lie
Those things will pass
They will shatter like walls
Made of glass

Then, Amy Grant came on at 9:00. She totally surprised me and ministered to my soul even more deeply. Got out at 11:00. Dropped off Laura at 12:30 and arrived home at 1:00. Talked to Mom and Dad. Went to bed at 1:30.

What a fantastic concert! The only thing better would have been to go with better company. Only a few days left, and a lot to do.

Saturday, August 10, 1985

Got up at 10:00. Worked on my photo album for a while. Had lunch. Peck called. He came over at 1:30. We chatted. He left at 2:30. I got ready to go out. Left at 3:00 with the whole family (except Amy). The five of us got to Grandma's house at 4:00. Dropped the boys off there. Dad, Mom and I met their best friends, Gary and Jorie at a Mexican restaurant. We had a great time talking and eating. I talked the most. Pastor Gary gave me some good advice about studying psychology (my new major).

"There are some helpful things in secular psychology—some insights you will glean. But I've seen too many people become corrupted by it as well, confused about the truth." Pastor Gary was utterly serious, which I needed.

"So, be careful. Be discerning. Look to Scripture as your final authority," he continued.

"Thank you for that. It's all so new to me. I will pay close attention," I replied.

Left at 7:30. We picked up the boys and got home at 9:00. Talked with Peck until 9:30. Worked on my photo album and watched the White Sox until 11:00. Watched Saturday Night Live until midnight. Bed.

Gary and Jorie are the coolest couple ever. I wish I could be like them one day—married and in ministry together.

Almost time for L-Day (Leaving Day).

I get to talk to Wendy tomorrow...and Robin too!

Sunday, August 11, 1985

Got up at 9:00. Showered. Left at 9:45 for church. Met Gram and Gramps there. A good sermon on prayer. Went to my favorite Italian place—Savoia's for lunch. It was my early birthday dinner! Got $40 from Gramps and had some great spaghetti. Got home at 1:15. Robin called and we planned our meeting times. Read the paper and worked on my photo album until 4:00. Talked to Wendy. Good solid talk. Peck called and we talked until 5:00. Worked on my photo album until 7:00. Finally finished! Ate dinner. Argued with Amy about my stereo. I'm so protective of my things! Peck came over at 8:00. Bry came over at 9:00 after our Yahtzee game. Played People Trivia and then Upwords until 11:15. They left. Bed at midnight.

Got to get out of here! I feel like I'm just wasting time.

Lord, forgive me. Am I doing your will?

Monday, August 12, 1985

Got up at 9:30. Showered and had breakfast. Read the paper and relaxed. Left at 11:30 with Mom and the boys. Went to the eye doctor first. Then, lunch at McDonald's. Afterwards, went to the store and bought some canned goods for school. Sold my coin collection for $232.40! That will help. At 2:00, went to Sears and bought my toiletries. At 3:00, had my dentist appointment. Got my teeth cleaned and a cavity filled. Picked up Amy at 4:30 and went home. Cleaned my room. Peck called. Got ready to go out.

Ate dinner at 6:45. Had a big argument with Amy again! We are wearing on each other's nerves. Went to Peck's house at 7:30. Met Bry and Jeff there too. Went to the movies to see "Real Genius." It was good. Dropped Jeff off and went back to Peck's house. Then came the real big argument of the day! (Peck and me vs. Bry)—until 11:30. Exasperating! We got nowhere. Drove home. Watched David Letterman. Packed until 1:30.

Bry! Devil, I'm so mad at you.

Glad to leave (sorry to say).

Milwaukee, Wisconsin

August 13, 1985

Tuesday, August 13, 1985

Got up. Showered. Had breakfast with the family at 8:15. Left at 8:45. Drove to the Milwaukee Zoo. Slept some of the way. Arrived at 11:00. Walked around. Picnicked at noon and had family devotions. Walked some more. Met Robin at 4:00 at the front gate. Drove to a restaurant and had pizza with her and my whole family. I felt bad for her.

The family left me with Robin at 5:30. Drove to her house in Cedarburg, outside of Milwaukee. Relaxed at her very nice house and talked. Watched TV. Her mom and dad came home and we met. We left at 8:15, got ice cream and drove around town. Went to the movies at 9:15 and saw "Mask." Good, but too long. Drove home at 11:15, very tired and had a headache. Bed at midnight.

I like it here. It's very quaint.

Should be a good couple of days.

Wednesday, August 14, 1985

Got up at 9:00. Showered. Robin's mom made us breakfast. Left at 10:15. We drove to downtown Milwaukee. Went to the Grand Avenue Mall and walked around. Had lunch at 12:30. Looked around some more and left. Went on a tour of the Miller Brewery at 1:30. It was fun and educational. I drank a small sample of Miller Lite at the end. Ick. Why do people drink beer? Left at 2:30 and took the scenic route back to her house. Home at 4:00. Snacked and watched TV.

Robin's dad came home at 6:30. Had a great family dinner together—and conversation. Kevin and Lynn (Robin's friends) came over and we played Trivial Pursuit. Her mom and dad won! After that, the four "kids" played Chutes and Ladders (how old are we?), then Mille Bornes (which lasted way too long). Said goodbyes at midnight. Robin and I hung out. Bed at 12:30.

It's fun up here in Wisconsin.

Can't wait to get to school again!

Thursday, August 15, 1985

Got up at 9:45. Showered. Had a light breakfast. Left at 11:00 with Robin and drove into town. Visited the winery and all the little shops around it. Nice time. Came back to her house at 12:45. Watched TV and had lunch (and wine). Picked up Kevin and Lynn at 2:00. Went and played putt-putt golf (Lynn won). Went to Toys-R-Us and shopped. Bought a Nerf hoop for my dorm room. Then, went to Tim's Custard and had a black cow (my favorite A&W

root beer float). Dropped Kevin and Lynn off. Last time to see them.

Back to Robin's house at 5:15. Watched TV. Robin's dad came home and the three of us left at 6:00. We picked up Sue (another friend) at 6:45 and went to County Stadium. Brewers vs. White Sox game! Sadly, the Sox lost, but I still had had fun. Back to Robin's at 11:45. Packed Robin's car. Got ready for bed, sleep by 12:15.

Milwaukee was fun. Time to go.

Almost time to see Wendy. Good or bad?

Crete, Illinois

August 16, 1985

Friday, August 16, 1985

Got up at 8:45. Showered and packed. Had breakfast and said goodbye to Robin's mom. Left at 10:10. Drove straight to my house, arriving at 12:45. Had lunch. Showed Robin around the Crete house—all my stuff, pictures, etc. Began packing. Walter (the new roommate) called. All is well, but our good friend Todd isn't coming back to ORU! Sad. Packed some more. Mom came home and I helped her with dinner. Chris (Amy's boyfriend) came over, then my long-lost friend Randy!

Had my birthday dinner: Spaghetti. What else? It was great. Opened my gifts: a plaque, two books, and a Polar Bear stuffed animal! Polar bears are my second favorite animals, right behind penguins. Drove to town and rented movies with Robin and Randy. Showed Randy pictures of my trip and had birthday cake. Watched "Micki and Maude" with Dad, Randy, and Robin. Robin went to bed at 10:15. Movie was over at 11:00. Randy and I caught up until 2:00 am! Said our goodbyes.

I have to finish packing!

It's nice to see Randy—he's on the ball, spiritually speaking.

Saturday, August 17, 1985

Got up at 7:30. Said goodbye to Mom and Dad. Almost fell back to sleep after my shower. Woke up Robin. Grandma came over at 9:30. Had breakfast. Finished packing until Noon. Robin and I drove around and saw the Chicago suburbs. Stopped in and saw my other grandma for awhile. Home at 1:00. Had lunch and watched a movie—"The Lonely Guy." Gramps watched it with us. Hung out. Then went to town and returned the movies. Peck called.

Robin and I went to his house at 6:45, then picked up Bry at 7:00. Went bowling at Stardust Lanes (Peck and I beat Bry and Robin twice). Peck and I went to his house and shot baskets until Robin and Bry came (half-hour later). We played croquet until 11:00. Sad last goodbyes to Peck and Bry and left. Back to my house at 11:45. Packed some more and went to bed at 12:30.

Off to Tulsa tomorrow! Looking forward to seeing Wendy.

I'm going to miss Peck a lot. He got me a mug and a book.

Still praying for Bry.

Glad to have an easy friend like Robin.

To be continued...in my Sophomore year!

www.ingramcontent.com/pod-product-compliance
Lightning Source LLC
Chambersburg PA
CBHW051502150726
47997CB00001B/88